THE
CLASSIC
CHINESE
COOK BOOK

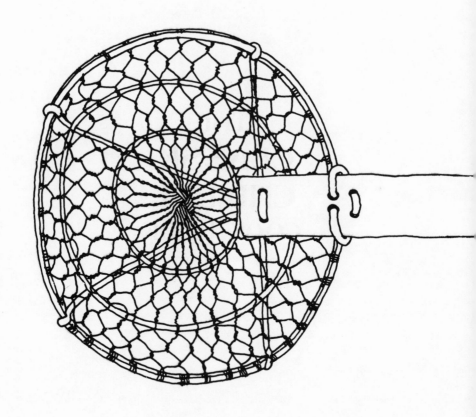

THE
CLASSIC
CHINESE
COOK BOOK

MAI LEUNG

Drawings by
CLAUDE MARTINOT

PERENNIAL LIBRARY

Harper & Row, Publishers, New York
Cambridge, Philadelphia, San Francisco, Washington
London, Mexico City, São Paulo, Singapore, Sydney

A hardcover edition of this book is published by Harper & Row, Publishers, Inc.

THE CLASSIC CHINESE COOK BOOK. Copyright © 1976 by Yuk Mai Leung Thayer. All rights reserved. Printed in the United States of America. No part of this book may be used or reproduced in any manner whatsoever without written permission except in the case of brief quotations embodied in critical articles and reviews. For information address Harper & Row, Publishers, Inc., 10 East 53rd Street, New York, N.Y. 10022. Published simultaneously in Canada by Fitzhenry & Whiteside Limited, Toronto.

First PERENNIAL LIBRARY edition published 1987.

Library of Congress Cataloging-in-Publication Data

Leung, Mai.
  The classic Chinese cook book.

  "Perennial Library."
  Includes index.
  1. Cookery—Chinese. I. Title.
TX724.5C5L478 1987   641.5'951   75-9354
ISBN 0-06-091414-9 (pbk.)

87 88 89 90 91 MPC 10 9 8 7 6 5 4 3 2 1

To
My husband, Nel,
our son, Nelson, Jr.,
our daughter, Mai-Ning,
and
to my new home, America

◊◊◊◊

CONTENTS

PREFACE

I was very pleased to learn from Sallie Coolidge, my attentive and suppor-
tive editor, that Harper & Row had decided to publish a paperback edition
of *The Classic Chinese Cook Book*. As I point out in the Introduction, this book
is the expression of many years of practice, research, and teaching. In the
eleven years since its publication, I have been deeply gratified by the public's
response both to the recipes themselves and to the vignettes of Chinese
culture by means of which I try to convey a taste of the Chinese sense of
life.

I am especially happy that, over the years, Chinese readers have found
that this book has brought to life for them the cuisine and culture of their
heritage. They have shared with me their delight that my recipes have en-
abled them to prepare at home the dishes their memories savored.

I cannot begin to name all the friends, students, and readers who have
taken the initiative to express their appreciation for this book. I hope these
words of thanks will be taken personally by each of them.

1987   MAI LEUNG

✿✿✿✿

ACKNOWLEDGMENTS

To the people and culture of China, I acknowledge my enduring indebtedness. The collective experience of my people has been my teacher and my benefactor. I had the good fortune to be born among them, to participate in their learning and experience.

I am especially grateful to my grandmother and mother, who encouraged my early ventures in the kitchen. To their spirits I bow deeply. I must also thank my father, who arranged to place me in the kitchens of several restaurants owned by his friends in Hong Kong.

During my youth, the cooks of my grandparents and parents stirred up my interest and basic skill in cooking, patiently tolerated my intrusions, and indulgently cleaned up my experiments. Of their simple and unassuming lives, I remain in awe.

Many kowtows go to Chef Tong Shui Lin, Chef Mui, Chef Lin, of Hong Kong; Chef Ng and Chef Chon of New York. I profoundly appreciate their hours of assistance and their generosity in sharing their special knowledge and skill in Szechwan and Peking cooking.

Also I would like to express my heartfelt appreciation to my dear friends who have assisted me in countless ways:

JoAnn Kitch gave valuable advice in the first stage of this book and then flew to my rescue as the deadline descended. Stephanie Bartlett and Gail Gilbert typed the manuscript. Without them I would still be buried in papers and ink. Jean Friedman, Barbara Grunes, and Joan Pirie Leclerc are treasured friends whose encouragement has been constant.

The cheerful welcome and good will of my friends on the staff of New York's Wing Woh Lung   永和隆   Grocery Store have enlivened my shopping and will continue to be a source of pleasure for me.

For the publication of this book, I am greatly indebted to Mrs. Harriet Fine, her daughter, Deborah Freundlich, my editor, and her son-in-law, Lawrence Freundlich, editor in chief of Harper's Magazine Press. I will always be grateful to Debbie for her appreciation of the essential nature of my book. Her assistance in shepherding it through the final stages has been a blessing. Many thanks go to Claude Martinot, whose exquisite drawings contribute so much.

I cherish deeply the thousands of hours spent with hundreds of students. It has been a joy to share with them the Chinese approach to cooking. Teaching them has helped me to learn how to present the information and instructions in this book.

My deepest appreciation, which is beyond words, is for my husband, Nel. Without his continued assistance and confidence, I could not have persevered.

❀❀❀❀

INTRODUCTION

This book is an undertaking of fourteen years of hovering over hot woks and sizzling oil, thousands of hours of research, as well as countless visits with chefs, cooks, and grocers. Yet when I look back at these pages, I hesitate to claim them as my own. For they are the expression of millions of cooks, stretching through thousands of years. Most of those I am indebted to have become faceless, nameless, and are gone; a few I have known and hold dear.

Few of them were celebrated or wealthy. Most have been humble, many poor, but they have been blessed with talent, creativity, and rich and exuberant spirits. Cooks in homes, food-hawkers on the streets, chefs in restaurants, it is these ordinary people who have raised our cuisine to its peak. In so doing, they have served, enriched, and expressed our life.

Past and present, these are my people, the ordinary people of China. It is they who have patiently taught me. It is their collective experience that enables me to express my own. In addition to these recipes, it is their spirit which I wish to convey in this book.

Here are over two hundred well-loved dishes from Szechwan, Hunan, and Peking, and from the east and south of China as well. All of these recipes have been tested and enjoyed by many hundreds of students and guests for nearly a decade.

I hope that with each meal you will share and love not only the abundant food of my people but also their spirit.

Madison, New Jersey
March 1975

Mai Leung

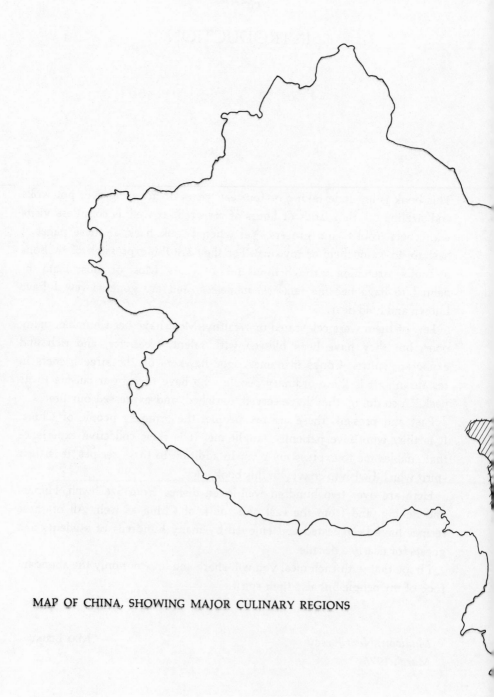

MAP OF CHINA, SHOWING MAJOR CULINARY REGIONS

BEFORE BEGINNING

1. Read the entire recipe carefully before preparing the ingredients and cooking.

2. Have all the ingredients prepared and organized as directed in the Preparation of Ingredients.

a. This sign * means that portion of the recipe can be prepared several hours in advance.

b. Ingredients such as meat, poultry, and seafood can be cut in advance. It is easier to cut meat and poultry if they are half-frozen (put them in the freezer for about 30 minutes). After they are cut, be sure to keep them covered and refrigerated before use.

c. Always cover the sauce mixture if it is prepared in advance. The vegetables, ginger, and scallions can also be cut hours ahead. Put them on a plate and wrap them to prevent drying.

3. All measurements should be exactly as in the recipe.

a. If the measure is by spoon, especially the sauce mixture, it should always be a level spoon. Level it with your finger or a knife.

b. Do not add more than the recipe asks for; adding a few more ounces of meat, poultry, or seafood to a stir-fried dish will make the dish bland and cause it to lose its taste. (If you need more than a recipe calls for, repeat the recipe.) To ensure making no mistake, weigh ingredients. Exact measurement is essential for the success of these recipes. A scale is an indispensable aid to satisfactory results.

4. Do not use double black soy sauce because the dishes will be a little too salty for you.

5. This book is based on cooking on a gas stove. Since an electric stove is usually hotter than a gas one, you might need to adjust the heat to medium-high or medium (see Stove, page 8).

Utensils, Cooking and Cutting Techniques

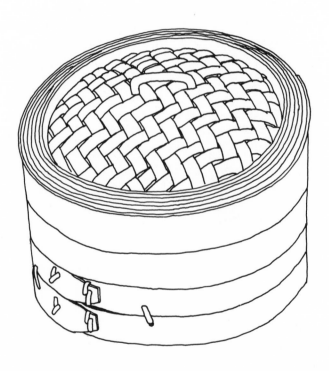

✿✿✿✿

UTENSILS

WOK WITH COVER AND COLLAR

The wok is a round-bottomed, formidable-looking Chinese cooking vessel. It has been used for many centuries and was designed for stir-frying to shorten cooking time and to save fuel. A few tablespoons of oil just barely cover a flat-bottomed skillet, but in the wok the same amount of oil forms a little pool, in which each piece of meat or vegetable has a chance to be immersed. Besides, the wok is almost an all-purpose cooking utensil. It can be used in many ways—to deep-fry, to stir-fry, to steam, to stew, to smoke, to poach. Once my grandmother even lifted it over my head with a prayer to stop me from growing too tall.

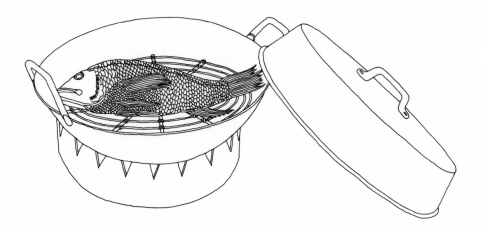

Woks come in different sizes, with matching covers, from 10 to 20 inches in diameter. The ideal size for family cooking is a 14- or 16-inch wok. The 10- or 12-inch one is too small to do Chinese cooking. Woks that are bigger than 16 inches are too large to use on your family stove. They are used by restaurants that have specially built high-heat stoves.

In China, most woks are made with cast iron or carbon steel. In the States, woks are made with carbon steel, aluminum, stainless steel, or some other material. For Chinese cooking, I prefer the cast iron or the carbon steel ones. They get hot easily but do not retain heat as long as the others, so that they serve well for the purpose of stir-frying.

In China, a wok sits comfortably on a specially built stove. But your gas or electric ranges are not built for a round-bottomed wok, and you need a metal collar for it to sit on.

A new cast iron or carbon steel wok comes with a layer of machine grease to protect it from rusting. Clean it thoroughly with hot water and a mild detergent. Dry it, then season it in this manner: place wok over medium heat. With a paper towel slightly dampened with vegetable oil, wipe wok constantly over heat for a few minutes. Rinse in hot water and dry thoroughly. Wipe and shine wok with the oiled towel. Now the wok is treated and will not rust. Such treatment will not be necessary before each use. Your wok may become blackened after a few uses—it is supposed to be that way. Do not try to brighten it by scouring. No strong detergent should be used on the wok. The round bottom makes cleaning easy, for there is no corner in which the food can stick. Hot water and a dish brush are sufficient to clean it. If you keep it dry after each use, and oil it occasionally, it will last forever.

For convenience in cooking the Chinese way, I strongly recommend the purchase of a wok. If you do not have a wok, a big skillet can also be used for a lot of Chinese cooking.

CLEAVER

The Chinese cleaver is quite a frightening piece of equipment. Its blade is broad and long, about 3 to 4 inches by 8 inches. The big, thick, heavy cleaver is for chopping meat with bones; it is called a "bone knife." The thin and light kind is for slicing meat and cutting vegetables. Cleavers are made of carbon steel and can be sharpened easily with a sharpening stone, which can be obtained in a hardware store. It takes only a few seconds to sharpen a cleaver. There is nothing more annoying than to have a dull knife skid on the meat!

Do not immerse your cleaver completely in water, for water can damage the wooden handle. Just clean the blade and wipe it thoroughly with a towel. Never leave a cleaver wet, for it will rust and stain.

The cleaver is a very talented piece of equipment. It does an excellent job in slicing and mincing meat, cutting vegetables, or chopping bones, and the end of its wooden handle can mash salted black beans. The broad flat blade can scoop out and carry food from the chopping board to other places. Another impressive little trick a cleaver can do is to help peel off a garlic skin in a split second. Put the garlic on a hard surface, and be sure your thumb is out of the way! Give it a whack with the flat of the cleaver blade. Now, you find that the skin comes off the crushed garlic with just a gentle pull.

Each kind of cleaver has its own function, however. So don't force a meat cleaver to chop bones, or use a bone cleaver to ax wood! You will just break its sharp edges and end its service.

Having a cleaver is pleasurable and helpful, but not absolutely necessary. Any sharp knife in your kitchen, a carving knife, a boning knife, or even a steak knife is adequate to help in preparing the meat of the Chinese meal.

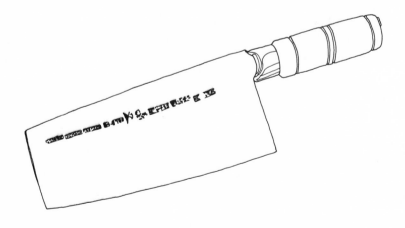

LADLE

For Chinese stir-fry cooking, ideally, the spatula and the ladle should work together like your right hand and left hand. While the ladle in your left hand swirls in the oil, soy sauces, or wine, the spatula in your right hand tosses and stirs. Both coordinate in harmony. However, on the American stove the wok does not rest securely enough on the collar. Therefore, one hand is needed to hold on to one of the handles to ensure steadiness. Otherwise you could easily end up having a floor full of food.

A Chinese ladle is not essential; a big spoon or a serving spoon will do.

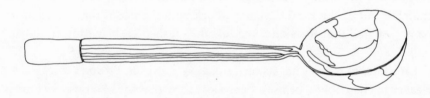

SPATULA

The Chinese spatula is very useful for tossing, stirring, or turning food in the wok. It has a low rim around the heel to catch gravy. However, a pancake turner will serve equally well.

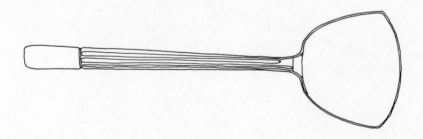

STEAMERS

The traditional Chinese steamers are bamboo and handwoven. They are round baskets with a solidly woven lid on top. In order to save fuel and time, the baskets containing food are stacked and steamed over a wok full of boiling water. Sizes of bamboo steamers vary from 4-inch dim sum steamers to 16-inch seafood or poultry steamers. The most practical size is the 10-inch one in which you can steam a wide range of foods.

Aluminum steamers are very popular. They are not as handsome as the bamboo ones, but they last longer.

However, there are ways to steam food without a steamer (see Steaming).

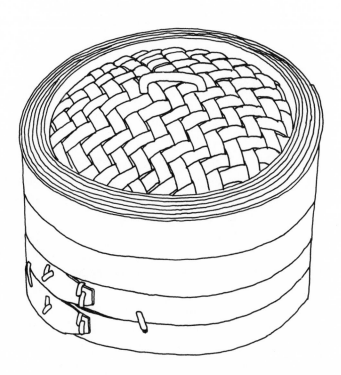

DEEP-FRY DRAINER

The Chinese drainer is woven by hand with shiny brass wires, connected to a bamboo handle. The basket diameter ranges from 4 to 8 inches. For family cooking, the small drainer is more useful than the large one. It is used for draining fried food, blanched meat, vegetables, noodles, or spaghetti. Once I even caught my children using it for catching crayfish!

If you have a big slotted spoon, the drainer is optional.

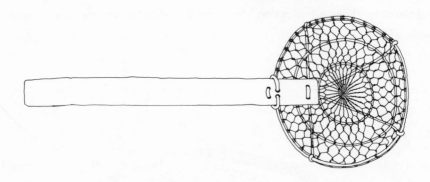

STOVE

The American gas stove is perfect for Chinese cooking. The heat can be controlled instantly. If you have an electric range, controlling the heat is not as smooth as with the gas stove. But it will work out just as well if you turn on two burners at different temperatures. You simply switch the wok to the other burner if the heat is too high or too low.

Beware of the electric stove with an automatically controlled burner. Do not use this burner to deep-fry, for it will not heat the oil to deep-fry temperature.

You can now buy a specially built wok for an electric stove. It is circular and has sloping sides like a regular wok, but has a flat bottom so that it can rest directly on the burner. The highest possible temperature can then be reached due to direct contact with the burner. You can also use a round-bottomed wok with a collar, but it is more difficult to reach high temperature. Or, if you like, for stir-frying, you can remove the collar and rest the wok directly on the burner, using one hand to hold a handle of the wok to steady it. For deep-frying, I suggest that you use a pot instead. A wokful of hot oil without a collar to steady it is too dangerous.

CHOPSTICKS

In Chinese, chopsticks means "quick little ones." If you want to see the quick little ones in action, drop into Chinatown at lunch or supper hours and watch the shopkeepers eat. You will see chopsticks moving at great speed, diving, lifting, and shoveling among the few dishes and the rice bowls.

Chopsticks are used not only for eating but also for stirring ingredients, beating eggs, cutting food, or even as a thermometer to test the oil temperature (see Cooking Techniques).

In the old days, the nobles and the rich used silver, gold, or even jade chopsticks. Silver chopsticks were used by a number of emperors who feared foes might put poison in their food. It was said that the tips of the silver chopsticks would turn black when in contact with poisoned food.

Many Chinese families use lacquered or ivory chopsticks for eating. The ivory ones are given as wedding presents. Like silver flatware, they are well cared for and are expected to last at least a lifetime.

Nowadays, plastic chopsticks are very popular. They are made to look like ivory. Do not use them or the lacquered or ivory ones for cooking or deep-frying, for they will bend or melt with the heat. For cooking, use chopsticks that are made of bamboo or other wood.

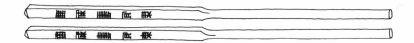

COOKING TECHNIQUES

STIR-FRYING

This unusual cooking method is uniquely Chinese. It is the most essential and frequently used technique in Chinese cooking. Experience, practice, and the training of your eyes, your nose, and even your ears are required for success in this cooking method. Preparation, organization, and concentration are also essential. Because it is very important for you to master this technique, I am going to explain it in detail.

To prepare for stir-frying, you should have all the vegetables or meat cut in advance. The shape and size of the ingredients are generally small and uniform. In most dishes, meat plays the leading role, and its size and shape determine the size and shape of the subordinate ingredients. For instance, in sweet and sour pork, the pork is cut into ¾-inch cubes, then the subordinate ingredients, such as bamboo shoots and green pepper, should be cut into the same size and shape as the pork. If it is a beef with noodles dish, and the beef is to be sliced, then the vegetables should be sliced like the beef. If it is a vegetable dish, such as stir-fry broccoli, the broccoli should be cut two times bigger than bite-size. A big piece of vegetable prevents overcooking and looks much prettier in the dish. All the recipes in this book have specific instructions about the sizes of the meat and vegetables.

After you have the meat and vegetables cut, organize all the ingredients and put them in bowls or on plates near the stove within reach. Now comes the most important part, the technique. Heat the dry wok until it is very hot. This takes from one to two minutes, depending on your stove and the weight of your wok. To know if the wok is hot enough, put your open palm about 3 inches above the bottom of the wok (not on it!). If your palm feels very warm, then the wok is hot enough for stir-frying. (Heating a dry wok before adding the oil prevents the food from sticking.) Swirl the oil in

10

around the rim of the wok, as if you were drawing a circle. Because of the shape of the wok, the oil will naturally run down to grease most of the wok, and it will heat on the way down. (If you use a skillet, spread the oil with a spatula.) Wait a few seconds to allow the oil to get hot but not smoking. Throw in the salt, scallions, ginger, and garlic. Do you hear the sizzling sound? And do you see the scallions, ginger, and garlic spinning around? If so, you are getting there! If not, heat the wok and oil longer next time.

Salt, scallions, ginger, and garlic are almost always put into the wok right after the oil and before the other ingredients. The hot oil draws out the fragrance and the flavor of these seasonings. When the aroma flows from the wok to the air, Chinese chefs call it "wok aroma." Now it is time for you to put in the vegetables or the meat. They are never put in at the same time. Toss and stir the food constantly and vigorously. Use not just your wrist, but your whole arm. You should hear a nice sound and rhythm each time the spatula hits the wok. The intense heat of the oil instantly seals in the flavor and juice of the meat. The color of the vegetables is not only preserved by the hot oil, but is enhanced. All this happens in less than three minutes. Very few stir-fry dishes take longer than five minutes because all the vegetables and meat are cut into small pieces.

Remember that the heat is still high, and your spatula has to stir and toss constantly. Keep your eyes on the color change of the meat or the vegetables. Let your nose experience the fragrance released by the spices. Allow your ears to listen to the various sizzling sounds of the food. Sense it, feel it. If the phone rings, don't answer it. Let the world stop for you for a few minutes.

Be careful not to overcook food. Prolonged cooking will toughen meat and destroy the beautiful green color and the crunchiness of vegetables.

What happens if you fail a few times at the beginning? Stir-frying is learned from experience. Remember the old Chinese saying, "Peking was not built in a day!"

DEEP-FRYING

It is very important to have the oil at the right temperature for deep-frying. If the oil is not hot enough, residues from meat and poultry will cloud it; also the food will absorb more oil and thus become soggy and greasy.

If it is too hot, the food will burn or get brown outside and not be cooked enough inside. On the other hand, if the oil temperature is just right, the food will be crisp and will use less oil.

Since the Chinese do not care about the exact temperature of the oil, a cooking thermometer is not used. We judge the oil by experienced eyes or test it by dropping in a piece of scallion. If the oil is right for deep-frying, the scallion will spin vigorously and sizzle noisily. If it sizzles gently and does not spin, the oil should be a little hotter.

Another easy testing method is to dip a dry bamboo chopstick into the oil. If a great many sizzling bubbles quickly gather around the chopstick, then the oil is ready for frying. If the bubbles surround the chopstick slowly, the oil is not quite ready. Be sure that the chopstick is dry. A wet chopstick does not work! If the oil is smoking, do not put in anything. Turn off the heat and let it cool.

Sometimes oil splatters. I found some students of mine uneasy about the hot oil. They throw in the food and run! But you don't need to be afraid. If you gently slide in the food, the oil will not splatter. To ensure that the oil will not fire single shots at you from time to time, be sure to dry the food thoroughly before slipping it in.

The oil left over from frying can be saved and reused (see chapter on ingredients, page 319).

BLANCHING IN WATER
(For Chicken and Vegetables)

For Chicken: Use 1 quart of boiling water for each cup of sliced, shredded, or diced raw chicken. Immerse chicken in boiling water. Turn off heat at once. Stir to separate pieces. Let chicken blanch in water for 1 minute. Pour into a colander. Rinse thoroughly in cold water to prevent further cooking. Drain. Use as required in recipes.

For Vegetables: Use 2 quarts of boiling water for each ½ pound of fresh vegetables. Immerse vegetables in boiling water. Turn off heat. Let vegetables stay in water for about 10 seconds. Pour into a colander. Rinse thoroughly in cold water to prevent further cooking. Drain. Use as required in recipes.

BLANCHING IN OIL
(For Meat, Poultry, and Seafood)

One of the unique Chinese cooking methods is to blanch food in oil. In Chinese it is called *yu-pao*. This method is different from deep-frying. The food is not fried for a long period to golden brown, but is removed from the oil immediately when it is just done. Usually the food is sliced or shredded into thin pieces before cooking. This method is mostly used by Chinese chefs. The purpose is to achieve the maximum tenderness, smoothness, and lightness of the food.

Use 2 cups of oil for each cup of food.

For Meat: Heat oil to deep-fry temperature (test it with a piece of scallion; it should spin and sizzle noisily) over medium heat. Add the meat. Quickly stir to separate pieces. As soon as the meat loses its redness (it takes less than a minute), remove it with a drainer. Drain, put aside, and use as required in the recipe. Save oil for blanching and cooking again.

For Poultry or Seafood: Over medium heat, heat oil to hot (test it with a piece of scallion; it should just sizzle quickly). Add poultry or seafood. Quickly stir to separate pieces. In about 30 seconds, the poultry should turn milky-white, the seafood whitish or pink. Remove with a drainer. Drain and use as required in the recipe. The oil may be saved for blanching and cooking again.

STEAMING

Steaming in bamboo or perforated metal steamer tray: Put food (buns, dumplings, poultry, meat, seafood, rice, eggs, etc.) on tray. If using rice, line steamer tray with cheesecloth, so that the rice will not fall through.

Use a wok or a pot that will contain the steamer tray, and pour in enough boiling water to reach about 1 inch below the tray. Return water to rapid boil, place tray over water, cover, and steam over high heat according to the time given in the recipe. (*Important:* Never start steaming food if water is not boiling rapidly.) If you have a large amount of food and two steamer trays, you may place food on both trays; place one tray on top of the other, cover the top tray, and steam. Add boiling water to maintain the water level as necessary during steaming.

Steaming on a wire rack: A cake rack will do the job. Place one layer of cheesecloth on rack; place food on cheesecloth. Use a wok or a pot that will hold the rack. Pour in about 1 inch of boiling water. Place one or two small, heavy, heatproof bowls—right side up—in wok or pot. (Lightweight bowls such as thin aluminum containers may float and swim around.) When the water is boiling vigorously, gently place the loaded rack on the bowls. Cover the wok or pot and steam over high heat according to the time given in the recipe. Add boiling water to maintain the water level as necessary during steaming.

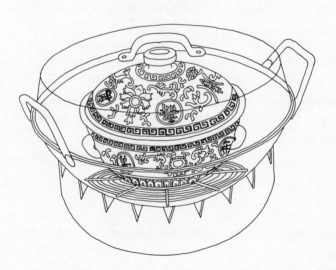

DRY STEAMING

Dry steaming is somewhat like the Western way of cooking food in a double boiler, in which the food is cooked but not touched by the steam.

The method of dry steaming is to put food into a tightly covered heatproof container. A china bowl, a clay pot, or a casserole will do, but a tight lid is essential. Put casserole into a big wok or pot which has a tight lid and can comfortably hold the covered casserole.

Put enough water into the wok or pot to come two-thirds up the side of the casserole. Put lid on wok or pot, and steam over medium-high heat. Add boiling water from time to time to maintain the water level.

This steaming process is usually slow; it takes from two to four hours or more. But the food will come out whole, very tender, and tasty.

RED COOKING

Red cooking refers to the process in which food is covered and cooked slowly over low heat for an extended period. The color of the food runs from brown to black, depending on how much black soy sauce is added. The Chinese prefer to call this method of preparation "red" cooking because, unlike black or brown, red is considered a happy color connoting celebration.

HOW TO TAKE OUT PART OF AN EGG WHITE

Open a hole as big as a blueberry on one end of the egg. Then turn over the egg and let one glob of egg white run out. One glob is about a third of an egg white, and 2 globs are about half of an egg white. To get a whole egg white, open a bigger hole (but not big enough to let the yolk fall out), and let the egg white run out completely, shifting the egg to prevent the yolk from covering the hole. To save washing a bowl, refrigerate the yolk in the shell.

CUTTING TECHNIQUES

Cutting and Slicing: Always cut meat, especially beef, against the grain, to achieve tenderness. Flank steak is the best beef to use, for its grain is clear. If you want to cut meat into paper-thin slices, it is easier to cut or slice it when it is half-frozen. The size of a slice varies according to the recipe.

Shredding: The size of a shred in general is the size of a matchstick, ⅛ inch wide, ⅛ inch thick, and 1 to 2 inches long. The only way to shred is to slice the meat or vegetable first, and then cut each slice into shreds.

Dicing and Mincing: Dicing means cutting ingredients into peanut-sized or pea-sized pieces. In mincing, ingredients are chopped into rice-sized pieces or cut so finely that they become a paste. The best way to dice or mince is to cut ingredients into slices (thickness according to the recipe), cut slices into strips, then dice or mince strips crosswise into desired size.

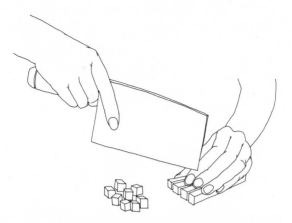

Cubing: Cubing means cutting the ingredients into small chunks. Follow the recipe for required size of cubes.

Double Scoring: Double scoring is mostly done to gizzards and kidneys. It is similar to the way a baked ham is scored, but the depth varies. For gizzards: score deeply at $\frac{1}{8}$-inch intervals from the center hump to $\frac{1}{8}$ inch from the base. For kidneys: score diagonally from the top at $\frac{1}{8}$-inch intervals to $\frac{1}{8}$ inch from the flat underside.

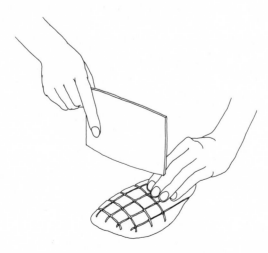

Dim Sum, Appetizers, and Cold Dishes

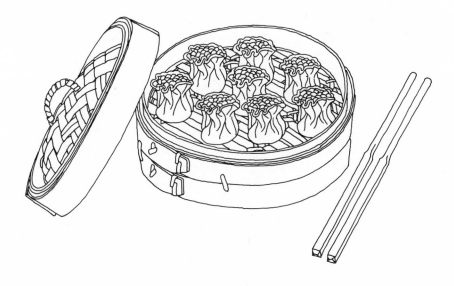

DIM SUM

If you go to China or Hong Kong someday, be sure to visit the teahouses and have some of their specialty, the famous dim sum.

Dim sum are small stuffed dumplings, pastries, and little cakes. In Chinese, the words *dim sum* roughly mean "point to those that please your heart."

The teahouses open early in the morning, depending on their location. Some open as early as 5:00 A.M. to accommodate the night-shift factory workers, but most start serving around 8:00 A.M. Since most Chinese do not make dim sum at home, preferring to have them in a teahouse, the teahouses are always full.

In most of the teahouses, young girls between eleven and fifteen are hired to parade the dim sum around the hall. Each girl carries a big tray in front of her, secured by shoulder straps. Stacks of small bamboo steamers containing various dim sum are piled on the tray. Each calls out the names of the dim sum she is carrying in a slow, singsong voice, "Hah . . . Gau . . . Shao . . . Mai. . . ." You sit there and chat over a cup of tea, one ear alert to the conversation and one ear to the singsong voice. A little signal and baskets of piping hot dim sum come right to your table. Dumplings stuffed with shrimp, pork, or crabmeat, pastry filled with sweets or meat, steamed stuffed buns, sweet cakes, and others are there for you to choose. All of them are fresh, handmade by many dim sum chefs and dozens of helpers who stayed up all night through dawn.

Dim sum are prepared only in sufficient quantity to last for one morning, so that there are no leftovers. Usually, by 11:30 A.M., most of them are gone. At noon, the menu will be changed, offering no dim sum, but noodles, rice, and other dishes.

In the teahouses, the only beverages served are various kinds of tea. We believe that tea helps digestion, relieves heartburn, clears our minds, and lifts our spirits.

For many Chinese, teahouses are not just for sipping tea and eating dim sum, but also places for doing business and making deals. They are also a very good place to read the newspapers, listen to gossip, make a friend, or pick an argument. That is how my father spends his mornings in Hong Kong: retirement, Chinese style.

茶葉蛋

TEA EGGS
makes 8

When the gusty cold wind from the North swept across the Great Wall, China's winter was bitingly cold. Evenings came early, and the nights seemed long. I remember that in those wintery nights nobody seemed to have things to do away from home. The little ones were half-asleep while the adults' mah-jongg game went on. We teens, in-between, had little to do. We did not mind, though, for we were listening, waiting for the voices of the food hawkers of the night. Suddenly, our hearts grew quiet as the bell and the familiar singsong voice drew near. "Tea eggs!" we called. "The egg man is here!" The mah-jongg stopped. Small legs flew out from beds and rushed to the door. Soon the steaming hot eggs disappeared; only the shells and the fragrance remained. The little ones went again to their beds, hoping to stay awake until the cake man arrived. The mah-jongg resumed. And then we—the not old and not too young—lingered on, waiting for the bamboo click—the noodle man—to come.

PREPARATION OF INGREDIENTS

8 hard-boiled eggs, unshelled

TEA MIXTURE (MIX IN A BOWL)*

> *4 teaspoons salt*
> *½ teaspoon five-fragrance powder*
> *4 teaspoons tea leaves (any dark-colored tea, such as lychee black or orange pekoe)*
> *3 cups hot water*
> *3 tablespoons black soy sauce*
> *1 tablespoon thin soy sauce*

DIRECTIONS FOR COOKING

1. Use a spoon to gently and evenly tap and crack each hard-boiled egg. *Do not peel them!*

2. Immerse eggs in tea mixture. Simmer for about 2 hours, adding water from time to time to cover eggs. Turn off heat, and let eggs stay in tea mixture for another couple of hours. During this time, the tea mixture will seep through the tiny cracks in the shell, leaving a delicate design on the eggs. Drain, peel, and serve hot or cold, whole or sliced. Or you may let your guests have the pleasure of peeling their own eggs.

鍋貼

KUO-TIEHS

(PEKING PAN-FRIED DUMPLINGS)
makes about 18

PREPARATION OF INGREDIENTS

½ pound Chinese celery cabbage

FILLING (MIX IN A BOWL)*

> *½ pound ground pork*
> *1 scallion: minced, including green part*
> *2 teaspoons pale dry sherry*
> *2 teaspoons thin soy sauce*
> *¼ teaspoon salt*
> *¼ teaspoon sugar*

2 cups all-purpose flour
about ½ cup cold water
about ¾ cup boiling water
about 6 tablespoons oil
Soy-Vinegar Dip (see recipe) or Soy-Chili Dip (see recipe)

DIRECTIONS FOR COOKING

1. Put celery cabbage on a steamer or a rack and steam over water for about 10 minutes or until tender. Mince cabbage, squeeze out excess water, then mix cabbage with filling mixture. Keep refrigerated before use.

2. Put 1 cup flour in a mixing bowl, and add cold water a little at a time. Mix and knead into a soft smooth dough. Put the second cup of flour in a separate mixing bowl. Add boiling water gradually. Mix and knead into a soft dough. Mix hot and cold doughs together and knead until homogenized—dough should be elastic and not sticky. Cover it with a slightly damp towel and let rest for about 15 minutes.

3. Roll dough into a long sausage, 1 inch in diameter. Pinch off pieces as big as the size of a walnut. Flour them slightly and roll them into small balls. With a rolling pin, roll each into a thin circle. Put about a tablespoonful of filling in the center of each circle. Make as illustrated.

4. Place kuo-tiehs on a floured tray and cover with a towel.

5. Put 2 tablespoons oil in a big skillet and spread it evenly. Line up the kuo-tiehs in skillet. Pour in enough cold water to come halfway up the sides of the kuo-tiehs. Cover and cook for about 3 minutes. Remove from heat and drain off liquid from skillet. (Do not remove kuo-tiehs from skillet, but tip the skillet and drain by opening the cover slightly.) Rearrange the kuo-tiehs. Add about 4 tablespoons oil to pan and spread it evenly. Cover and pan-fry over medium-low heat until kuo-tieh bottoms are crisp and brown (about 5 minutes). If they stick to the pan, usually it is because they are not browned enough, or the oil was not spread evenly. Serve hot with choice of dip.

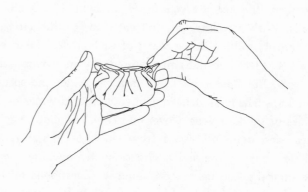

蝦餃

HAH GAUS
makes about 24

(CANTONESE STEAMED SHRIMP DUMPLINGS)

This is one of the favorite Cantonese teahouse dim sum. These walnut-sized dumplings are steamed and shrimp-filled. To the Cantonese, a true hah gau has paper-thin, translucent dough, with shrimp in it crisp and almost crunchy in the mouth.

Making hah gaus is time-consuming. It will seem a lot of work, little to eat, but well worth the effort. Hah gaus are generally served as a teatime snack or for breakfast, not as a full family meal. The Chinese seldom make them at home, preferring to have them occasionally in a teahouse. Making hah gaus needs practice and patience, for wheat starch, unlike white flour, has no elasticity. Do not give up if you fail the first time.

PREPARATION OF INGREDIENTS

1 cup wheat starch, sifted
¾ cup boiling water
1 tablespoon lard or oil

FILLING (MIX IN A BOWL. KEEP REFRIGERATED BEFORE USE)*

> *½ pound fresh shrimp: shell, devein, rinse in running cold water,*
>   *drain, pat dry, cut into peanut-sized pieces*
> *6 minced water chestnuts*
> *2 tablespoons minced pork fat or bacon fat*
> *½ teaspoon salt*
> *½ teaspoon sugar*
> *2 teaspoons sesame seed oil*
> *2 teaspoons pale dry sherry*

Soy-Sesame Oil Dip (see recipe)

DIRECTIONS FOR COOKING

1. Prepare the hah gau skins: Put wheat starch in a medium-sized bowl, and make a well in the center. Pour in boiling water, stirring quickly with a spoon. Add lard or oil, and knead dough until it is homogenized. Then roll dough into a 1-inch-diameter sausage. Cover with a warm damp towel and let it rest for about 15 minutes. Cut dough into chestnut-sized pieces and roll them into round marbles. Cover them with a towel.

2. Assemble the hah gaus: Oil one side of a cleaver or the blade of a broad knife. Press oiled blade on each marble of dough to make a thin circle. Put about 1½ teaspoons of filling in the center of each circle. Make hah gaus as illustrated in recipe for kuo-tiehs.

3. Place hah gaus on an oiled plate and cover.

4. Steam hah gaus over water for 10 minutes. Serve hot with dip.

燒賣

SHAO-MAIS
(CANTONESE STEAMED DUMPLINGS WITH PORK AND SHRIMP FILLING)
makes about 24

PREPARATION OF INGREDIENTS

24 wonton skins

FILLING (MIX IN A BOWL. KEEP REFRIGERATED BEFORE USE)*

> *½ pound ground pork*
> *3 Chinese dried mushrooms: soak in hot water until spongy,*
> *discard stems, mince caps*
> *½ pound fresh shrimp: shell, devein, clean with running cold*
> *water, pat dry, cut into peanut-sized pieces*
> *½ teaspoon sugar*
> *2 teaspoons sesame seed oil*
> *⅛ teaspoon ground pepper*
> *½ teaspoon salt*
> *1 tablespoon thin soy sauce*
> *1 teaspoon pale dry sherry*

Soy-Sesame Dip (see recipe)

DIRECTIONS FOR COOKING

1. Cut wonton skins into round circles. Put about 1 tablespoon of filling in the center of each circle. Gather sides around filling to form pleats. Squeeze the center of the dumpling. Press down the top to firm up the filling. Tap shao-mai gently to flatten bottom so it can stand up. You may make the shao-mais in advance and refrigerate them before steaming.

2. Grease the bottom of a steamer or a heatproof plate with oil. Arrange shao-mais on it. Cover and steam over boiling water for 15 minutes. Serve hot with dip.

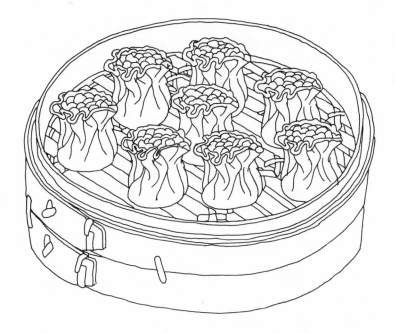

炸蘿蔔絲餅

ROADSIDE FRIED TURNIP FRITTERS
makes about 12

I first came upon these fritters when I was eight, in a small farming town whose name meant "river gate near the Pearl River." It was a school field trip. Like little ducklings, we were herded through a busy food marketplace where everybody was either cooking, selling, yelling, or eating. The air was thick with the smell of steamed clams, snails, noodles, and the sweet aroma from the spiced innards of pork and beef.

Somehow I found myself all alone, with a mouthful and a handful of these fritters, standing and watching the vendors' hands as they quickly ladled the batter into the hot oil and scooped out other fritters.

Besides my hand getting five smacks from the ruler, I had to stay in school until dusk, finishing ten pages of "I should obey the teacher," before I could go home. The face of the anxious teacher has long gone; only the memory of those fritters has remained.

Twenty-five years later, I found a woman cooking the same fritters on the roadside in Shatin, Hong Kong. I bought two dozen and chatted with her for two hours, learning about her grandchildren, her sons, and all about these fine fritters.

Here I give my thanks to this good woman and wish her well.

PREPARATION OF INGREDIENTS

about 1 pound Chinese white giant turnip: peel off skin, then use potato peeler to shave turnip into thin strips (to make 2½ cups)*
about 3 ounces raw sweet potato: peel and shave as with turnip (to make 1 cup)*
1 cup chicken broth (not condensed)
1 cup flour
1 cup cornstarch
½ teaspoon salt
2 Chinese pork sausages: mince into small pieces
⅔ cup shredded scallions: strips 1½ inches long, including green part
about 6 cups oil
Soy-Vinegar Dip (see recipe)

DIRECTIONS FOR COOKING

1. Combine all ingredients except oil and soy-vinegar dip in a bowl in the order listed. This batter can be prepared in advance and refrigerated.

2. Heat oil in wok over high heat to deep-fry temperature. Pour ¼ cup batter into hot oil to make one fritter. Deep-fry both sides to light golden color. Two or three fritters may be deep-fried at the same time, but too many fritters will lower the oil's temperature and lengthen the frying time. Remove batter crumbs from oil. The fritters should be crisp outside and soft inside. Drain on paper towels. Put in 275-degree oven to keep warm while other fritters are frying. Serve hot with dip.

炸香蕉夾

DEEP-FRIED SHRIMP-FILLED BANANA SANDWICHES, SOUTHERN STYLE
makes 9

PREPARATION OF INGREDIENTS

2 big peeled bananas: cut each into 3 sections across, then slice
each section into 3 lengthwise slabs
about 2 tablespoons cornstarch

FILLING (MIX IN A BOWL. KEEP REFRIGERATED BEFORE USE)*

 4 ounces fresh shrimp: shell, devein, rinse in cold water, pat dry
 1 slice bacon: cook until crisp, mince
 ½ teaspoon sesame seed oil
 ½ teaspoon thin soy sauce
 ⅛ teaspoon white pepper
 ½ teaspoon pale dry sherry

about 4 cups oil

BATTER (MIX UNTIL SMOOTH)

 ½ cup flour
 7 tablespoons water
 ¼ teaspoon salt
 ½ teaspoon baking powder
 1 tablespoon oil
 1½ teaspoons sesame seeds

DIRECTIONS FOR COOKING

1. Dust each slice of banana with cornstarch.

2. Like making a sandwich, spread some filling on a slice of banana and top with another banana slice.

3. Heat oil to deep-fry temperature. Dip each sandwich in batter, and put in hot oil to deep-fry until crisp and golden brown. (Do not deep-fry too many at one time because the oil temperature will be cooled off too quickly and the batter will not be crisp.) Serve hot at once.

蝦土司

SHRIMP TOAST
makes 32 pieces

PREPARATION OF INGREDIENTS

SHRIMP PASTE (MIX IN A BOWL. KEEP REFRIGERATED BEFORE USE)*

> ½ *pound fresh shrimp: shell, devein, wash in cold running*
>   *water, drain, dry, mince into fine paste*
> 1 *tablespoon minced fat pork or fat bacon*
> 1 *teaspoon pale dry sherry*
> 1 *beaten egg*
> 1 *pinch white pepper*
> ¼ *teaspoon salt*
> ¼ *teaspoon sugar*
> 1 *teaspoon thin soy sauce*
> ⅓ *cup minced water chestnuts*
> 1 *scallion: mince, including green part*
> 2 *teaspoons cornstarch*
> ½ *teaspoon sesame seed oil*
> ¼ *teaspoon five-fragrance powder*

8 *pieces thin white bread (thin diet bread is best): cut off crusts,*
   quarter bread, leave pieces out overnight to dry
32 *flat leaves parsley (optional)*
3 *tablespoons white sesame seeds (optional)*
about 4 cups oil for deep-frying

DIRECTIONS FOR COOKING

1. Spread shrimp paste on bread, more in the middle and less on the edges. Press on parsley leaf. Sprinkle the shrimp side with sesame seeds.

2. Heat oil to deep-fry temperature. Put toast in oil, shrimp side down. Deep-fry until golden brown. Drain on paper towel. Put in a warm oven to wait for the others to cook. Serve hot.

NOTE: *Shrimp toast can be frozen uncooked. Deep-fry while still frozen.*

蘑菇鳳肝脆角

CRISP TURNOVERS WITH MUSHROOM AND CHICKEN LIVER FILLING
makes 12

PREPARATION OF INGREDIENTS

about 3 tablespoons oil for stir-frying
1 scallion: cut into pea-sized pieces, including green part
4 ounces ground pork
2 cups thinly sliced fresh mushrooms
2 fresh chicken livers: put in boiling water for 20 seconds, cut
    into thin small pieces
⅓ cup minced water chestnuts

SAUCE MIXTURE (MIX IN A BOWL)*

   ¼ teaspoon salt
   2 tablespoons thin soy sauce
   ¼ teaspoon sugar
   1 tablespoon pale dry sherry
   ⅛ teaspoon ground pepper
   1 tablespoon cornstarch
   1½ tablespoons water

¼ teaspoon five-fragrance powder
½ teaspoon sesame seed oil
10 to 12 slices soft white bread: cut off crust, roll bread until
    thin with rolling pin, cover with damp towel
1 egg yolk
about 4 cups oil for deep-frying
Soy-Vinegar Dip (optional; see recipe)

DIRECTIONS FOR COOKING

1. Heat wok and add oil for stir-frying. When oil is hot, add scallions and ground pork, and stir-fry until pork is cooked. Add mushrooms and cook for about 30 seconds. Add livers and stir-fry until they just lose their redness. Add water chestnuts and mix well. Stir in sauce mixture and cook for 15 seconds. Add five-fragrance powder and sesame seed oil. Mix well and cool in refrigerator.

2. Put about 1½ tablespoons cooled filling in center of bread slice and fold in half. Moisten edges with egg yolk and press to seal. Use scissors to trim into shape of half-moon. Make the rest of the turnovers in the same manner. Heat 4 cups oil to deep-fry temperature. Deep-fry turnovers to golden brown. Drain on paper towels. Serve hot with or without dip.

炸餛飩

FRIED WONTONS WITH SHRIMP OR PORK FILLING
makes 40

This is an excellent appetizer and finger food for cocktail hours. But the Chinese always eat fried wontons with a sweet and sour dish, such as Sweet and Sour Pork (see recipe) rather than with plum sauce.

PREPARATION OF INGREDIENTS

40 wonton skins

FILLING (MIX IN A BOWL. REFRIGERATE BEFORE USE)*

> *6 ounces fresh shrimp (or ground pork): shell, devein, rinse in running cold water, pat dry, cut into peanut-sized pieces*
> *about ½ egg white*
> *1 scallion: cut into pea-sized pieces, including green part*
> *¼ cup minced bamboo shoots*
> *½ teaspoon sesame seed oil*
> *½ teaspoon pale dry sherry*
> *2 teaspoons thin soy sauce*
> *1 large pinch ground pepper*
> *¼ teaspoon salt*

about 4 cups oil for deep-frying
Plum Sauce Dip (see recipe)

DIRECTIONS FOR COOKING

1. Cover wonton skins with a damp cloth to keep them from drying.

2. Put about 1½ teaspoons of shrimp or pork filling in the middle of each skin. Moisten edges with water. Make wontons as illustrated.

3. Heat oil to deep-fry temperature. Deep-fry wontons, several at a time, until golden brown. Drain on paper towels. Serve hot or warm with dip.

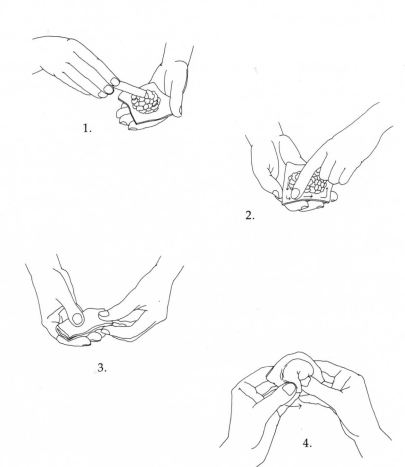

鷄絲蝦肉春卷

SPRING ROLLS WITH SHRIMP AND CHICKEN FILLING
makes 20

Egg rolls are similar to these spring rolls—except that spring rolls are purely Chinese, and egg rolls were created in the West by the Chinese for the Westerners. Once you taste spring rolls, you do not want egg rolls.

Spring rolls are filled with all sorts of delicious ingredients (not American cabbage), juicy and tasty. The skins are paper thin, like transparent crepes. They are made from marshmallowlike dough, adhered to a hot iron surface, and then peeled off by hand. Each one is 9 inches in diameter. When fried, they are crisp, smooth, and delicate.

Egg roll skins actually are machine-made noodle sheets, cut into 8-inch squares. If they are thin, after frying, they are also crisp, but not quite smooth, covered with tiny bubbles. The Chinese use egg roll skins only if spring roll skins are not available.

In many Chinese restaurants, especially the good ones, they prepare spring rolls as well as egg rolls. If you are Chinese, they give you spring rolls. The non-Chinese are presented with egg rolls.

PREPARATION OF INGREDIENTS

3 tablespoons oil for stir-frying
2 slices fresh ginger root, each as big and thick as a quarter
1 clove garlic: crush and peel

SHRIMP MIXTURE (MIX IN A BOWL. REFRIGERATE BEFORE USE)*

> *6 ounces fresh shrimp: shell, devein, rinse in running cold water,*
>   *pat dry, cut into peanut-sized pieces*
> *about ½ egg white*
> *1 teaspoon pale dry sherry*
> *¼ teaspoon salt*

8 Chinese dried mushrooms: soak in hot water until spongy,
  discard stems, cut caps into thin strips
6 water chestnuts: cut into thin strips
3 cups fresh bean sprouts or shredded Chinese celery cabbage
1 cup shredded bamboo shoots
2 scallions: cut into 1½-inch lengths, then shred

CHICKEN MIXTURE. BLANCH MIXTURE IN WATER [SEE COOKING TECHNIQUES].
DRAIN. (MIX IN A BOWL. REFRIGERATE BEFORE USE)*

> *8 ounces boned, skinless chicken breast: shred into matchstick*
>   *strips (to make 1 cup)*
> *1 teaspoon cornstarch*
> *¼ teaspoon salt*
> *⅛ teaspoon sugar*
> *about ½ egg white*

SAUCE MIXTURE (MIX IN A BOWL)*

> *1 tablespoon black soy sauce*
> *2 tablespoons thin soy sauce*
> *1 tablespoon sesame seed oil*
> *1 teaspoon cornstarch*
> *1 tablespoon water*
> *¾ teaspoon salt*

20 Shanghai spring roll skins or egg roll skins
1 egg yolk (if spring roll skins are used)
a small bowl of water (if egg roll skins are used)
about 4 cups oil for deep-frying
Plum Sauce Dip (see recipe) or Mustard-Oil Dip (see recipe) or
  Soy-Vinegar Dip (see recipe)

DIRECTIONS FOR COOKING

1. Heat wok over high heat. Swirl in 3 tablespoons oil for stir-frying. When oil is hot, slightly brown ginger and garlic and then discard them. Add shrimp mixture. Stir-fry briefly until shrimp just turn whitish (less than 20 seconds). Remove with a drainer; press shrimp with a spoon to drain oil back into wok. Put shrimp in a bowl.

2. Reheat oil remaining in wok over medium heat, and add mush-rooms. Stir-fry for about 15 seconds to draw out their flavor. Add water chestnuts, bean sprouts or celery cabbage, bamboo shoots, and scallions. Stir-fry for about 20 seconds. Add chicken mixture. Mix well. Stir in sauce mixture and return shrimp to wok. Stir-fry for 15 seconds or until chicken is thoroughly hot. Put on plate to cool in refrigerator before wrapping.* Clean and dry wok.

3. Put 2 to 3 tablespoons of filling on each spring roll or egg roll skin. Cover the remaining skins to keep them from drying out. Moisten edges and seal with egg yolk (for spring roll skins) or water (for egg roll skins). See illustrations.

4. Heat about 4 cups oil in wok to deep-fry temperature. Deep-fry spring rolls until golden brown. Drain on paper towels. Serve hot with dip.

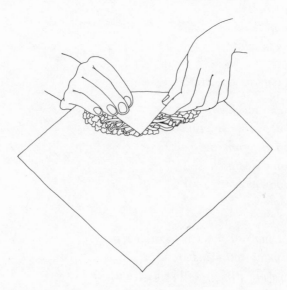

Above and opposite page:
Filling and rolling an egg roll.

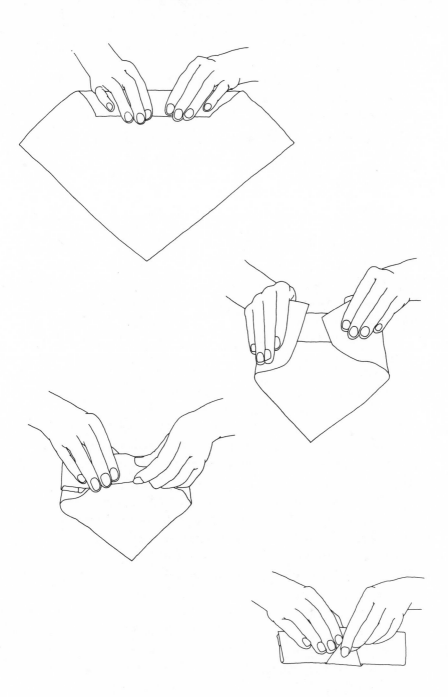

葱油大餅

SCALLION BREAD
makes two rounds of bread, each 10 inches in diameter and ½ inch thick

In many regions of China, steamed, pan-fried, or baked bread is often served in place of rice. Or it is simply eaten as a snack. This bread is crisp outside and soft inside.

PREPARATION OF INGREDIENTS

2 cups all-purpose flour (unsifted)
1 teaspoon salt
about ¾ cup boiling water
2 tablespoons baking powder
about ½ cup cold water
3 scallions: chop into pea-sized pieces, including green part
about ½ cup oil

DIRECTIONS FOR COOKING

1. In a mixing bowl, place 1 cup flour and salt and mix well. Make a well in the flour and pour in the boiling water. Mix and knead well.

2. In another mixing bowl, mix baking powder and remaining flour together; add cold water. Mix and knead well.

3. Combine hot and cold doughs and knead until they are homogenized. Put in a covered bowl and let rest at room temperature for at least 2 hours or more (the dough should become soft and sticky).

4. Sprinkle flour on a board. Divide dough into two equal portions, and roll each into a ball. With a rolling pin, roll each ball into a pancake ¼ to ⅓ inch thick and 10 inches in diameter. Sprinkle each pancake with chopped scallions, pressing them into dough.

5. Heat 3 to 4 tablespoons oil in a large skillet. Pan-fry scallion pancakes one at a time over low heat in the covered skillet. Turn once so that both sides are golden brown. Cut into large slices. Serve hot at once.

葱肉燒餅

SHAO-BINGS WITH SCALLION AND HAM FILLING
makes 14 to 16

In Chinese *shao* means "bake," and *bing* means "cake" or "biscuit." There
are many different kinds of shao-bings in China. Some are stuffed with
meat, some with scallions, others with a sweet. Some are plain, like your
hard rolls, and topped with sesame seeds. The stuffed ones are usually eaten
as a snack. The plain ones are eaten with a meat dish.

My family and I like the ones stuffed with scallions and ham best, for
they are good both as a snack for the children and to eat with meat.

PREPARATION OF INGREDIENTS

2 teaspoons active dry yeast
about 1 cup lukewarm water
1 tablespoon sugar
2 teaspoons sesame seed oil
3 cups sifted all-purpose flour

FILLING (MIX IN A BOWL)*

> *½ cup minced scallions including green part*
> *½ cup chopped Smithfield ham or cooked crisp bacon: mince*

1 tablespoon honey mixed in bowl with 1 tablespoon water
about ¼ cup white sesame seeds

DIRECTIONS FOR COOKING

1. In a mixing bowl, combine yeast and ½ cup lukewarm water. Stir
well. Add sugar, oil, and flour. Pour in remaining lukewarm water. Mix
and knead into a ball. Turn dough onto a floured surface and knead until
smooth and soft, not sticky. If dough is stiff or dry, wet your hands under
warm tap water and knead the dough until it is soft. If the dough is sticky,

dust it with a little flour, and knead until it feels smooth and silky. Put dough in a big clean bowl, and cover bowl with a piece of plastic wrap (it should not touch the dough) so that you can see the dough rise. This takes from 35 minutes to one hour, depending upon room temperature.

2. Turn on oven to 400 degrees while you are making shao-bings. Punch dough down and turn it out onto a floured surface. Knead well. Roll into a thick sausage and cut off pieces as big as a lime. Cover with a towel to keep from drying. Roll each piece between your palms into a round ball. With a rolling pin, roll ball into a circle about 2½ inches in diameter and not less than ¼ inch thick. Put about 2 teaspoons of filling in the center of the circle. Gather up the edges and pinch them together tightly. Smooth out pinch marks as you roll shao-bings between your palms into a round ball. Brush top generously with honey water, and press this side on the sesame seeds. Cover shao-bings with towel to prevent drying.

3. Arrange shao-bings seed side up on a greased cookie sheet or a pan lined with aluminum foil. Bake in oven for 15 minutes or until golden brown. Serve hot or warm.

Note: *Dough can be made a few hours ahead of time. Keep it in a covered bowl, then make it into shao-bings when you are ready.*

春卷皮及餛飩皮

EGG ROLL OR WONTON SKINS
makes 20 egg roll skins or 80 wonton skins

Making egg roll or wonton skins is not difficult, but it is time-consuming. The Chinese prefer buying the skins to making them at home. The skins from the markets are machine-made, usually thin and fresh. If you cannot obtain the skins in your area, here is the recipe for making them.

PREPARATION OF INGREDIENTS

3 cups all-purpose flour
½ teaspoon salt
2 eggs: beat until slightly foamy
¾ cup cold water

DIRECTIONS FOR COOKING

1. Put flour in a big mixing bowl. Add salt and mix well. Make a well in the center of the flour. Add eggs, and mix into the flour with your hands. Knead mixture while adding water gradually.

2. When mixture becomes a soft dough, turn it onto a floured surface. Knead until dough becomes homogenized and elastic. Put in a bowl, and cover with a slightly damp towel. Allow dough to stand at room temperature for about 45 minutes.

3. Turn dough onto a floured surface again. Divide dough into 20 equal portions. Roll each portion into a round ball and cover with a towel to prevent drying out.

4. Take one ball at a time, and roll it on a floured surface with a rolling pin until it becomes a very thin skin, almost transparent, approximately 8 inches in diameter. Dust the skin on both sides with flour, and let it stand uncovered at room temperature for about 30 minutes. (This is to allow the skin to stiffen slightly so that it will be easier to handle.) Cover the skin with a dry towel. These egg roll skins are now ready to be used. They can also be frozen in stacks (no need to separate them); thaw at room temperature before use.

5. If you want wonton skins, just quarter the egg roll skins, and trim them into 3-inch-square pieces.

醉鷄

DRUNKEN CHICKEN

(A COLD DISH)

6 to 8 servings

PREPARATION OF INGREDIENTS

2 whole chicken breasts (about 2 pounds) with skin and bones
2 teaspoons salt
½ teaspoon sugar
1 cup Chinese Shaohsing wine (or your favorite white wine)

DIRECTIONS FOR COOKING

1. Clean chicken breasts and pat dry. Cut breasts in half (you may bone the chicken, though the Chinese prefer it with bone). Rub breasts evenly with salt and keep in refrigerator overnight.

2. Place chicken breasts on rack over water, cover, and steam for about 15 minutes. Remove chicken and put in a dish.

3. Mix sugar with wine and pour it over chicken. Cover and soak chicken for one or two days or more before serving. Turn pieces from time to time to soak evenly. Drain chicken, place it on a chopping board, and chop the breasts, crosswise, into ½-inch pieces. Arrange the pieces on a serving plate. Serve cold or at room temperature.

NOTE: *The chicken in the wine sauce, covered and refrigerated, will keep at least a week.*

燻鷄

SMOKED CHICKEN, PEKING STYLE
(A COLD DISH)
about 8 servings

PREPARATION OF INGREDIENTS

RUBBING MIXTURE (COMBINE, THEN USE TO RUB CHICKEN INSIDE AND OUT. MARINATE IN REFRIGERATOR FOR 2 TO 3 HOURS)*

> *1 tablespoon pale dry sherry*
> *1 tablespoon salt*
> *2 teaspoons flower peppercorn powder*
> *1 teaspoon five-fragrance powder*
> *½ teaspoon sugar*

1 fresh chicken, 3½ pounds

SPICED WATER (COMBINE IN WOK)

> *12 cups water*
> *2 cinnamon sticks*
> *4 whole star anise*

1 chunk (big as a walnut) fresh ginger root: crush slightly
1 cup black soy sauce
2 tablespoons sugar
2 teaspoons salt

½ cup (loosely packed) light brown sugar
3 tablespoons dark-colored tea leaves, such as orange pekoe or
lychee black tea
1 tablespoon sesame seed oil mixed with 1 tablespoon thin soy
sauce

DIRECTIONS FOR COOKING

1. Simmer spiced water in wok for about 15 minutes. Add chicken. Cover and simmer over low heat for about 40 minutes, turning once, or until chicken is just done.

2. Remove chicken from wok. Drain; put aside. (The spiced water can be frozen and reused for the next chicken; discard the anise, ginger, and cinnamon sticks.)

3. Line a big wok with heavy aluminum foil. Sprinkle bottom of wok with brown sugar and tea. Arrange four bamboo chopsticks or metal skewers overlapping each other to form a tick-tack-toe design. Rest chicken on chopsticks, breast side up. Cover wok tightly. (The cover should be high enough to allow the smoke to circulate, and the chicken should be at least 1 inch above the smoking ingredients.)

4. Turn heat to high. Smoke chicken for 20 minutes. Turn off heat, but do not uncover. Allow the smoke to subside (about 15 minutes).

5. Remove chicken to a chopping board and chop as illustrated in the chapter on duck. Brush chopped chicken with sesame seed oil and soy sauce mixture. Serve chicken cold or warm.

NOTE: *This chicken can be prepared a day in advance.*

凍羊羔

JELLIED LAMB
(A COLD DISH)
about 4 servings

PREPARATION OF INGREDIENTS

1½ pounds lean lamb (or 1 pound lamb and ½ pound lean pork)
½ pound pork skin
1 teaspoon sugar
¼ cup black soy sauce
¼ cup Chinese Shaohsing wine or pale dry sherry
3 whole star anise
3 slices fresh ginger root, each as big and thick as a quarter
2 cloves garlic: crack and peel

DIRECTIONS FOR COOKING

1. Fill a big pot with about 10 cups of water and bring to a rolling boil. Immerse lamb and pork skin in water and bring to a boil. Cook over high heat for 2 minutes. Turn off heat. Remove lamb and pork skin from pot. Discard water.

2. Put lamb and pork skin in a medium-sized pot. Add 3 cups of water and all the remaining ingredients. Cover and simmer until lamb is tender. There should be about 1 cup of sauce remaining in pot. Discard pork skin, star anise, ginger, and garlic. Cut lamb into sugar-cube-sized pieces.

3. Put the cubed lamb and the sauce in a bread pan. Cover and put in refrigerator to jell for 4 to 6 hours.*

4. Slice jellied lamb into ¼-inch pieces. Arrange pieces slightly overlapping on a serving platter. Serve cold.

棒棒鷄

PONG-PONG CHICKEN, SZECHWAN STYLE
(HACKED CHICKEN, A COLD DISH)

2 to 4 servings

PREPARATION OF INGREDIENTS

2 big chicken breasts, with skin and bones
⅓ cup uncooked skinless peanuts
1 cup oil
1 cup sliced cucumber or shredded celery: keep refrigerated
⅓ cup shredded scallions, cut 1½ inches lengthwise, including
    green part
1 tablespoon finely minced fresh ginger root
1 tablespoon minced garlic
¼ teaspoon flower peppercorn powder

SAUCE MIXTURE (MIX TOGETHER SMOOTHLY IN A BOWL)*

3 tablespoons smooth peanut butter
2½ tablespoons black soy sauce
1½ tablespoons Chinese red vinegar
2 tablespoons sesame seed oil
1½ teaspoons sugar
1 to 2 teaspoons chili oil (see recipe)
1 tablespoon pale dry sherry
2 tablespoons water

DIRECTIONS FOR COOKING

1. Immerse chicken breasts in a large pot of cold water. Cover and bring water to a rolling boil. Turn heat down and simmer for about 10 minutes or until just done. Drain, bone, and cool. Discard water.*

2. Deep-fry peanuts in 1 cup oil until golden brown. Drain and cool. Put in plastic bag and crush coarsely with rolling pin. Put aside for later use.*

3. Arrange cucumber on serving platter and top with half the scallions.

4. Put chicken breasts on a chopping board. Cut them in half, then crosswise into ¼-inch pieces. Arrange chicken pieces on cucumber and scallions. Sprinkle with ginger, garlic, flower peppercorn powder, and crushed peanuts. Then evenly pour sauce mixture over them. Sprinkle remaining scallions on top. Toss before eating. Serve at room temperature.

鷄絲拌黃瓜

CHICKEN SHREDS AND CUCUMBER SALAD
about 8 servings

PREPARATION OF INGREDIENTS

*2 cups agar-agar: soak in cold water until soft, cut into 2-inch
    lengths
2 cups sliced cucumber: peel and cut in half, remove seeds, slice
    thinly
2 boned, skinless chicken breasts: cut into matchstick strips,
    blanch in water (see Cooking Techniques)
½ cup jellyfish skin (optional) soaked in cold water overnight,
    blanched in water as chicken, shredded in matchstick pieces
2 tablespoons oil*

SAUCE MIXTURE (MIX IN A SMALL BOWL NO LONGER THAN 30 MINUTES BEFORE
SERVING—OTHERWISE MUSTARD WILL LOSE ITS STRENGTH)

> *2 tablespoons Chinese red vinegar
> 2 tablespoons thin soy sauce
> 1 tablespoon sugar
> 1 teaspoon salt
> 2 teaspoons Colman's mustard powder
> ¼ teaspoon cayenne pepper
> 4 teaspoons sesame seed oil*

DIRECTIONS FOR COOKING

1. Arrange agar-agar on serving platter. Then arrange cucumber, chicken, and jellyfish skin on top. Chill.

2. In a small saucepan heat 2 tablespoons oil and pour in sauce mixture. Cook over low heat until sauce comes to a boil. Turn off heat. Pour sauce on the salad. Toss before serving.

燻魚

SMOKED FISH

(A COLD DISH)

about 6 servings

Although the Chinese call this smoked fish, the preparation does not actually include smoking the fish; when prepared, however, the fish looks as if it had been smoked.

This dish is usually eaten cold as an appetizer. Soft and crisp at the same time, the fish is salty yet sweet. It can be cooked ahead and it keeps well.

PREPARATION OF INGREDIENTS

MARINADE (MIX AND MARINATE FISH FOR SEVERAL HOURS IN REFRIGERATOR)*

> 3 tablespoons black soy sauce
> 1 tablespoon pale dry sherry
> ¼ teaspoon five-fragrance powder
> ¼ teaspoon salt
> 1 pound fresh fish with bone (perch, red snapper, or bass): cut
>   into pieces about 1 by 2 inches

SAUCE MIXTURE (MIX IN A SAUCEPAN)*

> 2 tablespoons sugar
> 1 tablespoon finely minced fresh ginger root
> 1 scallion: cut into pea-sized pieces, including green part
> ½ stick cinnamon
> 2 whole star anise
> 2 tablespoons black soy sauce
> 2 tablespoons pale dry sherry
> ⅓ cup water
> ¼ teaspoon five-fragrance powder

4 cups oil

DIRECTIONS FOR COOKING

1. Simmer sauce mixture over very low heat for about 15 minutes. (Keep an eye on it constantly; the sauce foams up and spills over easily.) Set aside.

2. Drain fish pieces and discard marinade.

3. Heat oil in wok to deep-fry temperature. Deep-fry fish, a few pieces at a time, over medium heat until they are crisp. (Do not turn them until they are stiff; otherwise they will fall apart.) Drain.

4. Soak fried fish in sauce mixture for about 10 minutes or more. Drain and serve cold.

Chicken and Egg Dishes

CHICKEN

I am told that years ago "a chicken in every pot" was an American dream. Now the dream seems to have come true, and chicken is the least expensive meat in this country. For the Chinese, "a chicken in every pot" is still a dream. Chicken does not come to their table every day. Rather, it is for special occasions such as birthdays, festivals, ancestor worshipings, and offerings.

In China, many families raise their own chickens. Even the boat people, living with their families on a 6-by-12-foot sampan, still have room for a few. In fact, the boat people's chickens are highly prized by many Chinese. Sometimes my family's cook, Ah Sahm, made a special trip to purchase these chickens. As a child, I used to go along with her.

The boat people raised and kept their chickens in small bamboo cages hung above the water along the boat's sides. The chickens were fed well with good grain, but they hardly had room to move. As a result, they grew fat and tender; even the bones were soft and fragile. This practice might sound inhumane to the non-Chinese, but to us, humans come first. When the tender, juicy, fragrant chicken came to the table, we enjoyed it with all our hearts and souls and clear consciences.

For the American, buying a chicken is a casual thing. You simply pick up a package and throw it in your shopping cart. But for many Chinese like Ah Sahm, buying a chicken was a display of skill, experience, and expertise. She thoroughly examined every part of the bird, as if she were choosing a beauty queen. The feathers had to be shining and dark colored. She felt the chicken's breast and blew the feathers on it, so that she could make sure that the skin was yellow. Then, she gently squeezed the bird's body and felt its bottom to be certain it was a full-grown female that had not yet laid eggs. It had to weigh around 4½ pounds. If all its qualities pleased her, then it was chosen.

In order to obtain the chicken's best flavor, she would not have it killed in the marketplace. Instead she took it home, alive and with feathers. Then she would kill it herself, just before cooking.

Like many Asians, I was thrilled to find that chicken was so plentiful and inexpensive in this country. But we all soon discovered that chicken here is less tasty. For some time I blamed it on the vitamin food that the chickens were fed. But then a few years ago, while we were living in Chicago, I stopped in Mr. Chang's Chinese grocery store in Chinatown and found him in the process of killing a few chickens. Now the chickens in Mr. Chang's hands reminded me of how a fresh-killed chicken's skin should look—very rich yellow! Not like those that came from the supermarkets—pale and grayish white.

My mind awoke, my heart lightened, my eyes flashed. Buddha must have experienced a similar awakening. He left his family life to serve our souls. I left Mr. Chang's store with a 4-pound chicken to fill a few stomachs. The chicken was prepared following the Pure Cut Chicken recipe (see page 69), without any makeup, only its own beauty. It was the first good chicken I found in America!

Chickens lose their flavor quickly. Therefore, the difference in taste between a fresh-killed chicken and a supermarket one is great. In America, chickens spend a great length of time waiting to be plucked and then rinsed. Then there is a long wait in the cold compartment before they are trucked to the markets, and then another wait to be packed and sold. By the time the chicken reaches your mouth, it has come a long way and the flavor is tired.

So what can we do? There are so few chickens alive with feathers near our neighborhood. If you have an idea like mine of raising your own chickens, be sure to check with your local police. "No chicken coop allowed in the backyard!" our local police and my neighbors told me firmly. So, we just have to take what we can get and show our skill. I was taught that a good cook should be able to make a banana peel fit for a king. And here I present many recipes which will make chickens fit not only for kings but also for gods in heaven and mortals on earth.

TIPS FOR BUYING CHICKEN

Shop in markets that specialize in chicken. Avoid buying on Monday because you are likely to pick up chickens left over the weekend. Always buy roasting chicken; fryers are not mature enough to have full flavor. Choose one that weighs about 4 to 4½ pounds, has rich yellow skin, and is plump and round-chested. Cook chicken on the same day that you purchase it.

紙包鷄

PAPER CHICKEN
about 6 servings

PREPARATION OF INGREDIENTS

3 whole boned, skinless chicken breasts: cut into 1- by 2½-inch pieces

MARINADE (MIX AND MARINATE CHICKEN FOR NO LONGER THAN AN HOUR)

1 tablespoon finely minced fresh ginger root
2 tablespoons thin soy sauce
2 tablespoons black soy sauce
2 tablespoons Chinese Shaohsing wine or pale dry sherry
1 teaspoon sugar
2 tablespoons sesame seed oil
½ teaspoon ground pepper
1 teaspoon minced garlic
1 teaspoon Chinese red vinegar
2 teaspoons hoisin sauce
½ teaspoon Colman's mustard powder

12 scallions (white parts only): cut into 2-inch pieces, then halve
6 Chinese dried mushrooms: soak in hot water until spongy,
    discard stems, cut caps in half
12 pieces 10-by-10-inch rice paper or waxed paper
4 cups oil

DIRECTIONS FOR COOKING

1. Wrap 2 pieces of marinated chicken, 2 pieces of scallion, and 1 piece of mushroom in rice paper or waxed paper (see illustrations). Repeat until 12 packages are made.

2. Heat oil in wok over high heat to deep-fry temperature. Deep-fry chicken packages a few at a time for about 5 minutes; turn once. Drain on a rack. Keep warm in low oven while frying the rest. Place on a serving platter. Serve hot. Let your family and guests have the pleasure of opening them.

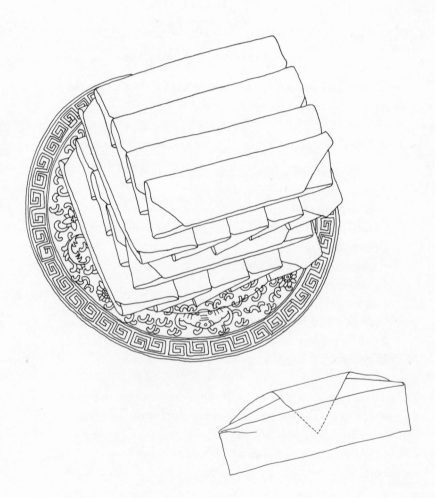

貴妃鷄

IMPERIAL CONCUBINE CHICKEN
6 to 8 servings

"Imperial Concubine" refers to Yang Huei Fei, the favorite concubine of Emperor Ming of the Tang Dynasty, A.D. 618–907. It was said that she was plumply beautiful, a woman of extravagance, imperious. Living behind the palace wall, she was one of the emperor's three thousand concubines. Her beauty dazzled the old king; he no longer attended to state affairs, but wined and dined, enjoying Yang Huei Fei's songs and dances.

Then An Lu Shan, who governed the Northern Frontier, revolted. The king's army blamed Yang Huei Fei for weakening the country; they refused to advance unless she was executed. The old king, helpless, could only grieve as she was led away.

It was said that she was also fond of wine. When this dish, containing a good amount of wine, was created decades ago, it was named to honor this imperial lady.

PREPARATION OF INGREDIENTS

2 to 2½ pounds chicken wings (or legs and thighs): disjoint
3 tablespoons oil
2 slices fresh ginger root, each as big and thick as a quarter
2 scallions: cut into 1½-inch lengths, including green part
10 Chinese dried mushrooms: soak in hot water until spongy,
  discard stems
½ cup bamboo shoots cut into paper-thin slices

SAUCE MIXTURE (MIX IN A BOWL)*

   ¼ teaspoon salt
   2 tablespoons thin soy sauce
   2 tablespoons black soy sauce
   ⅓ cup Chinese Shaohsing wine or pale dry sherry
   ½ teaspoon sugar

about 1 cup clear chicken broth (not condensed) or water

DIRECTIONS FOR COOKING

1. Heat a big pot of water to a boil. Blanch chicken in water for 1 minute. Remove chicken, place in a colander, and rinse with cold running water. Drain. Pat dry with paper towels.

2. Heat a 4- to 5-quart pot over medium heat. Swirl in the oil. When oil is hot, add ginger and scallions and brown slightly. Add chicken and evenly brown pieces. Put in mushrooms, bamboo shoots, and sauce mixture. Mix well. Add half the broth. Cover and cook over medium-low heat for 30 to 40 minutes or until chicken is tender. During cooking, add remaining broth if needed. There should be about ¾ cup sauce. Serve hot.

NOTE: *This dish may be cooked a day ahead. Reheat on stove over low heat.*

醬爆鷄丁

CHICKEN WITH WALNUTS IN HOT BEAN SAUCE
2 to 4 servings

PREPARATION OF INGREDIENTS

1 cup oil for deep-frying
¼ cup raw walnuts: rinse in hot water, drain, and dry on paper
  towels
1 slice fresh ginger root, as big and thick as a quarter
1 clove garlic: crush and peel

CHICKEN MIXTURE (MIX IN A BOWL)*

  1½ boned, skinless chicken breasts: cut into ½-inch cubes
    (to make 1 cup)
  1 teaspoon pale dry sherry
  ⅓ egg white
  ½ teaspoon thin soy sauce
  1 teaspoon cornstarch

2 dried chili peppers: tear into small pieces, do not discard seeds
4 Chinese dried mushrooms: soak in hot water until spongy,
  discard stems, cut caps into small squares

½ cup quartered water chestnuts
½ cup bamboo shoots cut into ⅓-inch cubes
½ cup green or red bell pepper cut into ½-inch pieces
1 scallion cut into pea-sized pieces, including green part

SAUCE MIXTURE (MIX IN A BOWL)*

6 teaspoons ground bean sauce
4 teaspoons hoisin sauce
4 teaspoons black soy sauce
½ teaspoon sugar
4 teaspoons pale dry sherry

2 teaspoons sesame seed oil

DIRECTIONS FOR COOKING

1. Heat oil for deep-frying in wok over high heat. Deep-fry walnuts until golden brown. Drain on paper towels.*

2. Remove all but 4 tablespoons oil from wok. Heat oil, slightly brown ginger and garlic, then discard. Add chicken mixture. Stir-fry until chicken just turns white. Remove from wok to bowl.

3. Keep wok hot over high heat. Add chili peppers. Stir-fry for a few seconds. Drop in mushrooms and cook for about 10 seconds. Add water chestnuts, bamboo shoots, pepper, and scallion. Stir-fry for about 30 seconds. Stir in sauce mixture. Return chicken to wok, mix well and cook until sauce begins to bubble. Swirl in sesame seed oil. Put on a serving platter. Top with walnuts. Serve hot.

五香鷄塊

FIVE-FRAGRANCE CHICKEN PIECES
6 to 10 servings

PREPARATION OF INGREDIENTS

*4 whole boned chicken breasts, with or without skin: pound with
back edge of cleaver, cut into pieces 1½ by 2 inches*

MARINADE (MIX AND MARINATE CHICKEN IN A BOWL FOR AN HOUR OR A LITTLE
LONGER. TURN PIECES FROM TIME TO TIME)*

> *2 teaspoons salt*
> *1 teaspoon sugar*
> *½ teaspoon five-fragrance powder*
> *1 tablespoon black soy sauce*
> *1 tablespoon thin soy sauce*
> *1 tablespoon Chinese Shaohsing wine or pale dry sherry*
> *2 teaspoons finely minced fresh ginger root*

about ⅔ cup cornstarch
about 4 cups oil
double recipe Soy-Vinegar Dip (see recipe)

DIRECTIONS FOR COOKING

Dredge marinated chicken pieces in cornstarch. Heat oil in wok over high
heat to deep-fry temperature. Deep-fry chicken pieces, a few at a time,
until golden brown. Drain on paper towels. Serve hot with dip.

蠔油鮮菇鷄翼

CHICKEN WINGS AND MUSHROOMS IN OYSTER SAUCE
4 to 6 servings

PREPARATION OF INGREDIENTS

*2 pounds chicken wings: disjoint each wing into 3 parts, rinse in
   cold water, pat dry*
1 tablespoon black soy sauce
2 tablespoons cornstarch
4 cups oil for deep-frying
1 tablespoon oil for stir-frying
1 tablespoon minced garlic
1 teaspoon finely minced fresh ginger root
2 scallions: cut into 1-inch lengths, including green part

SAUCE MIXTURE (MIX IN A BOWL)*

> *4 tablespoons oyster-flavored sauce*
> *1 tablespoon black soy sauce*
> *½ teaspoon sugar*
> *2 tablespoons Chinese Shaohsing wine or pale dry sherry*

*½ pound fresh mushrooms: cut each in half or leave whole if
   small*
½ cup water

DIRECTIONS FOR COOKING

1. Mix chicken and black soy sauce together, then add cornstarch.

2. Heat 4 cups oil in wok over high heat to deep-fry temperature.
Deep-fry half the chicken wings until they turn golden brown. Remove
with a drainer to a bowl. Deep-fry remaining chicken.

3. Remove all the oil from wok. Clean and dry wok.

4. Heat wok over high heat. Swirl in 1 tablespoon oil for stir-frying.

When oil is hot, drop in garlic, ginger, and scallions. When garlic turns golden, swirl in sauce mixture. Stir and cook for about 5 seconds. Return chicken wings to wok. Add mushrooms. Mix well. Add water. Mix well. When sauce comes to a boil, turn heat to medium. Cover and cook, stirring from time to time, for 25 minutes. Put on a serving platter. Serve hot.

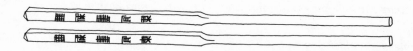

杏仁鶏丁

CHICKEN WITH ALMONDS
4 to 8 servings

PREPARATION OF INGREDIENTS

1 cup oil
⅓ cup uncooked, skinless almonds: rinse, dry on paper towels

CHICKEN MIXTURE (MIX IN A BOWL)*

> *1½ boned, skinless chicken breasts: cut into ½-inch cubes*
> *(to make 1 cup)*
> *¼ teaspoon salt*
> *½ egg white*
> *1 pinch of white pepper*
> *⅛ teaspoon sugar*
> *1 teaspoon cornstarch*

2 slices fresh ginger root, each as big and thick as a quarter
1 clove garlic: crush and peel
4 Chinese dried mushrooms: soak in hot water until spongy,
*   discard stems, cut caps into ½-inch squares*
½ cup ⅓-inch pieces green or red bell pepper
½ cup ⅓-inch cubes pineapple

½ cup quartered water chestnuts
⅓ cup ⅓-inch cubed bamboo shoots
1 scallion cut into pea-sized pieces, including green part

SAUCE MIXTURE (MIX IN A BOWL)*

4 tablespoons thin soy sauce
2 teaspoons black soy sauce
1 teaspoon sugar
2 tablespoons pale dry sherry
1 tablespoon sesame seed oil
1 teaspoon cornstarch

DIRECTIONS FOR COOKING

1. Heat oil in wok over high heat to deep-fry temperature. Deep-fry almonds until golden brown. Drain on paper towels.

2. Reheat oil in wok. Add chicken mixture and stir to separate pieces. Blanch chicken briskly until it just turns white. Remove with slotted spoon.

3. Remove all but 1 tablespoon of oil from wok. Heat oil, and add ginger and garlic. Brown them slightly and discard. Add mushrooms, pepper, pineapple or bamboo shoots, and water chestnuts. Stir-fry for about 1 minute. Return chicken to wok. Add the scallion and stir-fry for about 30 seconds. Stir in sauce mixture. Mix well and stir-fry for another 30 seconds. Put on a serving platter. Top with almonds. Serve hot.

椰子鷄

COCONUT CHICKEN
6 to 8 servings

This dish belongs to my aunt in Macau with whom I stayed for a year. Macau, an old Portuguese colony connected to mainland China, is an hour away from Hong Kong by boat. Ninety-five percent of the population is Chinese, and their cooking, culture, and customs remain purely Chinese. Only occasionally, a few Chinese restaurants would offer some dishes that had the flavor of the colonials, such as coconut chicken. My aunt learned to prepare this dish from a chef who was captivated by her charming smile; very few could resist giving her their secrets.

The Chinese fondness for coconut is similar to the Westerners' love for chocolate. It is the dominant flavor in candies and ice cream, and is so much a part of our lives that we hardly realize it is mainly imported.

PREPARATION OF INGREDIENTS

3 cups oil

CHICKEN MIXTURE (MIX IN A BOWL. REFRIGERATE BEFORE USE)*

> *3 whole chicken breasts: bone, but leave skin on, pound meat side with back of cleaver, cut into 1-inch-square pieces*
> *1 egg white: beat slightly*
> *2 teaspoons cornstarch*
> *1 teaspoon sesame seed oil*
> *⅛ teaspoon white pepper*

SAUCE MIXTURE (MIX IN A BOWL)*

> *½ cup Philippines unsweetened coconut milk*
> *⅓ cup light cream*
> *1 teaspoon salt*
> *1 tablespoon pale dry sherry*
> *¼ teaspoon sugar*
> *1 tablespoon melted lard*

1 tablespoon flour
2 egg whites: beat until stiff

DIRECTIONS FOR COOKING

1. Heat oil in wok over high heat. Add chicken mixture. Stir to separate pieces, and blanch briskly until chicken just turns white. Remove with a drainer to a baking dish.

2. Preheat oven to 375 degrees.

3. Remove all oil from wok. Clean and dry wok, then heat it over medium heat. Pour in sauce mixture. Stir in flour. Stir and cook until sauce thickens. Pour sauce over chicken and top with beaten egg whites.

4. Bake chicken in oven for 20 minutes or until egg whites turn golden brown. Serve hot.

脆皮檸檬鷄

CRISP LEMON CHICKEN
2 to 4 servings

PREPARATION OF INGREDIENTS

2 *large whole chicken breasts: bone but leave on skin, pound meat side with back of cleaver*

MARINADE (MIX AND MARINATE CHICKEN IN A BOWL FOR AN HOUR OR LONGER)*

    1 egg: beat well
    ¼ teaspoon salt
    1 teaspoon pale dry sherry
    ¼ teaspoon sugar
    juice from ½ lemon

½ cup cornstarch for dredging
2 tablespoons oil for stir-frying
1 teaspoon finely minced fresh ginger root
2 teaspoons minced garlic
¼ cup shredded scallions: 1½ inches long, including green parts
8 very thin slices lemon without skin
¼ cup thinly shredded red or green bell pepper

SAUCE MIXTURE (MIX IN A BOWL AND COVER)*

    ¼ teaspoon salt
    4 teaspoons white vinegar
    4 teaspoons sugar
    2 tablespoons thin soy sauce
    4 teaspoons pale dry sherry
    ½ cup clear chicken broth (not condensed)

2 teaspoons cornstarch mixed with 2 teaspoons water
1 teaspoon lemon extract
4 cups oil for deep-frying
Scallion Brushes (see recipe) or slices of lemon for garnish

DIRECTIONS FOR COOKING

1. Put cornstarch for dredging on a plate. Generously and evenly dredge marinated chicken. Put chicken flat on a plate and set aside.

2. Heat a small pan over medium heat. Swirl in 2 tablespoons oil for stir-frying. When oil is hot, add ginger, garlic, and half the scallions. Stir to cook until garlic turns golden. Add lemon slices and shredded pepper. Immediately pour in sauce mixture. When sauce just starts to bubble, add cornstarch water, stirring constantly until sauce is thickened. Add lemon extract. Mix well. Cover to keep warm.

3. Heat 4 cups oil in wok over high heat to deep-fry temperature. Slide breasts into hot oil and deep-fry until golden brown. Remove and drain.

4. Put chicken breasts on a chopping board and chop crosswise into half-inch pieces. Arrange pieces neatly on a serving platter. Sprinkle chicken with remaining shredded scallions.

5. Discard lemon slices from sauce. Pour sauce over chicken. Garnish platter with lemon slices, scallion brushes, parsley, or other greens. Serve hot.

炒龍鳳片

HAPPY UNION
2 to 4 servings

The Chinese sometimes honor the shrimp by calling it "dragon" and the chicken by calling it "phoenix." Chinese dragons symbolized manliness, wisdom, strength, and kindness. It was said that because they were so wise, they never truly revealed themselves, but appeared disguised as fish, shrimp, or other creatures. The phoenix symbolized femininity, serenity, grace, and beauty. When dragon and phoenix meet, it represents the happy union of men and women.

PREPARATION OF INGREDIENTS

CHICKEN MIXTURE (MIX IN A BOWL)*

> *1 whole boned, skinless chicken breast: slice paper-thin*
> *⅛ teaspoon salt*
> *½ teaspoon thin soy sauce*

½ egg white
1 tablespoon cornstarch

½ pound bok choy or broccoli: cut into bite-sized pieces
4 tablespoons oil
4 to 6 ounces fresh shrimp: shell, devein, split in half, clean
   under cold running water, pat dry
2 slices fresh ginger root, each as big and thick as a quarter
1 clove garlic: crush and peel
2 scallions: cut into 1½-inch lengths, including green part
4 Chinese dried mushrooms: soak in hot water until spongy, discard stems

SAUCE MIXTURE (MIX IN A BOWL)*

½ cup clear chicken broth (not condensed)
2 teaspoons oyster-flavored sauce
1 teaspoon sesame seed oil
1½ teaspoons thin soy sauce
⅛ teaspoon ground pepper
1 teaspoon pale dry sherry
½ teaspoon salt

1 tablespoon cornstarch mixed with 2 tablespoons water

DIRECTIONS FOR COOKING

1. Separately blanch chicken mixture and bok choy or broccoli in water (see Cooking Techniques). Drain and put on a plate.

2. Heat wok over high heat until almost smoking. Add 2 tablespoons oil. When oil is hot, add shrimp. Stir-fry for a few seconds until shrimp turn white-pink. Remove with a drainer or slotted spoon to a bowl.

3. Keep wok hot. Add remaining 2 tablespoons oil. When oil is hot, add ginger and garlic. Discard them when they are golden brown. Add scallions and mushrooms. Stir-fry for about 15 seconds and then stir in sauce mixture. When sauce begins to boil, return the chicken, bok choy, and shrimp to wok. Mix well and cook for about 30 seconds. Stir in cornstarch water. Stir constantly until sauce thickens. Serve hot.

豉油鷄

SOY SAUCE CHICKEN
4 to 8 servings

PREPARATION OF INGREDIENTS

2 tablespoons oil for searing
1 fresh chicken, 3½ to 4 pounds: rinse in cold water, pat dry
3 slices fresh ginger root, each as big and thick as a quarter
1 clove garlic: crush and peel
2 scallions: cut into 1½-inch lengths, including green part

SAUCE MIXTURE (MIX IN A BOWL)*

½ cup black soy sauce
¼ cup Chinese Shaohsing wine or pale dry sherry
4 teaspoons sugar
2 whole star anise

1 cup water
1 tablespoon sesame seed oil

DIRECTIONS FOR COOKING

1. Heat wok over high heat. Swirl in 2 tablespoons oil for searing. When oil is hot, sear chicken evenly until it is shiny yellow. Remove chicken from wok.

2. Reheat oil in wok. Drop in ginger, garlic, and scallions, and brown them slightly. Pour in sauce mixture. When sauce begins to boil, return chicken to wok and add water. Cover wok, turn heat to low and simmer chicken for 20 minutes. Turn chicken. Cover and simmer for another 20 minutes or until chicken is just done. Pierce the thigh, and if the juice runs clear, then it is done.

3. Drain chicken. Discard ginger, garlic, scallions, and star anise. Put chicken on a chopping board. Brush it with sesame seed oil. Chop chicken with bones as illustrated in chapter on duck. Pour sauce over chicken. Serve hot.

焗柱候鶏

CHICKEN IN HOISIN SAUCE
4 to 8 servings

PREPARATION OF INGREDIENTS

4 tablespoons oil for searing
1 fresh chicken, 3 to 4 pounds: rinse, pat dry
2 teaspoons finely minced fresh ginger root
2 tablespoons minced garlic

SAUCE MIXTURE (MIX IN A BOWL)*

6 tablespoons hoisin sauce
1 teaspoon salt
1 tablespoon sugar
2 tablespoons black soy sauce
1 tablespoon pale dry sherry
1 tablespoon oyster-flavored sauce

½ cup boiling water
1 teaspoon sesame seed oil

DIRECTIONS FOR COOKING

1. Heat wok over high heat until it is hot. Swirl in oil for searing. When oil is hot, sear chicken evenly until it is shiny yellow. Remove chicken from wok.

2. Keep oil hot. Slightly brown ginger and garlic. Stir in the sauce mixture. When sauce begins to boil, return chicken to wok and roll it around to coat it with the sauce. Pour in water. Cover and simmer over low heat for about 20 minutes. Turn chicken and add a little more boiling water if sauce is drying out. Cover and simmer for another 20 minutes.

3. Place chicken on a chopping board and brush it with the sesame seed oil. Chop chicken with bones as illustrated in chapter on duck. Pour sauce over chicken. Serve hot.

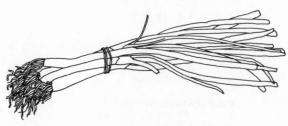

東江鹽焗雞

SALT ROAST CHICKEN
4 to 6 servings

Nobody could make this chicken better than our Elder Old Aunt. We never knew her by any name other than Elder Old Aunt. She was always there, and she was always old. My grandfather's elder sister, she had no family of her own. She sat in silence, with her lips tightly locked, and seldom spoke—except when we were haled before our parents for misbehavior; then she would add more crimes from her silent files. Among the children, she was called "the silent toad." My grandfather had taught her city manners, but she often forgot. The servants laughed because she made noise when she ate, and sometimes licked her bowl.

A few times a year, upon request, she would prepare this chicken for a special treat. She would ignore the compliments that followed and eat without a word. When she was ninety-two, somehow she knew that her time had come. She went back to her native village to lie next to her long-dead husband and her ancestors.

I learned how to cook this chicken from grandmother, who learned from Elder Old Aunt. I hope in heaven she knows that we savor her chicken, and regret, as we grow older, that we never searched her silence, which soundlessly still tolls.

PREPARATION OF INGREDIENTS

6 pounds kosher salt
1 fresh chicken, 4 pounds: rinse, thoroughly dry inside
*   and out with paper towels, rub outside with 2 teaspoons salt*
cheesecloth, enough to wrap chicken
⅓ cup shredded scallions for garnishing
double recipe Ginger-Scallion Dip (see recipe)

DIRECTIONS FOR COOKING

1. Pour the kosher salt into a big wok. Cover and heat over medium-high heat for 30 minutes; stir and turn salt from time to time.

2. Wrap chicken in one layer of cheesecloth, overlapping cheesecloth slightly at side of chicken. Tie knots at neck and tail.

3. Dig a well in the salt. Put in chicken, breast side down. There should be a lot of salt between wok and chicken. Pile salt over chicken, covering it completely. Cover the wok. Roast chicken over medium-high heat for 1½ hours.

4. Test chicken by piercing thigh with skewer or small knife. If juice runs clear, it is done. Remove chicken from wok and put on a tray. Brush off salt with pastry brush. Cut cheesecloth, then remove chicken and put on chopping board.

5. Chop off legs and wings with cleaver. Arrange them on a serving platter. With your fingers, tear chicken breast, skin and meat, as well as the back, into big strips as long as a finger. Arrange in the middle of the platter, garnish with scallions and serve warm. Serve dip in individual dishes for each person.

白切鷄

PURE CUT CHICKEN WITH GINGER-SCALLION DIP
4 to 6 servings

This dish and the salt roast chicken in the preceding recipe are the most famous dishes of Tung Kung cooking, which developed along the East River (Tung Kung) of Kwangtung Province. This good unadorned style of cooking and serving chicken is true art—simple and pure.

PREPARATION OF INGREDIENTS

4 whole star anise
2 tablespoons salt
¼ cup Chinese Shaohsing wine or pale dry sherry
¼ cup oil
2 chunks (each the size of a pecan) fresh ginger root: crush slightly
2½ gallons water
1 fresh chicken, 4 pounds: rinse, pat dry
¼ cup shredded scallions for garnishing
double recipe Ginger-Scallion Dip (see recipe) or
  Oil-Oyster Sauce Dip (see recipe)

DIRECTIONS FOR COOKING

1. Add star anise, salt, wine, and ginger to the water in a large pot (a lobster or stock pot) and bring to a rapid boil. Immerse chicken in water to cover completely. Cover pot and bring water to a boil again. (It will take a few minutes.) As soon as the water boils rapidly, turn off the heat. Do not uncover for at least 2 hours. Do not peek, even once, at the chicken during the entire 2 hours because the heat and hot steam cooking the chicken must not be allowed to escape. The chicken can stay in the water for up to 3 hours.

2. Fifteen minutes prior to serving the chicken, turn heat to medium and bring the water to a boil; simmer for 3 minutes. Turn off heat. Drain chicken and put it on a chopping board. Chop off legs and wings with a cleaver. Place them on a serving platter. Chop remaining chicken with bones as illustrated in chapter on duck, or carve as you would a turkey. Garnish with scallions. Serve hot. Serve dip in individual dishes for each person.

蘑菇鷄片

MOO GOO GAI PAN
4 to 8 servings

Moo goo means "button mushrooms" and *gai pan* means "chicken slices."

PREPARATION OF INGREDIENTS

½ cup canned straw mushrooms: rinse in cold water, drain
1 cup canned or fresh button mushrooms: rinse in cold water, drain
½ cup canned baby corn: cut each ear in half lengthwise
2 teaspoons Chinese Shaohsing wine or pale dry sherry
2 cups clear chicken broth (not condensed)
2 cups oil

CHICKEN MIXTURE (MIX AND MARINATE IN A BOWL)*

2 whole boned, skinless chicken breasts: trim and cut into paper-thin slices when half-frozen

1 tablespoon cornstarch
½ egg white
1 teaspoon pale dry sherry
¼ teaspoon salt
¼ teaspoon sugar

1 teaspoon minced garlic
1 scallion: cut into 1½-inch lengths, including green part, then
 shred

SAUCE MIXTURE (MIX IN A BOWL)*

1 tablespoon thin soy sauce
½ teaspoon sugar
2 teaspoons Chinese Shaohsing wine or pale dry sherry
¾ cup clear chicken broth (not condensed)

1 tablespoon cornstarch mixed with 1 tablespoon water
1 teaspoon sesame seed oil

DIRECTIONS FOR COOKING

1. Put straw mushrooms, button mushrooms, corn, 2 teaspoons wine, and 2 cups chicken broth in a saucepan and bring to a boil. Remove from heat and let sit for half an hour. Drain vegetables. (Reserve broth if desired, for use at a later time.)

2. Heat 2 cups oil in wok to deep-fry temperature. Add chicken mixture. Stir to separate pieces. Blanch chicken briskly until pieces just turn white. Remove with a drainer or slotted spoon to a bowl.

3. Remove all but 2 tablespoons oil from wok. Heat oil over medium-high heat, and add garlic and scallion. When garlic turns a light golden color, add mushrooms and corn. Stir and cook for 15 seconds. Swirl in sauce mixture and bring to a boil. Pour in cornstarch water. Cook, stirring constantly, until sauce is clear and thickened. Return chicken to wok. Stir-fry briefly. Swirl in the sesame seed oil. Put on a serving platter. Serve hot.

酥炸鷄球

PUFFED CRISP CHICKEN BALLS
6 to 8 servings

PREPARATION OF INGREDIENTS

BATTER

> ¼ teaspoon salt
> 1 tablespoon baking powder
> 1 cup all-purpose flour
> 5 tablespoons oil
> about ⅔ cup cold water
> 4 teaspoons white sesame seeds
> 3 tablespoons finely minced scallions

3 whole boned, skinless chicken breasts: pound with back of cleaver,
  cut into 1-by-2-inch pieces

MARINADE (MIX AND MARINATE CHICKEN IN A BOWL FOR 30 MINUTES OR MORE)*

> ½ teaspoon salt
> ¼ teaspoon sugar
> 1 big pinch of ground pepper
> 1 teaspoon pale dry sherry
> ½ teaspoon five-fragrance powder
> 1 tablespoon thin soy sauce
> 1 tablespoon cornstarch
> 1 egg white

4 to 6 cups oil for deep-frying
Soy-Vinegar Dip (see recipe)

DIRECTIONS FOR COOKING

1. Add salt and the baking powder to flour. Mix well. Add 5 table-spoons oil, a little at a time, until flour becomes somewhat like pie dough. It should stick together. Add water, a little at a time to break up dough until it becomes a thick batter. Add sesame seeds and scallions. Mix well.

Important: To test the consistency of the batter, dip a piece of chicken in the batter and hold it up. The batter should drip off the chicken slowly.

2. Heat oil in wok over high heat to deep-fry temperature. Roll a piece of chicken in batter to form a ball, and deep-fry until golden brown. A few pieces can be deep-fried at the same time. Drain and put in a warm oven. Deep-fry the rest of the chicken pieces in the same manner. Transfer to a serving platter. Serve hot with dip.

咖喱鷄

CHINESE CURRIED CHICKEN
6 to 8 servings

As they adopted Buddhism, the Chinese took Indian curry and made it their own. Because of the superiority of Chinese soy sauces, and the Chinese capacity to bring out the best flavor of ingredients, many Indians prefer Chinese curried dishes. If you follow the directions below, your curry's fragrance can be sensed a block away. Close your bedroom doors and open a few windows, or you'll wake up tasting curry for days.

PREPARATION OF INGREDIENTS

3 tablespoons oil
3 whole chicken breasts with skin and bone: chop into 1½-inch pieces
1 tablespoon minced garlic
2 teaspoons finely minced fresh ginger root
2 onions: cut lengthwise into narrow strips

SAUCE MIXTURE (MIX IN A BOWL)*

2 tablespoons curry paste
1 teaspoon curry powder
¼ teaspoon cayenne pepper
2 tablespoons black soy sauce
1 teaspoon sugar
2 tablespoons pale dry sherry
¼ teaspoon salt

2 medium-sized potatoes: peel, cut into walnut-sized pieces
½ cup water

DIRECTIONS FOR COOKING

1. Heat wok over high heat. Swirl in oil. When oil is hot, add chicken pieces. Pan-fry until chicken skin turns golden. Remove chicken with drainer to a bowl.

2. Reheat remaining oil in wok over medium heat. Drop in garlic, ginger, and onion. Stir-fry until garlic just turns golden. Swirl in sauce mixture. Stir and cook until sauce begins to bubble. Return chicken to wok. Add potatoes. Swirl in water. Mix well. Turn heat to low. Cover and cook for about 20 minutes, stirring and turning chicken pieces from time to time. When done, the chicken should be tender and the dish saucy. Serve hot.

湘江鷄球

HUNAN CHICKEN IN GINGER AND TOMATO SAUCE
2 to 6 servings

The Chinese name for tomato is "barbarian vegetable." It was imported from the West and has been growing in China for hundreds of years.

Eating raw tomatoes is still considered foreign by many Chinese, but using tomato sauce in cooking has been a common practice. Combined with soy sauce and other Chinese seasonings, tomato sauce completely loses its acid taste. Its sweetness and its beautiful redness remain, giving the dish a very rich color and a very fresh taste.

Hunan is famous for its peppery dishes, but there are some dishes of Hunan that are not hot. Here is one.

PREPARATION OF INGREDIENTS

2 cups oil

CHICKEN MIXTURE (MIX IN A BOWL)*

*1½ boned, skinless chicken breasts: cut into ½-inch cubes
(to make 1 cup)
½ egg white
1 tablespoon cornstarch*

*2 scallions: chop into pea-sized pieces, including green part
1 teaspoon finely minced fresh ginger root*

SAUCE MIXTURE (MIX IN A BOWL)*

*1 teaspoon black soy sauce
4 teaspoons sugar
2 teaspoons white vinegar
1 tablespoon tomato ketchup
2 teaspoons pale dry sherry
¼ teaspoon salt*

1 teaspoon cornstarch mixed with 1 teaspoon water

DIRECTIONS FOR COOKING

1. Heat oil in wok over high heat to deep-fry temperature. Add chicken mixture. Stir to separate pieces. Blanch chicken briskly until it just turns white. Remove with drainer or slotted spoon to a bowl.

2. Remove all but 2 tablespoons of oil from wok. Heat the oil, then drop in scallions and ginger. Stir-fry until they are slightly brown. Add sauce mixture and stir to heat. Stir in cornstarch water, and cook until sauce is thickened. Return chicken to wok, and stir to reheat. Put on a serving platter. Serve hot.

宮保鷄丁

KUNG-BAU CHICKEN WITH PEANUTS
2 servings

Ding Kung-Bau was a government official, "Guardian to the Heir Apparent." Kung-Bau was his title; Ding was his family name. It was said that he liked to serve this peppery dish when in Szechwan. If your palate does not match Ding Kung-Bau's, the hot pepper can be reduced.

PREPARATION OF INGREDIENTS

2 cups oil
⅓ cup raw skinless peanuts

CHICKEN MIXTURE (MIX AND MARINATE IN A BOWL)*

> *1½ boned, skinless chicken breasts: cut into ⅓-inch cubes*
> *(to make 1 cup)*
> *1 tablespoon cornstarch*
> *¼ teaspoon salt*
> *¼ teaspoon sugar*
> *½ egg white*

4 dried chili peppers: tear into small pieces, do not discard seeds
1 tablespoon finely minced fresh ginger root
2 scallions: cut into pea-sized pieces, including green part

SAUCE MIXTURE (MIX IN A BOWL)*

> *2 tablespoons black soy sauce*
> *2 tablespoons Chinese Shaohsing wine or pale dry sherry*
> *2 teaspoons Chinese red vinegar or cider vinegar*
> *½ teaspoon salt*

½ *teaspoon sugar*

2 *teaspoons sesame seed oil*

½ *teaspoon cornstarch*

1 *tablespoon water*

DIRECTIONS FOR COOKING

1. Heat oil in wok and deep-fry peanuts until golden brown. Drain on paper towels.

2. Reheat oil in wok and add chicken mixture. Stir to separate pieces. Briskly blanch chicken pieces until they just turn white. Remove with a drainer or slotted spoon to a bowl.

3. Remove all but 2 tablespoons oil from wok. Heat oil. Slightly brown chili peppers. Add ginger and scallions, and stir-fry until they turn golden. Stir in sauce mixture. Cook and stir until sauce is thickened. Put chicken back into wok. Mix well. Stir-fry briefly to reheat. Add peanuts. Mix well and put on a serving platter. Serve hot.

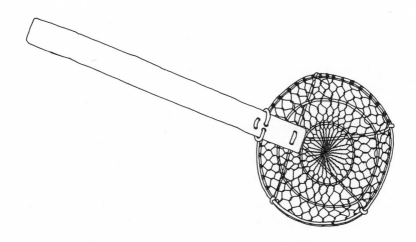

成都辣鷄

SZECHWAN CHENG TU CHICKEN
4 to 8 servings

Cheng Tu is the capital of Szechwan. This is one of its famous peppery dishes.

PREPARATION OF INGREDIENTS

2 cups oil

3 whole chicken breasts: bone, but leave on skin, cut into 1-inch squares

1 to 2 dried chili peppers: tear into small pieces, do not discard seeds

1 teaspoon finely minced fresh ginger root

½ teaspoon flower peppercorn powder

1 tablespoon minced garlic

2 scallions: cut into pea-sized pieces, including green part

SAUCE MIXTURE (MIX IN A BOWL)*

    1 tablespoon Szechwan sweet bean sauce or ground bean sauce

    2 teaspoons Szechwan chili bean sauce

    1 tablespoon Chinese red vinegar

    1 tablespoon pale dry sherry

    ½ teaspoon sugar

    1 tablespoon black soy sauce

    ¼ teaspoon cayenne pepper

    ½ cup clear chicken broth (not condensed)

1 medium green or red bell pepper: cut into 1-inch squares

1 teaspoon cornstarch mixed with 1 teaspoon water

DIRECTIONS FOR COOKING

1. Heat oil in wok to deep-fry temperature. Add chicken, stir, and blanch until half done (about 15 seconds). Remove with drainer to a bowl.

2. Remove all but 2 tablespoons oil from wok. Heat oil, then drop in chili peppers, ginger, peppercorn powder, garlic, and scallions. As soon as garlic turns golden, stir in sauce mixture. Add bell pepper. Mix well. Return chicken to wok. Cover and cook over medium heat for 10 minutes. Stir in cornstarch water. Stir and cook until sauce thickens. Put on a serving platter. Serve hot.

腰果珍肝

CHICKEN LIVERS WITH CASHEW NUTS
2 to 6 servings

PREPARATION OF INGREDIENTS

½ cup oil for deep-frying
⅓ cup uncooked cashew nuts: rinse in hot water, dry on paper towels
4 tablespoons oil for stir-frying
1 scallion: cut into pea-sized pieces, including green part
2 slices fresh ginger root, each as big and thick as a quarter
4 Chinese dried mushrooms: soak in hot water until spongy,
* discard stems, cut into ½-inch squares*
½ cup ½-inch pieces red or green bell pepper
⅓ cup quartered water chestnuts
⅓ cup bamboo shoots: cut into small cubes
7 chicken livers: cut each into 8 pieces

SAUCE MIXTURE (MIX IN A BOWL)*

1 tablespoon black soy sauce
1 teaspoon thin soy sauce
¼ teaspoon sugar
1 tablespoon Chinese Shaohsing wine or pale dry sherry
¼ teaspoon salt

1 teaspoon cornstarch mixed with 2 teaspoons water

DIRECTIONS FOR COOKING

1. Heat ½ cup oil in small pot to deep-fry temperature. Deep-fry cashew nuts to golden brown. Drain on paper towels.

2. Heat wok over high heat. Swirl in 4 tablespoons oil for stir-frying.

When oil is hot, add scallion and ginger. Discard ginger when it turns light brown.

3. Keep heat on high. Add mushrooms and stir-fry for about 30 seconds. (Mushrooms need more heat than other vegetables to draw out the flavor.) Add remaining vegetables and stir-fry for about 20 seconds. Remove vegetables with a drainer or a slotted spoon. Let oil drain back into wok. Put vegetables in a bowl.

4. Reheat oil in wok until oil is very hot, but not smoking. Add chicken livers and stir-fry until they lose their red color and are almost cooked through. Stir in sauce mixture and thicken it with the cornstarch mixture. Mix well with the livers. Return vegetables to the wok and stir-fry briefly to reheat. Put on a serving platter and sprinkle cashew nuts on top. Serve hot.

網油肝卷

CHICKEN LIVERS WRAPPED IN CAUL
4 to 8 servings

PREPARATION OF INGREDIENTS

2 sheets of caul (lace fat), about 8 by 7 inches

STUFFING (MIX IN A BOWL. REFRIGERATE BEFORE USE)*

8 chicken livers: cut into thin slices
8 ounces ground pork
2 scallions: cut into pea-sized pieces, including green part
½ teaspoon five-fragrance powder
1½ tablespoons black soy sauce
½ teaspoon sugar
½ teaspoon salt
1 teaspoon sesame seed oil
1 tablespoon pale dry sherry
2 teaspoons chopped fresh coriander (leaves only)
2 tablespoons cornstarch

BATTER (BEAT TOGETHER WITH A BEATER UNTIL SMOOTH)

2 tablespoons water chestnut powder
2 egg whites

Soy-Vinegar Dip (see recipe)

DIRECTIONS FOR COOKING

1. Lay caul on a flat surface. Divide stuffing into two equal portions, and place one portion on a sheet of caul lengthwise, approximately 2 inches in diameter, near the edge of the sheet. Roll the stuffing in the caul and tuck in both ends to look like a thick sausage. Seal with the batter. Then brush batter all over the sausage. Repeat with the other in the same manner.

2. Broil sausages on the upper rack under the broiler for about 12 minutes, turning once, or until sausages are golden brown and livers and pork are just cooked.

3. Cut sausages into 1-inch pieces crosswise. Put on a serving platter. Serve hot with dip.

滑蛋蝦球

SHRIMP FU YUNG EGGS
4 to 6 servings

Fu yung is the name of a flower in China. Its color is white or a pretty light yellow, resembling the color of an omelet. Therefore, many Chinese egg dishes are called fu yung eggs or eggs fu yung.

PREPARATION OF INGREDIENTS

4 tablespoons oil for stir-frying
⅓ cup chopped scallions: in pea-sized pieces, including green part
⅓ cup frozen green peas
6 water chestnuts: dice each into 6 pieces

continued

SHRIMP MIXTURE (MIX IN A BOWL. REFRIGERATE BEFORE USE)*

6 ounces fresh shrimp: shell, devein, cut into halves lengthwise,
rinse in cold water, pat dry
½ egg white
¼ teaspoon salt
1 pinch of white pepper
½ teaspoon pale dry sherry
1 teaspoon cornstarch

4 teaspoons thin soy sauce

EGG MIXTURE (MIX IN A BOWL)*

5 beaten eggs
½ teaspoon sugar
¼ teaspoon salt
1 tablespoon sesame seed oil

DIRECTIONS FOR COOKING

1. Heat wok over high heat, and swirl in oil for stir-frying. When oil is hot, drop in scallions and stir-fry for about 10 seconds. Then add peas and water chestnuts, and stir-fry briefly to heat through.

2. Keep heat on high. Add shrimp mixture. Stir-fry until shrimp turns whitish-pink (about 1 minute). Swirl in soy sauce and mix well. Swirl in egg mixture. Do not stir! Turn heat to medium-low. When egg begins to set around the edge, lift cooked edge and allow uncooked egg to run under. Repeat this procedure until egg is cooked but still moist. Put on a serving platter. Serve hot.

雪山蝦仁

SHRIMP SOUFFLÉ
about 4 servings

PREPARATION OF INGREDIENTS

3 tablespoons oil
1 scallion: cut into pea-sized pieces, including green part

SHRIMP MIXTURE (MIX IN A BOWL. REFRIGERATE BEFORE USE)*

> 1 cup (8 ounces) shelled fresh shrimp: clean and dry
> ½ egg white
> ½ teaspoon pale dry sherry
> 1 teaspoon cornstarch
> 1 pinch white pepper
> ¼ teaspoon salt

SAUCE MIXTURE (MIX IN A BOWL)*

> ½ teaspoon salt
> 1 teaspoon pale dry sherry
> ½ teaspoon sugar
> ½ teaspoon sesame seed oil

4 egg whites: beat until foamy

DIRECTIONS FOR COOKING

1. Heat wok over high heat, then swirl in oil. When oil is hot, add scallion. Stir-fry about 10 seconds. Add shrimp mixture. Stir-fry until shrimp turn light pink. Stir in sauce mixture. Mix well.

2. Turn heat to low. Pour in egg whites. When egg begins to set around the edge, lift cooked edge and allow uncooked egg to run under. Repeat this procedure until the egg is cooked but still moist. Put on a serving platter. Serve hot.

蝦肉蛋卷

CREPES WITH SHRIMP FILLING
about 6 servings

PREPARATION OF INGREDIENTS

6 tablespoons oil

CREPE MIXTURE (BEAT UNTIL FOAMY)

> *4 eggs*
> *1 egg yolk*
> *¼ teaspoon salt*

FILLING (MIX IN A BOWL. REFRIGERATE BEFORE USE)*

> *1 pound fresh shrimp: shell, devein, rinse in cold water, pat dry,*
> *mince into paste*
> *4 ounces ground pork*
> *3 scallions: mince, including green part*
> *1 teaspoon pale dry sherry*
> *1 egg white: beat until slightly foamy*
> *½ teaspoon salt*
> *½ teaspoon sugar*
> *⅛ teaspoon white pepper*
> *2 teaspoons sesame seed oil*
> *1 tablespoon thin soy sauce*

Soy-Vinegar Dip (see recipe)

DIRECTIONS FOR COOKING

1. Heat a medium-sized skillet over medium heat. Add 1 tablespoon oil. When oil is hot, add one-fourth of the crepe mixture and spread it thinly and evenly. Turn heat to low, and fry both sides of crepe to a golden color. Put on a plate to cool. Make the other three crepes in the same manner, adding a tablespoon of oil if necessary. Separate with wax paper.

2. Evenly spread one-fourth of the filling on each crepe. Then roll each as you would a jelly roll.

3. Heat a skillet and pour in remaining 4 tablespoons oil. When oil is hot, carefully place stuffed crepes in skillet. Cover and pan-fry over medium-low heat for about 5 minutes or until they are golden brown. Cut crosswise into slices ½ inch thick. Arrange on a serving platter. Serve hot with dip.

芙蓉蟹粉

CRABMEAT FU YUNG EGGS ON FRIED NOODLES
about 6 servings

PREPARATION OF INGREDIENTS

4 cups oil
2 ounces bean thread noodles

EGG MIXTURE (MIX IN A BOWL AND BEAT WITH CHOPSTICKS OR WIRE WHISK TO MIX EGG WHITES AND YOLKS THOROUGHLY. DO NOT OVERBEAT OR USE EGGBEATER)*

    6 medium-sized eggs
    1 tablespoon cornstarch
    ½ teaspoon salt
    ½ teaspoon sugar
    4 tablespoons water

CRABMEAT MIXTURE (MIX GENTLY IN A BOWL JUST BEFORE COOKING)

    6 ounces fresh or frozen crabmeat: if frozen, thaw and drain on
      paper towels, leave in big chunks
    ⅛ teaspoon white pepper
    ¼ teaspoon salt
    2 teaspoons pale dry sherry
    2 teaspoons sesame seed oil

2 scallions: cut into 1-inch-long thin shreds including green part
2 slices cooked crisp bacon: chop into rice-sized pieces

DIRECTIONS FOR COOKING

1. Heat oil in wok over high heat to deep-fry temperature. Test oil by dropping in a piece of noodle; if noodle pops up, turns white, and floats immediately to the surface, then the oil is right. Deep-fry half the noodles at a time. They will pop up and turn into a white nest instantly; quickly turn over the noodle nest and deep-fry the other side. Turn off heat. Drain noodles on paper towel. Crumble slightly and arrange on a serving platter.

2. Keep oil hot. Quickly mix egg mixture, crabmeat mixture, and scallions together. Stir gently so as not to break up the crabmeat too much. Pour half the mixture into hot oil. Stir gently. As soon as mixture is set, looking like a mass of yellow clouds, scoop it out with a drainer or a slotted spoon. With a spoon, press to squeeze off excess oil. Put in bowl and cover to keep hot. Turn heat to medium-high (because by now the oil is too cool to cook remaining eggs). Stir and fry the rest of the mixture in the same manner. Drain thoroughly.

3. Transfer cooked eggs and crabmeat onto noodles and top with chopped bacon. Serve hot at once.

西施蛋

HSI SHIH EGGS
about 4 servings

Hsi Shih was one of the most beautiful women in our history. This dish is colored red, black, green, and yellow, and supposedly is as beautiful as she was—thus it has always been called Hsi Shih eggs.

PREPARATION OF INGREDIENTS

3 tablespoons oil

EGG MIXTURE (MIX IN A BOWL)*

> *4 eggs: beat until slightly foamy*
> *1 tablespoon sesame seed oil*
> *2 preserved eggs: discard shell, cut into ¼-inch pieces*
> *2 tablespoons sweet red preserved ginger cut into pea-sized pieces*

¼ *teaspoon sugar*

½ *teaspoon salt*

⅛ *teaspoon white pepper*

¼ *cup chopped scallions: in pea-sized pieces, including green part*

DIRECTIONS FOR COOKING

1. Heat wok over high heat. Swirl in oil and spread around. When oil is hot, swirl in egg mixture. Do not stir!

2. Turn heat to medium-high. When egg begins to set around the edge, lift cooked edge and allow uncooked egg to run under. Repeat this procedure until egg is cooked but still moist. Put on a serving platter. Serve hot.

蛋黃魚餅

EGG YOLK FISH CAKES WITH SOY-VINEGAR DIP
about 4 servings

Egg white is often added to poultry, seafood, and other ingredients to make them smooth and velvety. You may wonder what to do with all the yolks. The following two recipes are marvelous with egg yolks.

PREPARATION OF INGREDIENTS

2 *quarts boiling water*

2 *tablespoons pale dry sherry*

1 *slice fresh ginger root, as big and thick as a quarter*

½ *pound fish fillet (sole or flounder)*

6 *egg yolks*

2 *scallions: cut into pea-sized pieces, including green part*

1 *teaspoon sesame seed oil*

1 *teaspoon Chinese red vinegar or cider vinegar*

½ *teaspoon salt*

⅛ *teaspoon white pepper*

4 *to 6 tablespoons oil for pan-frying*

Soy-Vinegar Dip (see recipe)

DIRECTIONS FOR COOKING

1. Put water, sherry, and ginger in a medium-sized pot and bring to a boil. Add fish, and cook over medium heat for about 3 minutes or until just done. Drain fish. Discard water and ginger. Chop fish coarsely.

2. Mix chopped fish in a bowl with egg yolks, scallions, sesame seed oil, vinegar, salt, and pepper.

3. Heat a skillet, add about 2 tablespoons oil, and spread it evenly. Spoon a heaping tablespoon of the egg yolk and fish mixture into skillet to make one cake. (You may make four to five cakes at the same time.) Fry cakes until both sides are golden brown. Put on a serving plate and place in a warm oven to keep hot. Fry others in the same manner, adding more oil when needed. Serve hot with dip.

溜黃菜

STIR-FRIED EGG YOLKS
2 to 4 servings

PREPARATION OF INGREDIENTS

6 egg yolks
2 scallions: cut into pea-sized pieces, including green part
6 water chestnuts: chop coarsely
¼ teaspoon sugar
¼ teaspoon salt
1 teaspoon thin soy sauce
1 teaspoon sesame seed oil
¼ teaspoon white pepper
3 tablespoons oil for stir-frying

DIRECTIONS FOR COOKING

1. Mix all the ingredients in a bowl except the 3 tablespoons oil for stir-frying.

2. Heat wok over high heat, then swirl in oil and spread it around. When oil is hot, pour in egg yolk mixture. Turn heat to medium, and stir-fry slowly until mixture is soft and firm, not runny. Serve hot.

Duck and Squab

DUCK

There are many kinds of ducks in China, the most famous of which is Peking duck. Though I had been roasting Peking ducks regularly and knew that they were force-fed by hand, before my recent trip to Hong Kong, I had never seen how it was done. During that time I called on Ah Lin, who, with her husband, Chou Ming, had a poultry farm in the New Territories near Hong Kong. They supplied Peking ducks as well as other kinds to various restaurants and barbecue stores in Hong Kong.

Ah Lin had been with my grandmother for thirteen years, for Grandmother had bought her when she was six years old, then married her to a fine man, Chou Ming, at the age of nineteen. She was now close to sixty, noisy as usual, but plumper and with more gold teeth each time I saw her. Her laughter rang through the valley, and her gold teeth shone in the hot Hong Kong sun. She gave me a big hearty welcome with a little good scolding. "Growing older, but not wiser! First messing yourself up in those restaurant kitchens, wasting the good life in all that cooking! Now, all the way from America to see the ducks! Here they are! Fifteen hundred of them!"

A mass of ducks was fenced in around a creek and a few shallow muddy ponds. Many of them were called mud ducks and rice ducks, I was told. Honestly, I could not tell the difference.

But the dazzling swanlike ones were unmistakably Peking ducks—snow-white feathers, orange beaks, feet, and crests. They were big and heavy, but carried themselves with imperial dignity. Peking ducks are not only beautiful-looking, but their meat is fragrant and delicate, and their rich fatty skins are excellent for roasting. Besides, they grow easily, attaining four pounds in two months. But they can reach six to eight pounds if they are force-fed with special food.

I saw that the Peking ducks prepared for restaurants were caged in seven groups. The cages were just big enough for them to stretch a little because too much exercise reduces their fat and toughens their flesh. Each day they were force-fed twice and were allowed to have only a twenty-minute swim. The rest of the time they stayed in the cages and grew fat.

I had missed the 6:00 A.M. feeding, and waited now for the afternoon feeding. Chou Ming and his three helpers had been busy preparing a lot of short and stout noodles, made of wheat, corn, and millet flours, a special diet for the caged ducks.

Each person squatted near a cage with a bucketful of noodles. Ah Lin swiftly pulled out a duck and held it gently between her legs. With her left hand holding the duck head, beak up, her right hand opened the duck's mouth and pushed in the noodles at the same time. Each duck got about eight noodles.

Because the whole operation seemed smooth and simple enough, I volunteered to help. But the duck was so much stronger than I thought. She quacked loudly and kept flapping her wings while I was pulling her out, then decided to fly when I tried to put her between my knees. When I finally got her mouth opened, I was practically sitting on her. I was so scared and shaken that I just had no heart to stuff anything into that snakelike neck. Chou Ming kindly took over my duck while Ah Lin rocked back and forth gasping with laughter.

Ducks in America are good, especially the Long Island ducklings. They are young and plump, juicy and tender, perfect for Peking roasted duck and other kinds of roasted dishes.

Fresh ducks usually are available only in some poultry shops. Be sure to ask for a young duckling and have its oil sac removed.

If you prefer to pick your own on a duck farm, and you can't tell an old duck from a young one, here are some hints from Ah Lin: "Choose the ones that have sparkling eyes, warm feet, feathers full and tidy, breasts thick and round."

I must tell you, though, that somehow Ah Lin's hints did not work very well for me. Once I went to a small duck farm near Chicago. I felt dozens of breasts, held dozens of feet. I wound up with a pair of duck-dirt shoes, a bodyful of feathers, and six chewy, gamy old ducks.

Since ducks do not lose their flavor easily, the frozen ones in most markets are almost as good as the fresh-killed. Choosing a frozen duck is easy because they are all guaranteed young ducklings. Just do not pick ones with the skin punctured during shipping and handling. Allow 10 to 12 hours to thaw out at room temperature or 24 hours in the refrigerator.

DUCK FAT

Duck fat is even tastier than chicken fat. It especially enhances vegetables if used to stir-fry them. It is not easy to obtain rendered duck fat from the market, but there are two ways to prepare it yourself:

1. Remove duck fat from cavity and cut it into peanut-sized pieces. Heat a wok. When it is hot, add 1 teaspoon vegetable oil and duck fat. Cook over medium-low heat until the fat particles become golden brown cracklings. Turn off heat. Remove the cracklings with a slotted spoon. Cool rendered fat before pouring into a jar. Cover; it will keep for weeks in the refrigerator. Also, it can be frozen.

2. When you roast a duck, save all the pan drippings and pour into a bowl. Cover and put in the refrigerator overnight. The rendered fat becomes creamy white and floats to the top. Skim off the fat from the top, and discard the liquid drippings below. Put in a covered jar. It will keep for weeks in the refrigerator. It also can be frozen.

SCALDING DUCK

In order to obtain a beautiful crisp skin, the duck has to be scalded in hot water with honey, ginger, wine, and vinegar. The honey will give the duck's skin a glossy, reddish-brown color; the wine, vinegar, and hot water draw out some fat from the skin to make a crispier skin, and the ginger helps to take away the gamy odor.

14 cups water
4 tablespoons honey
4 slices fresh ginger root, each as big and thick as a quarter
½ cup white vinegar
½ cup Chinese Shaohsing wine or pale dry sherry
1 duck

Put water, honey, ginger, vinegar, and wine in a wok or large pot and bring to a boil.

Tie the duck by the neck or by its wings and dip it in the boiling honey water. Ladle the water to scald the duck on both sides for about 2 minutes altogether. Drain and dry duck thoroughly with paper towels.

NOTE: *The honey water can be frozen and reused for one more duck; discard ginger and skim off residues and fat before use.*

BONING FOWL

The end we want to achieve in this process is to remove the carcass and main bones from the fowl while leaving the skin and flesh whole and intact. It is not as difficult to do the boning as it is to describe it. I hope the magnificent illustrations will make it clear.

1. Cut off neck 2 inches from base. Slit neck skin to base. With a sharp boning knife, working close to the bone, carefully separate the flesh from the bone so as not to pierce the skin. When you reach the wing, disjoint the main wing bone from the shoulder; cutting close to the main bone, remove it, leaving the wing intact.

2. Keep the knife close to the bone and work down to the lower part of the body, leaving the carcass separated from the flesh and skin.

3. When you reach the legs, in the same fashion as for the wings, detach and remove the thigh bones, leaving the legs intact.

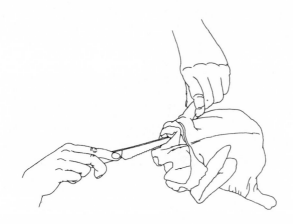

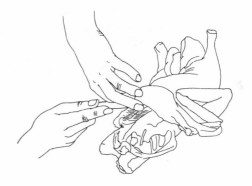

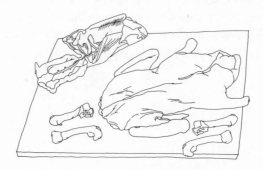

4. Remove carcass from body and save it to make soup (see recipe) or for some other use.

5. Lay out the boned fowl. If there are a few knife punctures, do not be discouraged. Just mend them with needle and thread. If you boned the fowl in less than 20 minutes, I bow to you.

CUTTING COOKED POULTRY FOR SERVING

1. Place fowl breast side up. With a heavy cleaver, chop off head and split it into halves lengthwise. Chop neck into bite-sized pieces, set aside.

2. Cut fowl into halves lengthwise from chest down to back. Disjoint wings and legs. Split fowl's halves lengthwise along the back bones. Chop back bones crosswise into bite-sized pieces; chop breast sides in the same manner.

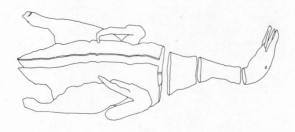

3. Reshape back bones in the center of a platter and arrange breast side pieces on them. Place head (optional), neck pieces, wings, legs, and tail at their original places to reshape the fowl. Garnish the platter with scallion brushes (see recipe), parsley, or greens.

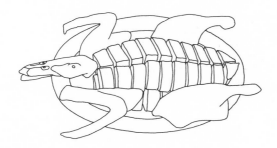

SKEWERING DUCK

Grasp the skin around the cavity. Insert a 5-inch skewer (a section of a coat hanger will do) at the tail. Stitch the cavity closed. Tie a string under the skewer and around the stitched cavity firmly but not too tightly.

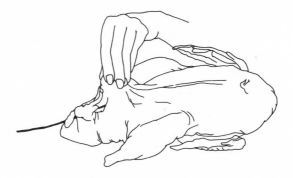

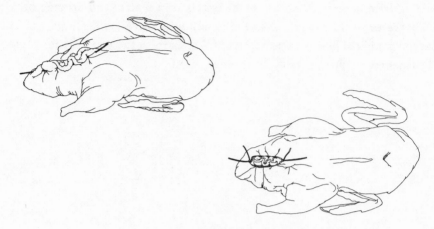

廣東燒鴨

CANTONESE ROAST DUCK
4 servings

This duck originated in a few small villages near Canton, but the village that prepared it best was Guh Jeng, meaning Old Well, the home of my grandmother. It was there that my grandmother was engaged to my grandfather when she was eight and was married to him when she was barely sixteen, never seeing him until the wedding day. She was born in the late Ching Dynasty, survived two revolutions and two world wars, but never learned to read or write. A tiny, uncomplicated woman with a kind and generous heart, she received everything that life brought her, good or bad. To all her grandchildren, she was a blanket of protection, embracing all our little woes and pains while we were growing up. During her eighty-three years, she never saw America or tasted a hot dog, but through her beloved Tarzan movies and my husband, she loved this faraway country.

Life comes and life goes, and quietly she went. She left me beautiful memories—and this delicious duck.

PREPARATION OF INGREDIENTS

1 fresh 5-pound duckling with head on: remove fat in cavity,
*   rinse duck and pat dry*
14 cups water

4 tablespoons honey
4 slices fresh ginger root, each as big and thick as a quarter
½ cup white vinegar
½ cup pale dry sherry

STUFFING (MIX IN A BOWL)*

1 tablespoon ground bean sauce
2 teaspoons *sugar*
1½ teaspoons salt
½ teaspoon five-fragrance powder
1 tablespoon minced garlic
2 teaspoons minced, soaked dried tangerine peel
2 tablespoons Chinese Shaohsing wine or pale dry sherry
2 tablespoons water

about 1 tablespoon thin soy sauce

DIRECTIONS FOR COOKING

1. Scald duck according to directions for scalding. Hang it in an airy place to dry for at least 8 hours.

2. Stuff duck. Then sew up the cavity with skewer and thread (see preceding page).

3. Place a big roasting pan, containing an inch of water, on the bottom of a gas oven or on the lowest rack of an electric oven to catch the drippings and prevent them from burning.

4. Preheat oven to 400 degrees.

5. Put duck directly on oven rack with breast side up. (If a gas oven, put duck on middle rack. If electric, put duck on upper rack.) Roast for 1½ hours. Remove duck and put on a chopping board.

6. Remove skewer and thread. Scoop out stuffing (mostly sauce) and put in a small saucepan. Measure ½ cup of the drippings (avoiding the grease) and mix with the stuffing. Add soy sauce **and sugar** to correct taste. Heat sauce over low heat until it comes to a boil. Cover and simmer over very low heat.

7. Cut duck as illustrated in this chapter. Pour sauce over duck. Serve hot.

脆皮窩燒鴨

CRISP BONELESS PRESSED DUCK

6 to 8 servings

PREPARATION OF INGREDIENTS

BROTH MIXTURE (MIX IN A BOWL)*

> 3 quarts water
> 3 slices fresh ginger root, each as big and thick as a quarter
> 2 teaspoons five-fragrance powder
> 2 tablespoons salt
> ⅓ cup black soy sauce
> ⅓ cup pale dry sherry

1 duckling, 4½ to 5 pounds: cut in half lengthwise from breast
   to back
1 egg white: beat until slightly foamy
⅓ cup water chestnut powder: sift
6 cups oil
⅓ cup uncooked walnuts

SAUCE MIXTURE (MIX IN A BOWL)*

> 1 tablespoon pale dry sherry
> 2 teaspoons white vinegar
> 1 teaspoon black soy sauce
> 5 teaspoons sugar
> juice from 1 orange
> ½ cup clear chicken broth (not condensed)
> 1 teaspoon finely minced fresh ginger root
> 2 tablespoons Grand Marnier liqueur or ½ teaspoon orange
>   extract
> 1 tablespoon plum sauce

1 tablespoon cornstarch mixed with 1 tablespoon water

DIRECTIONS FOR COOKING

1. Pour broth mixture into wok and bring it to a rapid boil. Immerse duck in broth. Cover and cook over medium-low heat for 1½ hours, turning duck from time to time.

2. Remove duck gently to a flat surface. Dry with towel. Remove breastbone and backbone from duck, but leave wings and drumsticks intact. Work gently so that the skin will not be torn.

3. Brush egg white evenly on the boned duck. Then generously sprinkle on water chestnut powder. Pat down powder with your fingers.*

4. Steam duck on rack over water for about 20 minutes or until the water chestnut powder is cooked (transparent). Put on a rack until dry and cool.*

5. Heat oil in wok over high heat to deep-fry temperature. Deep-fry walnuts to golden brown. Drain and cool on paper towels, then crush coarsely with a rolling pin. Set aside.

6. Reheat oil in wok to deep-fry temperature. Deep-fry duck over high heat until both sides are golden brown (about 15 minutes). Drain on a rack.

7. While the duck is frying, heat sauce mixture in a saucepan over medium-low heat. Stir and cook until sauce begins to bubble, then thicken it with cornstarch water. Simmer over very low heat until duck is ready.

8. Cut off wings and drumsticks. Chop duck into 1-by-1½-inch pieces. Arrange pieces on a serving platter. Pour sauce over duck and top with walnuts. Serve hot.

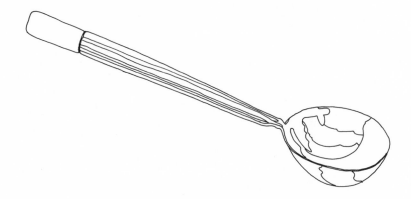

脆皮八宝鸭

STUFFED BONELESS EIGHT-JEWEL DUCK
6 to 8 servings

PREPARATION OF INGREDIENTS

*1 duckling, 4 to 5 pounds (if frozen, allow 10 to 12 hours to
thaw at room temperature): bone as illustrated in this chapter
3 tablespoons oil
⅓ cup soaked Chinese dried mushrooms: discard stems, cut caps
into ¼-inch squares
½ cup chopped lean pork: in pea-sized pieces
1 Chinese pork sausage or ½ cup Cantonese barbecued pork: cut
into pea-sized pieces
1 tablespoon dried shrimp: soak in very hot water to soften, mince
1 cup shelled chestnuts (dried or fresh): boil in water until soft
¼ cup water chestnuts: cut into pea-sized pieces
¼ cup shelled ginkgo nuts (canned may be used): split into halves
¼ cup dried lotus seeds: cook in water until tender*

SAUCE MIXTURE (MIX IN A BOWL)*

*1 tablespoon black soy sauce
1 tablespoon thin soy sauce
2 tablespoons sesame seed oil
⅛ teaspoon white pepper
¼ teaspoon five-fragrance powder
½ teaspoon sugar
1 tablespoon pale dry sherry*

*¾ cup glutinous rice: soak overnight until plump, steam over
water for 10 minutes or until done, loosen and put aside
2 teaspoons salt
Soy-Sesame Oil Dip (see recipe)
Five-Fragrance Salt Dip (see recipe)*

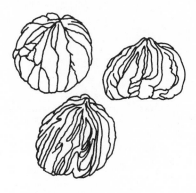

DIRECTIONS FOR COOKING

1. Scald boned duck according to directions for scalding. Hang duck to air-dry for at least 8 hours.

2. Heat wok until it is hot. Add 3 tablespoons oil. When oil is hot, add mushrooms and lean pork, and cook until pork is done. Add sausage or barbecued pork and shrimp; stir-fry for about 2 minutes. Put in chestnuts, water chestnuts, ginkgo nuts, and lotus seeds. Stir in sauce mixture. Add rice and mix until all of it is glazed with sauce. Put this stuffing in a bowl to cool in the refrigerator.*

3. When duck is air-dried, rub it inside with 2 teaspoons of salt. If it is a frozen duck and the head has been removed, sew together neck skin with thread. Stuff duck with stuffing (do not pack it too tightly or it might burst). Close the cavity with thread and skewer (see Skewering Duck).

4. Place a big roasting pan, containing an inch of water, on the bottom of a gas oven or the lowest rack of an electric oven to catch the drippings and prevent them from burning.

5. Preheat oven to 400 degrees.

6. Put duck directly on oven rack with breast side up. (If a gas oven, put duck on middle rack. If electric, put duck on upper rack.) Roast duck for 1½ hours. Remove from oven.

7. Put duck on a big oval serving platter. Remove thread and skewer. Cut off wings and legs. Cut duck into ½-inch pieces crosswise and then cut it down the middle lengthwise. (Cut carefully, disturbing the stuffing as little as possible.) Serve hot with dips.

芋頭鴨

TARO DUCK
about 8 servings

PREPARATION OF INGREDIENTS

1 duckling, 4½ to 5 pounds (if frozen, allow 10 to 12 hours to
   thaw at room temperature)
1 tablespoon black soy sauce
6 cups oil

SAUCE MIXTURE (MIX IN A BOWL)*

>   6 tablespoons red bean curd cheese
>   2 tablespoons sauce from red bean curd cheese
>   ¾ cup clear chicken broth (not condensed)
>   1 tablespoon Chinese Shaohsing wine or pale dry sherry
>   ½ teaspoon five-fragrance powder
>   2 tablespoons sugar
>   3 scallions: cut into pea-sized pieces, including green part
>   2 teaspoons finely minced fresh ginger root
>   ¼ cup coarsely chopped fresh coriander (leaves only)

1 pound taro: peel and cut into slices ⅓ inch thick, 1 inch wide,
   and 1½ inches long
1 teaspoon cornstarch mixed with 2 teaspoons water

DIRECTIONS FOR COOKING

1. Brush duck's skin with black soy sauce.

2. Heat oil in wok to deep-fry temperature. Deep-fry duck until both sides are golden brown (about 3 minutes). Remove from wok. Drain.

3. Sew together neck skin with thread if it is a frozen duck. Stuff duck with half the sauce mixture. Put remaining sauce mixture in a small saucepan for later use. Close the cavity with thread and skewer (see Skewering Duck). Put duck on a big heatproof plate. Arrange taro on the plate around the duck. Cover and steam for 1½ hours. Add boiling water from time to time to maintain the water level.

4. When duck is done, put it on a chopping board. Remove thread and skewer. Scoop out stuffing and put it in the saucepan with the remaining sauce mixture. Heat sauce over low heat until it comes to a boil. Stir in cornstarch water. Stir and cook until sauce thickens. Cover and simmer over very low heat to keep it hot.

5. Cut duck as illustrated in this chapter. Put taro pieces around duck. Pour sauce over taro and duck. Serve hot.

樟茶鴨

SZECHWAN SMOKED DUCK
6 to 8 servings

PREPARATION OF INGREDIENTS

2½ *tablespoons salt*

2 *teaspoons flower peppercorn powder*

2 *teaspoons five-fragrance powder*

1 *duckling, 4½ to 5 pounds (if frozen, allow 10 to 12 hours to*
  thaw): remove fat from cavity, rinse duck in cold water, pat dry

1 *tablespoon black soy sauce*

1 *tablespoon pale dry sherry*

continued

SMOKING INGREDIENTS (MIX IN A BOWL)*

> *½ cup tea leaves (any dark-colored tea, such as orange pekoe or*
> *lychee black tea)*
> *2 tangerine peels or 1 orange peel: tear into quarter-sized pieces*
> *¼ cup brown sugar*
> *1 tablespoon ground cinnamon*
> *1 handful camphor wood chips (optional)*

6 cups oil
Scallion Brushes (see recipe) or parsley (optional)
Five-Fragrance Salt Dip (see recipe)

DIRECTIONS FOR COOKING

1. Mix salt, flower peppercorn powder, and five-fragrance powder in a bowl. Rub duck inside and out with this mixture. Let duck stand in refrigerator for 10 to 15 hours.

2. Mix black soy sauce and sherry in a bowl, and brush it over the duck's skin an hour before smoking the duck.

3. Line a big wok with heavy aluminum foil. Sprinkle the bottom of the wok with the smoking ingredients. Arrange four bamboo chopsticks or metal skewers overlapping each other to form a tick-tack-toe design. Rest duck on chopsticks, breast side up. Cover wok tightly. (The cover should be high enough to allow the smoke to circulate, and the duck should be at least 1 inch from the smoking ingredients.)

4. Turn heat to high. Smoke duck for 30 minutes. Turn off heat, but do not uncover. Allow smoke to subside (about 10 minutes).

5. Steam smoked duck over water, breast side up, for 1½ hours. Cool on a rack for at least an hour.*

6. Heat oil in wok over medium-high heat. When oil is hot, deep-fry smoked duck until both sides are evenly light brown. Drain.

7. Cut duck as illustrated in this chapter. Garnish with scallion brushes or parsley if you like. Serve duck warm with dip, divided into individual dishes for each person.

香酥鴨

SZECHWAN CRISP SPICED DUCK
6 to 8 servings

From this duck's appearance, it would seem as if the cook has had a bad day or has played a joke on the diners. The duck's breast sinks into its body. The pale brown skin is dull and dry. But it is really a beauty in disguise: the skin is crisp and luscious, the meat is fragrant, and even the bones are crunchy and tasty. This duck is for the true gourmet!

PREPARATION OF INGREDIENTS

1 duckling, 4½ to 5 pounds (if frozen, allow 12 hours to thaw)

MARINADE (MIX IN A BOWL)*

> *1 tablespoon flower peppercorn powder*
> *1 teaspoon five-fragrance powder*
> *1 tablespoon finely minced fresh ginger root*
> *1 tablespoon pale dry sherry*
> *2 tablespoons thin soy sauce*
> *½ teaspoon sugar*
> *1½ tablespoons salt*

6 cups oil
Lettuce, Scallion Brushes (see recipe), or parsley
Flower Peppercorn and Salt Dip (see recipe)

DIRECTIONS FOR COOKING

1. Clean and dry duck. Remove fat from the cavity. With both hands, press down on duck's breast to flatten the breastbone.

2. Rub duck inside and out with the marinade. Cover and marinate in the refrigerator for 8 to 10 hours.

3. Steam duck in a steamer or on a rack over water for 2½ hours, adding boiling water from time to time to maintain the level. Drain and air-dry duck on rack for several hours.

4. In a wok, heat oil over high heat to deep-fry temperature. The oil should cover half the duck. Deep-fry duck over medium heat for about 30 minutes, turning twice. When done, the duck is stiff and the skin is dull light brown. Drain.

5. Chop duck (including the bones) as illustrated in this chapter. Garnish with lettuce, scallion brushes, or parsley. Serve hot or warm with dip.

NOTE: *After you marinate and steam the duck, you may freeze it. Thaw at room temperature, then deep-fry it.*

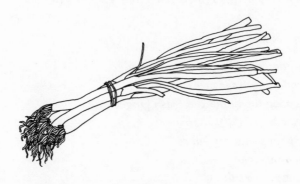

北京鴨

PEKING DUCK
6 to 8 servings

Never has a dish had such publicity! Never has a duck spread its wings so far! It all began around the year 1855 in Peking. Pen Yee Inn, a restaurant specializing in chicken and duck dishes, created the method which made Peking duck a star. The dish was purely for the very rich, and the primary interest was the crisp skin.

The traditional way to prepare Peking duck is unbelievable. It required a student of the Peking cuisine three months of training just to learn to kill and dress the duck correctly. A hole was opened under each wing to remove the innards so as to keep the duck's skin whole and unbroken. In order to make the skin crisp but not hard, rich but not oily, air was blown in from the duck's throat to separate the skin from the meat. Then the duck was dipped in hot water with honey, wine, vinegar, and ginger. The hot water and the wine helped to draw out some fat; the honey gave the skin a glossy, reddish-brown color when it was roasted; the vinegar stiffened the skin; and the ginger took away the gamy odor. Then the duck was hung in an airy cool place for between 12 and 24 hours to air-dry the skin. Finally, hanging by the neck, it was roasted in a huge drumlike clay oven with charcoal or coal burning below. An even skin was acquired by shifting the duck's position many times. Controlling the heat and the timing required an experienced cook.

Then the glistening, crisp brown skin, cut and arranged on a preheated platter, was served with warm pancakes, accompanied by scallion brushes and sauce. The tender meat, not the primary concern, was served as a separate side dish. And the carcass was used for soup.

Honestly, if you had to go through all this killing, dressing, and blowing in order to eat Peking duck, you'd probably opt for a peanut butter and jelly sandwich instead! Fortunately, living in the West has some advantages. With modern gas and electric ovens, and the young and plump Long Island ducklings, preparing Peking duck is quite simple. So never mind all the noises and words about the special skill and the long and hard preparation. The following method is very simple. All you need is a duck under 5 pounds.

PREPARATION OF INGREDIENTS

14 cups water

4 tablespoons honey

4 slices fresh ginger root, each as big and thick as a quarter

1 Long Island duckling, 4½ to 5 pounds (if frozen, allow 12 hours to thaw at room temperature): remove fat from cavity

½ cup Chinese Shaohsing wine or pale dry sherry

½ cup white vinegar

Mandarin Pancakes (see recipe)

24 Scallion Brushes (see recipe)

Hoisin Sauce Dip (see recipe) or Bean Sauce Dip (see recipe)

DIRECTIONS FOR COOKING

1. Scald duck according to directions for scalding (page 93).

2. Hang duck in a cool and airy place to dry for 10 hours.

3. Have the Mandarin pancakes covered and ready to be reheated. Prepare the scallion brushes and the dip.

4. Preheat oven to 400 degrees. Put duck, breast side up, directly on an oven rack. (If a gas oven, put duck on middle rack. If electric, put duck on upper rack.) Put a big roasting pan with about 1 inch of cold water on the bottom of gas oven or on the lowest rack of electric oven to catch drippings and prevent them from burning. Roast duck breast side up for 1½ hours.

5. Ten minutes before the duck is done, fold pancakes in quarters or in halves. Put them, slightly overlapping each other, on a steamer or a rack. Steam over boiling water for 3 minutes or until pancakes are hot. You may also wrap pancakes in a stack with aluminum foil and heat them in a 275-degree oven for 10 minutes or until all the pancakes are warm. Arrange pancakes on a platter just before serving.

6. When duck is done, drain off juice in its cavity, being careful not to let juice wet the crisp skin. Put duck on chopping board. Cut off legs and wings. Remove skin with a sharp knife or with scissors. Cut skin into 1-by-2-inch pieces and arrange them in one layer on a heated platter. Garnish with some of the scallion brushes. Slice duck meat and cut into pieces as big as the skin. Place them on another preheated platter, and arrange legs and wings beside the meat to look like a duck. Garnish with remaining scallion brushes.

7. Bring the dip, duck meat, duck skin, and pancakes to the table at the same time.

8. Give each person a plate. Unfold a pancake and put a piece of meat topped with a piece of skin in the middle of the pancake. Take a scallion brush and paint the skin with ¼ to ½ teaspoon sauce dip. Place the scallion brush on the pancake holding the sauced duck meat and skin, roll the edges of the pancake into a package, and eat.

NOTE: *Be sure that you place a pan with an inch of water in the oven to catch the drippings. One of my students had a small fire in his oven be-*

cause he used a shallow pan with very little water. No damage was done, except his duck and his guests all took on a little smoky flavor.

Make the Mandarin pancakes days or weeks ahead and freeze them so that you don't have all your preparation in one day.

Save or freeze the carcass for soup (see recipe).

醬油鴨

RED-COOKED DUCKLING WITH LETTUCE IN SOY SAUCE
4 to 6 servings

PREPARATION OF INGREDIENTS

8 cups water
1 duckling, 4 to 5 pounds (if frozen, allow 10 to 12 hours to
    thaw): remove fat from cavity, rinse duck thoroughly, pat dry

SAUCE MIXTURE (MIX IN A BOWL)*

   ¾ cup black soy sauce
   ⅓ cup pale dry sherry
   about 3 cups water
   4 tablespoons sugar
   1 whole star anise
   3 pieces fresh ginger root, each as big and thick as a quarter
   ½ stick cinnamon, about 2 inches long

½ head iceberg lettuce: separate leaves

DIRECTIONS FOR COOKING

1. Bring water to a boil. Put in duck and blanch for 3 minutes, turning from time to time. Remove duck, discard water, and dry duck thoroughly with a towel.

2. Put duck, breast side down, in a Dutch oven. Pour in sauce mixture. Cover and cook over medium-low heat for about 1½ hours or until duck is very tender. Turn it from time to time, and add more water if needed.

3. Discard anise, ginger, and cinnamon stick. Skim off fat, reserving 3 tablespoons.

4. Spoon sauce on duck for a few minutes to color the skin. There should be 1 to 1½ cups of sauce left in the pot.

5. Heat reserved fat from duck in wok. Add lettuce and stir-fry until it turns clear and soft. Transfer it to a serving platter.

6. Put duck on chopping board. Chop or carve into appropriate-sized pieces, and arrange them on the cooked lettuce. Pour some sauce on duck. Serve hot.

炸五香鴿子

CRISP SQUABS WITH FIVE-FRAGRANCE SALT
about 4 servings

PREPARATION OF INGREDIENTS

2 squabs: split and clean, pat dry with paper towels

MARINADE (MIX IN A BOWL)*

> *½ teaspoon salt*
> *1 tablespoon black soy sauce*
> *1 teaspoon sugar*
> *1 tablespoon Chinese Shaohsing wine or pale dry sherry*
> *½ teaspoon five-fragrance powder*
> *¼ teaspoon white pepper*
> *2 teaspoons Chinese red vinegar*
> *2 tablespoons minced scallions*

about 4 cups oil
Five-Fragrance Salt Dip (see recipe)

DIRECTIONS FOR COOKING

1. Rub squabs with marinade. Cover and let sit for about 4 hours.

2. Rest squabs on a rack in an airy place and let dry for at least 2 hours.

3. Heat oil in wok over medium heat. When oil is hot, deep-fry squabs for 10 minutes on each side over medium heat. Drain on paper towels.

4. With a cleaver chop squabs into pieces about 1 inch wide and 2 inches long. Serve hot with dip, divided into individual dishes for each person.

Pork

PORK

Chinese pigs look very different from their American cousins. They are darker and much softer-looking; their backs curve in a great deal, and their bellies nearly touch the ground. They are no great beauties, but they are good-natured. It does not take much good food or care for them to grow and get fat. Chinese country people treat pigs with much affection. If you visit the countryside or a Chinese village, you can see pigs wandering around the household almost like pets.

During the Second World War, food was scarce in many villages. Some families could not afford to raise a pig by themselves; a few families used to share in raising one or two. Each day, they took turns feeding the pigs, so one could see the animals being walked back and forth between families.

These pigs were usually slaughtered just before the Chinese New Year. The meat, the intestines, the feet, and even the bones were equally divided. It was a big occasion for many families. With great care, they treated their shares in endless ways—some for roasting, some for salting, some for smoking, some for sausages.

In an agricultural country such as China, meat is hardly a part of the daily diet. The desire for animal fat is accordingly great among many Chinese. For this, pork does wonders. It keeps many stomachs from getting rusty. Moreover, since cows are used to work in the fields, beef is of low quality. Therefore, pork is the most popular meat among the Chinese. When we say meat, we mean pork.

As I mentioned, pigs are good-natured. And so is their flesh. Pork gets along well with almost everything—all kinds of vegetables, meat, and even seafood. Above all, pork is tasty, tender, juicy, and sweet. No matter how you cut it or cook it, it is always good!

木樨肉

MOO SHU PORK
4 to 8 servings

PREPARATION OF INGREDIENTS

4 eggs
¼ teaspoon salt
5 tablespoons oil
1 thin slice fresh ginger root
2 scallions: shred into 1½-inch lengths, including green part
5 Chinese dried mushrooms: soak in hot water until spongy,
discard stems, shred caps into matchstick strips

PORK MIXTURE (MIX AND MARINATE IN A BOWL)*

8 ounces lean pork: shred into matchstick strips (to make 1 cup)
½ teaspoon pale dry sherry
1 teaspoon thin soy sauce
1 teaspoon cornstarch
¼ teaspoon sugar
⅛ teaspoon pepper

⅓ cup dried cloud ears: soak 15 minutes or until soft, pinch off
hard parts, tear remainder into halves
25 dried lily buds: soak 15 minutes or until soft, break off tough
parts, tear remainder into halves lengthwise
1 cup tightly packed, thinly shredded (crosswise) Chinese celery
cabbage
½ cup bamboo shoots shredded into matchstick strips

SAUCE MIXTURE (MIX IN A BOWL)*

2 tablespoons black soy sauce
1 tablespoon thin soy sauce
½ teaspoon sugar

½ teaspoon salt

2 teaspoons pale dry sherry

4 tablespoons water

1 teaspoon cornstarch

1 ounce bean thread noodles: soak in hot water until soft, cut
about 4 inches long with scissors

1 tablespoon sesame seed oil

Mandarin Pancakes (see recipe); steam until hot or reheat in
oven wrapped in foil

DIRECTIONS FOR COOKING

1. Beat eggs with salt. Heat wok until hot. Swirl in 2 tablespoons oil. When oil is hot, add eggs and cook them as you would scrambled eggs. Do not overcook—eggs should be smooth and moist. Cut eggs into chunks about the size of sugar cubes. Set aside.

2. Heat wok until hot. Swirl in 3 tablespoons oil. When oil is hot, brown ginger, then discard it. Keep wok hot. Throw in scallions and mushrooms, and brown them slightly. Add pork mixture, and stir-fry until meat is no longer pink. Add cloud ears and lily buds, then cabbage and bamboo shoots. Cook over medium-high heat until they are heated thoroughly. Stir in sauce mixture and cook for 15 seconds. Add cooked egg chunks and bean thread noodles. Toss to mix well. Add sesame seed oil. Mix. Put on serving platter and serve hot with Mandarin pancakes.

To eat, put 2 to 3 spoonfuls of Moo Shu pork in the center of a heated pancake, and fold pancake into a package.

NOTE: *This dish can be cooked in advance without the eggs. Scramble eggs and add chunks just before you reheat.*

珍珠丸子

STEAMED GIANT PEARLS
4 to 6 servings

PREPARATION OF INGREDIENTS

2 tablespoons dried shrimp (optional): soak in hot water to soften, mince

1 pound ground pork (ask your butcher to grind it only once)

6 Chinese dried mushrooms: soak in hot water until spongy, discard stems, mince caps

6 water chestnuts: mince

2 teaspoons cornstarch

1½ tablespoons thin soy sauce

2 teaspoons sesame seed oil

¼ teaspoon salt

½ teaspoon sugar

1 big pinch white pepper

6 tablespoons glutinous rice: soak in cold water at least 4 hours or until plump, drain just before use, put on plate, pat dry with towels

Chili-Oil Dip (see recipe) or Soy-Chili Dip (see recipe)

DIRECTIONS FOR COOKING

1. Mix together all the ingredients except rice and dip. Do not over-mix or the meatballs will be tough. Form mixture into 18 to 20 walnut-sized meatballs.

2. Roll meatballs in rice until well coated.

3. Arrange meatballs in a bamboo steamer or on a wire rack lined with a piece of cheesecloth. Cover and steam over water for 20 minutes. Serve hot with dip.

NOTE: *Meatballs can be rolled in advance. Do not coat them with rice until just before steaming, or the rice will dry out and become hard in the middle when cooked.*

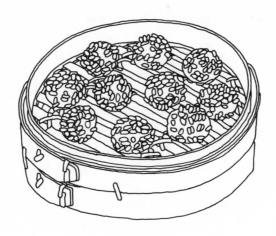

紅燒元蹄

RED-COOKED FRESH HAM

4 to 6 servings

PREPARATION OF INGREDIENTS

2 tablespoons oil
4 slices fresh ginger root, each as big and thick as a quarter
2 cloves garlic: crush and peel
2 scallions: cut into 1½-inch lengths, including green part
about 4 pounds fresh uncured ham

SAUCE MIXTURE (MIX IN A BOWL)*

> *½ cup black soy sauce*
> *2 tablespoons thin soy sauce*
> *¼ cup Chinese Shaohsing wine or pale dry sherry*
> *4 tablespoons sugar*
> *½ teaspoon salt*

about 5 cups boiling water
1 stick cinnamon
3 whole star anise
½ head iceberg lettuce: separate leaves and break into large pieces

DIRECTIONS FOR COOKING

1. Heat a Dutch oven and pour in oil. When oil is hot, add ginger, garlic, and scallions. Brown them slightly. Add the ham and sear it evenly.

2. Turn heat to medium-low. Pour in sauce mixture. Add 1 cup of boiling water, cinnamon stick, and star anise. Cover and simmer until ham is very tender (about 4 hours). Check ham from time to time during cooking, and add additional boiling water by the cupful as needed. There should be 1½ to 2 cups of sauce left in the pot at the end of the cooking time.

3. Discard ginger, garlic, cinnamon stick, and star anise. Skim off fat, reserving 3 tablespoons.

4. Heat reserved fat in wok. Add lettuce and stir-fry until it turns clear and softens. Transfer to a serving platter.

5. Slice the ham and arrange the pieces on lettuce. Spoon sauce over ham. Serve hot.

NOTE: *This dish can be precooked and reheated on stove.*

葱爆三樣

PEKING SLICED PORK, CHICKEN, SHRIMP, AND SCALLIONS
about 4 servings

PREPARATION OF INGREDIENTS

3 to 4 cups oil

CHICKEN AND PORK MIXTURE (MIX IN A BOWL)*

> *8 ounces lean pork: cut into paper-thin slices while half-frozen*
> *1 boned, skinless chicken breast: cut into pieces same as pork*
> *1 tablespoon brown sugar*
> *1 tablespoon black soy sauce*
> *2 tablespoons cornstarch*

SHRIMP MIXTURE (MIX IN A BOWL. REFRIGERATE BEFORE USE)*

> *4 ounces fresh shrimp: shell, devein, rinse in cold water, pat dry*
> *⅓ egg white*
> *¼ teaspoon salt*
> *1 pinch white pepper*

6 scallions: cut into 1½-inch pieces, including green part
2 teaspoons minced garlic

SAUCE MIXTURE (MIX IN A BOWL)*

1 tablespoon ground bean sauce
1½ tablespoons black soy sauce
3 tablespoons Chinese Shaohsing wine or pale dry sherry
2 teaspoons brown sugar

DIRECTIONS FOR COOKING

1. Heat oil in wok to deep-fry temperature. Add chicken and pork mixture. Stir to separate pieces. Blanch briskly until chicken turns white and pork loses its pink color. Remove with a drainer to a bowl.

2. In the same hot oil, briskly blanch shrimp mixture until shrimps just turn white-pink. Remove with a drainer to a bowl.

3. Remove all but 2 tablespoons oil from wok. Heat oil, then add scallions and garlic. When garlic turns golden, swirl in sauce mixture. Stir and cook until sauce begins to bubble. Return chicken, pork, and shrimp to wok. Mix and stir-fry for about 15 seconds. Put on a serving platter. Serve hot.

紅燒獅子頭

RED-COOKED LION HEADS
4 to 8 servings

The Chinese take the naming of their dishes as seriously as the naming of their children. The chicken is known as Phoenix, snake or shrimp becomes Dragon, and these big, fancy meatballs are called Lion Heads. The lion is the symbol of power, protector of humans and deities against evil spirits. The lion's roar signifies the voice of Buddha. Therefore, sculpted lions are often seen guarding the temples and official buildings in China.

The hearts of the celery cabbage are the manes of the lions. Since it is too costly to use just the heart of the cabbage in the United States, you may use the other parts of the celery cabbage also.

This is a northern dish, very tasty, meaty, with a lot of gravy for rice.

PREPARATION OF INGREDIENTS

PORK MIXTURE (MIX IN A BOWL. DO NOT OVERMIX OR MEATBALLS WILL BE TOUGH)*

> 1 pound ground pork
> 5 Chinese mushrooms: soak in hot water until soft, drain, discard
>   stems, and mince
> 1 tablespoon cloud ears: soak in hot water until soft, drain, mince
> 1/3 cup minced water chestnuts
> 1/4 cup minced bamboo shoots
> 2 scallions: mince, including green part
> 1 tablespoon pale dry sherry
> 2 tablespoons black soy sauce
> 1/2 teaspoon sugar
> 1/8 teaspoon pepper
> 1 1/2 tablespoons cornstarch

2 tablespoons oil
1 1/2 pounds Chinese celery cabbage hearts: cut into big pieces

SAUCE MIXTURE (MIX IN A BOWL)*

> 1 tablespoon pale dry sherry
> 1 tablespoon thin soy sauce
> 1 teaspoon sugar
> 3/4 cup chicken broth (not condensed)

1 tablespoon cornstarch mixed with 1 tablespoon water
1/4 teaspoon salt or to taste

DIRECTIONS FOR COOKING

1. Form pork mixture into 4 big peach-sized meatballs.

2. Heat a flat skillet. Add oil. When oil is hot, put meatballs in and turn heat to medium. Brown meatballs evenly, then remove them to a plate.

3. Leave oil in skillet, and add the cabbage. Turn on heat and stir-fry for a minute. Transfer cabbage to a 3- to 4-quart pot. Stir in sauce mixture and mix well. Put meatballs on top of cabbage. Cover and simmer for 20 to 30 minutes or until cabbage is soft.

4. Transfer meatballs and cabbage to a serving bowl, placing cabbage at the bottom and meatballs on top. Leave liquid in the cooking pot. Stir cornstarch water into liquid and cook until thickened. Salt to taste. Pour sauce over meatballs and cabbage. Serve hot.

NOTE: *This dish can be cooked in advance and reheated on stove.*

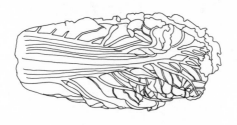

炸五香肉扒

DEEP-FRIED FIVE-FRAGRANCE PORK CHOPS
2 to 4 servings

PREPARATION OF INGREDIENTS

*6 pork chops: cut each in half and pound with back edge of
   cleaver (leave bone in)*

MARINADE (MIX IN A BOWL AND MARINATE PORK CHOPS FOR 30 MINUTES OR
   LONGER; TURN FROM TIME TO TIME)*

> *¼ cup black soy sauce*
> *1 tablespoon brown sugar*
> *1 tablespoon Chinese Shaohsing wine or pale dry sherry*
> *½ teaspoon five-fragrance powder*
> *½ teaspoon finely minced fresh ginger root*
> *2 scallions: mince finely, including green part*

about ¼ cup cornstarch
about 3 cups oil

DIRECTIONS FOR COOKING

1. Put cornstarch on a plate and lightly dredge marinated pork chops in it.

2. Heat oil to deep-fry temperature. Deep-fry pork chops, a few at a time, until they are golden brown. Drain on paper towels. Serve hot.

咕嚕肉

SWEET AND SOUR PORK
4 to 6 servings

Everybody seems to say that his or her sweet and sour pork is the best. I am afraid that I am going to say the same thing. The most elegant and delicious sweet and sour pork is prepared the way my aunts, my grandmothers, and their cooks prepared theirs. They never put ketchup in the sauce, but used shan jah beng. These little wafers give the sweet and sour sauce a very delicate flavor and a natural clear red color; therefore, no red food coloring is needed. But if shan jah beng is not available, you may substitute 2 tablespoons ketchup for it.

For this dish, choose pork marbled with some fat (such as pork butt), so it will be crisp after frying. Lean pork will come out dry and tough.

PREPARATION OF INGREDIENTS

about ¾ cup cornstarch

PORK MIXTURE (MIX IN A BOWL)*

> *about 12 ounces raw pork: cut into ¾-inch cubes (to make 1½*
> *cups), pound with back edge of cleaver or heavy knife*
> *1 teaspoon pale dry sherry*
> *1 egg, beaten*
> *⅛ teaspoon salt*
> *1 big pinch pepper*

2 tablespoons oil
⅓ cup water chestnuts, each cut in half
¼ cup bamboo shoots cut into small sugar-cube-sized pieces

¼ cup red or green bell pepper cut into ½-inch squares
⅓ cup canned pineapple chunks

SAUCE MIXTURE (MIX IN A BOWL. ALLOW TO SIT FOR AN HOUR OR MORE)*

 ⅓ cup canned pineapple juice
 1 tablespoon thin soy sauce
 1 tablespoon black soy sauce
 ¼ cup white vinegar
 1 ounce shan jah beng: separate wafers so they will
    dissolve easily
 ¼ cup sugar
 1 teaspoon minced garlic
 ½ cup water

1½ tablespoons cornstarch mixed with 2 tablespoons water
about 4 cups oil for deep-frying

DIRECTIONS FOR COOKING

1. Put cornstarch on a plate and roll pork mixture in it until cubes are no longer sticky. Put pork on plate, and after it absorbs cornstarch, roll in cornstarch again.

2. Heat a small saucepan over low heat. Add 2 tablespoons oil, water chestnuts, bamboo shoots, pepper, and pineapple. Pour in sauce mixture. Cook, stirring constantly, over medium-low heat until sauce bubbles gently. Stir in cornstarch water. Stir and cook until sauce is thickened. Turn heat to very low to keep sauce hot.

3. Heat about 4 cups oil to very hot, almost smoking. Deep-fry pork until pieces float to the top and turn a light golden color (about 5 minutes). Remove pork with drainer or slotted spoon and put on a serving platter. Pour sauce over pork. Serve piping hot immediately.

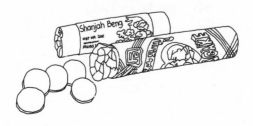

糖醋丸子

MEATBALLS IN SWEET AND SOUR SAUCE
about 4 servings

PREPARATION OF INGREDIENTS

PORK MIXTURE (MIX IN A BOWL. DO NOT OVERMIX OR MEATBALLS WILL BE TOUGH)*

> *1 pound ground pork: use pork with some fat so it will be crisp*
>   *and juicy*
> *1 tablespoon minced scallion*
> *1 tablespoon black soy sauce*
> *1 teaspoon pale dry sherry*
> *¼ teaspoon sugar*
> *¼ teaspoon salt*
> *1 egg, beaten*
> *1 tablespoon cornstarch*

about ¼ cup cornstarch
about 3 cups oil for deep-frying

SAUCE MIXTURE (MIX IN A BOWL)*

> *¼ cup white vinegar*
> *1 ounce shan jah beng or 3 tablespoons ketchup*
> *2 tablespoons sugar*
> *2 tablespoons thin soy sauce*
> *½ cup water*

1 tablespoon oil
1 tablespoon cornstarch mixed with 1 tablespoon water
4 scallions: shred into 1½-inch pieces, including green part
1 teaspoon sesame seed oil

DIRECTIONS FOR COOKING

1. Form pork mixture into walnut-sized meatballs.

2. Lightly roll meatballs in the ¼ cup cornstarch.

3. Heat oil in wok to deep-fry temperature. Deep-fry meatballs until light gold. Drain on paper towels. Keep them hot in warm oven.

4. Heat 1 tablespoon oil in a small saucepan. Stir in sauce mixture. When sauce begins to bubble, stir in cornstarch water. Stir and cook until thickened. Add scallions and sesame seed oil. Pour over meatballs. Serve hot.

糟溜肉扒

PORK CHOPS IN SPICED WINE SAUCE
about 4 servings

PREPARATION OF INGREDIENTS

2 pounds pork chops: pound each with back edge of cleaver,
   chop each into 3 pieces (leave bone in)

MARINADE (MARINATE PORK CHOPS IN A BOWL)*

   1 tablespoon Chinese Shaohsing wine or pale dry sherry
   1 tablespoon thin soy sauce

about ½ cup cornstarch
about 4 cups oil
2 scallions: cut into pea-sized pieces, including green part
1 tablespoon minced garlic

SAUCE MIXTURE (MIX IN A BOWL)*

   2 tablespoons black soy sauce
   1 teaspoon sugar
   1 tablespoon Chinese red vinegar or cider vinegar
   ½ teaspoon Chili Oil (see recipe)
   4 tablespoons sweet wine sauce (sauce only) or **orange** *liqueur*
   1 tablespoon Chinese Shaohsing wine or pale dry sherry

1 teaspoon cornstarch mixed with 2 teaspoons water

DIRECTIONS FOR COOKING

1. Lightly dust marinated pork chops with cornstarch. Set aside.

2. Heat oil in wok to very hot. Deep-fry pork chops, a few pieces at a time, to golden brown. Drain and keep hot in a 350-degree oven.

3. Remove all but 2 tablespoons oil from wok. Heat oil over high heat, then drop in scallions and garlic. When garlic turns golden, immediately stir in sauce mixture. Cook and stir until sauce bubbles gently. Add cornstarch water. Stir until sauce is thickened. Turn off heat.

4. Arrange pork on a serving platter and pour sauce evenly over chops. Serve hot.

魚香肉絲

SZECHWAN SPICED PORK SHREDS
2 servings

PREPARATION OF INGREDIENTS

4 tablespoons oil

PORK MIXTURE (MIX IN A BOWL)*

   ½ pound lean pork: shred into matchstick strips
   2 teaspoons cornstarch

1 teaspoon finely minced fresh ginger root
2 teaspoons minced garlic
3 scallions: cut into strips 1½ inches long, including green part
2 dried chili peppers: tear into small pieces, do not discard seeds
½ cup shredded bamboo shoots
½ cup water chestnuts
*⅓ cup dried cloud ears: soak in hot water until soft, tear each
   in half*

SAUCE MIXTURE (MIX IN A BOWL)*

   1 tablespoon black soy sauce
   1 tablespoon Szechwan sweet bean sauce or ground bean sauce
   1 tablespoon pale dry sherry
   2 teaspoons Chinese red vinegar or cider vinegar

¼ teaspoon salt
1 ¼ teaspoons sugar
1 teaspoon sesame seed oil
½ cup water

2 teaspoons cornstarch mixed with 1 tablespoon water

DIRECTIONS FOR COOKING

1. Heat wok over high heat. Swirl in the 4 tablespoons oil. When oil is hot, add pork mixture and stir-fry until meat is no longer pink. Remove with a drainer, leaving oil in wok.

2. Keep wok hot. Add ginger, garlic, scallions, and chili peppers, and brown them slightly. Throw in bamboo shoots and cloud ears. Stir-fry for about 30 seconds. Add sauce mixture and cornstarch water. Cook and stir until it bubbles gently. Add pork and stir-fry for about a minute. Put on a serving plate. Serve hot.

燒排骨

CANTONESE BARBECUED SPARERIBS
4 servings

Mr. Ng was a very good barbecue chef. He worked for a grocery store in New York's Chinatown. He was about fifty-five, noisy, and his face was full of expression when he talked. Fascinated by that face, I often did not hear what he said. He seemed to be forever arguing with his fellow workers, then a minute later he forgot. He laughed, he yelled, he joked, all in the same breath. Each week he barbecued about 150 ducks and at least 300 pounds of spareribs and pork. And yet he still found time to jest and quarrel. If he was not in a jubilant mood, he splashed the marinade and pushed the ducks around.

Since he did not speak English or write it, he seldom ventured out of Chinatown. His whole world was his family and his kin. He felt that he was my uncle simply because I had lived in the village where he was born. He thought that anybody who could write English was very smart; therefore, I was the scholar of his heart. I have met many cooks and chefs like Mr. Ng; many of them are not as noisy, and some are even shy. They all work long hours but never lose their steam. They own very little, but are extravagant spirits. Such persons humble one.

PREPARATION OF INGREDIENTS

3 to 4 pounds uncut spareribs

SAUCE MIXTURE (MIX IN A BOWL)*

> *2 teaspoons minced garlic*
> *⅔ cup hoisin sauce*
> *⅓ cup black soy sauce*
> *6 tablespoons light corn syrup or honey*
> *4 tablespoons Chinese Shaohsing wine or pale dry sherry*

GLAZE (MIX IN A BOWL)*
> *1 tablespoon thin soy sauce*
> *4 tablespoons honey*

DIRECTIONS FOR COOKING

1. Marinate ribs in sauce mixture at least 4 to 6 hours or overnight.

2. Heat oven to 375 degrees.

3. Put ribs directly on oven rack. (If it is a gas oven, put rack in the middle of the oven. If electric, put rack in upper part of the oven.) Put a big pan with ½ inch of cold water on the bottom of a gas oven or on the lowest rack of an electric oven to catch drippings and prevent them from burning. The ribs and the pan with water should be 9 to 10 inches away from each other; otherwise the water will steam the ribs, causing them to lose their barbecued flavor.

4. Cook ribs for about 45 minutes. Generously brush upper side of ribs with the glaze, and catch the drippings with a plate. Cook ribs for another 2 minutes. Turn ribs and glaze the other side in the same manner. Cook for 2 more minutes.

5. Put ribs on chopping board, cut into strips, and serve hot or cold.

NOTE: *You may freeze cooked ribs in aluminum foil. Thaw, then reheat in slow oven.*

义燒肉

CANTONESE BARBECUED PORK
8 to 10 servings

This famous barbecued pork is a Cantonese specialty. Eat it cold or hot as you like. Since most Chinese families do not have ovens or grills, barbecued pork is prepared mostly in restaurants, barbecue shops, and some grocery stores. They dye the pork red, the color of happiness.

To the Chinese, it is a dish for many occasions: for a special family treat, for a picnic, or for the drop-in guests who do not leave at dinner time.

For this recipe, it is best to use boneless loin roast, shoulder or rib end. If you use tenderloin, it will come out a little too dry.

PREPARATION OF INGREDIENTS

3 to 4 pounds boneless pork: cut into strips 1 inch thick and
2 inches wide

MARINADE (MIX IN A BOWL)*

2 teaspoons minced garlic
3 tablespoons sugar
5 tablespoons black soy sauce
⅓ cup hoisin sauce
½ cup Chinese Shaohsing wine or pale dry sherry
2 tablespoons ground bean sauce

GLAZE (MIX IN A BOWL)*

2 tablespoons honey
2 teaspoons sesame seed oil
3 tablespoons thin soy sauce

DIRECTIONS FOR COOKING

1. Put pork strips in a pan. Spoon marinade over pork evenly, and refrigerate for 8 hours or more. Turn pork from time to time.

2. Preheat oven to 375 degrees.

3. Spear pork strips lengthwise with skewers and put them directly on an oven rack. (If it is a gas oven, put rack in middle of oven. If electric, put rack in upper part of oven.) Put a big pan with ½ inch of cold water on bottom of gas oven or on lowest rack of electric oven to catch the drippings and prevent them from smoking. Roast for 20 minutes. Turn skewers and roast for another 20 minutes.

4. Generously brush upper side of pork strips with the glaze, catching the drippings with a plate. Roast pork strips for 5 minutes. Turn skewers and glaze other side of pork in the same manner. Roast for another 5 minutes. Turn off heat.

5. Remove barbecued pork from skewers. Cut into thin slices. Brush slices with the remaining glaze, if there is any, or the drippings you caught while brushing. Serve pork hot, warm, or cold.

NOTE: *You may freeze barbecued pork strips for fried rice and other recipes.*

胡桃炸肉丁

PORK DINGS AND WALNUTS
2 to 4 servings

PREPARATION OF INGREDIENTS

3 cups oil

PORK MIXTURE (MIX IN A BOWL)*

> *1 pound lean pork: slice ¼ inch thick, pound lightly, cut into*
> > *⅔-inch squares*
> *2 tablespoons cornstarch*
> *½ tablespoon brown sugar*
> *1 tablespoon black soy sauce*

⅓ cup uncooked walnuts: put in colander, rinse in hot water, drain, pat dry
4 scallions: chop into pea-sized pieces, including green part

SAUCE MIXTURE (MIX IN A BOWL)*

1 tablespoon black soy sauce
2 teaspoons pale dry sherry

DIRECTIONS FOR COOKING

1. Heat oil in wok to deep-fry temperature. Deep-fry half the pork mixture at a time until pieces are golden brown. Drain.

2. Keep oil hot over medium-low heat. Deep-fry walnuts. Drain.*

3. Remove all but 2 tablespoons of oil from wok. Heat oil, then add scallions and sauce mixture. Stir quickly. Immediately put pork back into wok and add walnuts. Mix well. Serve hot.

東坡扣肉

TUNG PO PORK
about 6 servings

Tradition attributes this way of preparing pork to Su Tung-po (1036–1101), one of China's greatest poet-statesmen. For centuries, the Chinese have loved his poems, admired his genius, wit, and courage. A high official in the government, he was arrested, tried, and banished from the capital for his advocacy of the common people in his writings. From 1094 to 1097 he spent his second exile in Huichow, the home of my father. Poor in cash but rich in heart, the poet turned exile into contentment, devoting his leisure to moonlight, poetry, cooking, and praising cinnamon wine. Finding Huichow lushly beautiful and the people kind and hospitable, he built a house to make it his permanent home.

It was said that his enemies in court heard that he was having a good time, whereupon they banished him further to Hainan, an impoverished island off southern China. He remained there until a new emperor restored him to full honor and high office. But soon after, on his journey home, he died. A thousand years have passed, but we still prepare his delicious, succulent pork, and fondly savor his luminous and generous spirit in our hearts.

PREPARATION OF INGREDIENTS

1½ pounds boneless pork butt or pork belly: leave whole
2 tablespoons black soy sauce
3 cups oil

SAUCE MIXTURE (MIX IN A BOWL)*

> 3 tablespoons Chinese Shaohsing wine or pale dry sherry
> 2 tablespoons salted black beans: wash in hot water, drain
> 4 tablespoons black soy sauce
> 1 tablespoon sugar

2 tablespoons oil
½ pound watercress (pinch off tough stalks, wash, drain) or
  ½ head iceberg lettuce (separate leaves)
1 teaspoon cornstarch mixed with 1 teaspoon water

DIRECTIONS FOR COOKING

1. Bring a big pot of water to a boil. Immerse pork. Cover and cook over medium heat for 30 minutes. Rinse pork in cold water, pat dry, and cut into 2-inch cubes. Roll cubes in 2 tablespoons black soy sauce. Put on a cake rack to drain.

2. Heat oil to deep-fry temperature. Deep-fry pork for about a minute or until nicely browned. Immediately immerse browned pork in a big bowl of cold water to cool for about 30 minutes.

3. Remove pork from water and put in a medium-sized casserole with a cover. Pour sauce mixture over pork and cover.

4. Put a heatproof bowl in the middle of a wok or a big pot, then place a heatproof plate on the bowl. Place the covered casserole of pork on the plate. Pour boiling water into wok to reach the level of the plate, then cover wok. Dry-steam over medium heat for 4 hours until pork is very tender, adding boiling water to wok from time to time to maintain water level.

5. When pork is nearly done, heat another wok or skillet. Swirl in 2 tablespoons oil. When oil is hot, stir-fry watercress or lettuce until just softened. Drain and put on a serving platter.

6. Spoon pork cubes onto watercress or lettuce. Heat sauce in casserole and thicken it with cornstarch water. Pour sauce over pork. Serve hot.

生菜包

MY MOTHER'S LETTUCE PACKAGES
(MINCED PORK AND SMOKED OYSTERS WITH
WALNUTS AND NOODLES WRAPPED IN LETTUCE)

6 to 8 servings

This dish is beautiful and delicious. It has been a treasure to me and my students. Unlike most persons who prepare lettuce packages with only minced pork or chicken and water chestnuts, my mother added smoked fat juicy Chinese oysters to be stir-fried with the minced pork, chopped water chestnuts, and bean sprouts. She lined the serving platter not only with lettuce leaves, but also with crisp noodles. She then placed the cooked oyster and pork mixture on the noodles surrounded by the lettuce; finally she sprinkled the dish with golden-brown walnuts.

My mother created this dish when she was about forty-seven. Never considering herself a good cook or special in anything, she was an unassuming woman, painfully shy. But in her village, she was the first college graduate and the village's only female to marry according to her own choice. During the Second World War, she wrote countless letters for neighbors and friends, since she was the only woman in the area who could write. At least twice a week she read her favorite legends to the villagers. Under the little oil lamp, men and women would laugh or silently weep at the stories conveyed by her lyrical voice.

When she departed, scores of unexpected people came. "Who was this woman, that so many mourn?" someone asked. She was neither nobility nor a celebrity, but a good departing soul whom they did not want to let go. She was fifty-four years of age.

continued

PREPARATION OF INGREDIENTS

1 head Boston lettuce: detach leaves, wash, dry
about 4 cups oil
1 ounce bean thread noodles
⅓ cup walnuts
1 teaspoon minced garlic
2 scallions: cut into pea-sized pieces, including green part
1½ cups (12 ounces) ground pork (ask butcher to grind it only once)
1 can (3⅔-ounce) smoked oysters in olive oil or cottonseed oil:
    drain, mince oysters coarsely
1 cup chopped water chestnuts in pea-sized pieces
1 cup coarsely chopped fresh bean sprouts or iceberg lettuce

SAUCE MIXTURE (MIX IN A BOWL)*

1 tablespoon thin soy sauce
2 tablespoons oyster-flavored sauce
¼ teaspoon sugar
¼ teaspoon cayenne pepper
1 teaspoon pale dry sherry
1 teaspoon sesame seed oil

2 teaspoons cornstarch mixed with 1 tablespoon water

DIRECTIONS FOR COOKING

1. Arrange Boston lettuce in a circle around the edge of a large serving platter.

2. Heat oil in wok to deep-fry temperature. Loosen bean thread noodles by pulling them apart. Test oil with a piece of noodle. If it pops up immediately, the oil is hot. Plunge noodles into oil. The noodles instantly become a white nest. Turn nest over and fry on the other side. (This takes less than 10 seconds.) Drain on paper towels.

3. Use the same oil to deep-fry the walnuts. Drain on paper towels. Put walnuts in plastic bag, crush them coarsely with a rolling pin. Set aside.

4. Slightly break the noodles into smaller pieces, and put in the center of the platter.

5. Remove all but 2 tablespoons of oil from wok. Heat oil, then slightly brown garlic and scallions. Add ground pork. Stir-fry until pork is no longer pink. Add oysters and stir-fry with pork for a minute. Add water chestnuts and iceberg lettuce or bean sprouts. Swirl in sauce mixture and mix well. Stir in cornstarch water and cook for a minute. Carefully place over the noodles, then top with the walnuts. Serve hot.

To eat, put 2 to 3 spoonfuls of meat and oysters with noodles in the center of a piece of Boston lettuce. Fold lettuce into a package.

煲生仔薑

CHILDBIRTH GINGER
(PIG'S FEET, EGGS, AND GINGER IN SWEET VINEGAR)
makes 8 to 14 bowls

In Kwangtung Province, after a woman gave birth to a child, it was the duty of a mother-in-law to prepare a big pot of this ginger for her daughter-in-law to regain her strength. The vinegar drew out the bone marrow of the pig's feet. The eggs, representing birth, turned dark brown while soaking in the vinegar. The ginger became sweet and mild. The sauce was the essence that the new mother had to drink. It was sweet, vinegary, gingery, and savory. No woman would refuse it.

The supply of the ginger, pig's feet, and eggs had to last for a month. And many extra pots had to be prepared in order to share with relatives, neighbors, and friends. Distant neighbors, who sensed the aroma of the sweet vinegar, could bring bowls containing red envelopes with a little money for good luck; then their bowls would be filled with great pleasure.

The daughter-in-law was proud to be served this ginger dish, for it showed that her mother-in-law cared. It gave the new mother face and pride that she could show her relatives and friends that she was in a good family and was being well treated.

Unfortunately, in some families, if a girl was born instead of a boy, the disappointment was so great that no ginger was served, or only a small amount might be prepared. My grandmother still sighed, at the age of seventy-eight, because her ginger was accompanied by no eggs and no pig's feet. For she had given birth to a girl—my mother.

PREPARATION OF INGREDIENTS

*2 pounds fresh ginger root: peel, break into small chunks, crack
and flatten slightly with flat side of cleaver*

*2 pig's feet with hocks (about 2½ pounds): ask butcher to split
them in half lengthwise and chop crosswise into 1-inch pieces;
blanch in a big pot of boiling water for a minute, drain, discard
water*

2½ cups Chinese sweet vinegar

¼ cup white vinegar

1 cup water

½ teaspoon salt

8 hard-boiled eggs: remove shells

DIRECTIONS FOR COOKING

1. Bring a big pot of water to a rapid boil. Add ginger and boil over
medium heat for 20 minutes to reduce hotness of ginger root. Drain in
colander. Discard water.

2. Choose a 6-quart pot or a clay pot (be sure it can be used on stove),
and add blanched pig's feet, ginger, sweet vinegar, white vinegar, water,
and salt. Cover and cook over medium-low heat for about 1½ hours, or
until pig's feet are tender. Stir from time to time while cooking. There
should be about 2 cups of liquid left in pot at end of cooking time. Immerse
eggs in sauce. Cover and allow the pot to stand for at least a day. Reheat on
stove over low heat before serving hot.

NOTE: *This dish is never served as a meal, but is eaten between meals.
Serve the new mother two small bowls a day for a month—whether she
gave birth to a girl or a boy.*

魚香腰花

SZECHWAN KIDNEYS IN CHILI SAUCE
2 to 4 servings

PREPARATION OF INGREDIENTS

8 tablespoons oil for oil-blanching

KIDNEY MIXTURE (MIX TOGETHER JUST BEFORE USE)

> *1½ pounds pork kidneys: cut into halves lengthwise, trim off white vessels in center, rinse kidneys in running cold water, double-score them (see Cutting Techniques), cut into pieces about ½ inch wide, soak pieces in cold water for 20 minutes, rinse with cold water, drain in colander, refrigerate in colander before use*
> *2 teaspoons pale dry sherry*
> *¼ teaspoon ground pepper*
> *1 tablespoon cornstarch*

2 tablespoons oil for stir-frying
1 teaspoon finely minced fresh ginger root
2 teaspoons minced garlic
2 scallions: cut into pea-sized pieces, including green part
2 dried chili peppers: tear in pieces, do not discard seeds

continued

SAUCE MIXTURE (MIX IN A BOWL)*

> 2 teaspoons Szechwan sweet bean sauce or ground bean sauce
> 1 tablespoon Chinese red vinegar
> 1 tablespoon black soy sauce
> 2 tablespoons Chinese Shaohsing wine or pale dry sherry
> 2 teaspoons sugar
> ¼ teaspoon cayenne pepper

5 water chestnuts: chop coarsely
2 tablespoons dried cloud ears: soak in hot water until soft,
   discard tough parts, tear into halves
1 teaspoon cornstarch mixed with 2 teaspoons water
2 teaspoons sesame seed oil
½ teaspoon flower peppercorn powder (optional)

DIRECTIONS FOR COOKING

1. Heat oil for oil-blanching in wok over high heat to deep-fry temperature. Add kidney mixture. Stir to separate. Cook kidneys briefly until they almost lose their redness (they are not quite done yet). Remove kidneys to a colander to drain.

2. Discard all the oil in wok. Clean and dry wok.

3. Heat wok over high heat. Swirl in oil for stir-frying. When oil is hot, drop in ginger, garlic, scallions, and chili peppers. When garlic turns golden, swirl in sauce mixture, add water chestnuts, and cloud ears. Stir and mix until sauce begins to bubble. Return kidneys to wok. Stir-fry for about 15 seconds. Stir in cornstarch water. Stir constantly until sauce is thickened. Add sesame seed oil and flower peppercorn powder. Mix well. Put on a serving platter. Serve hot.

Beef and Lamb

✿✿✿✿

BEEF AND LAMB

Two-thirds of the beef and lamb dishes in this book are from the west and north of China. Many of these dishes have strong Moslem, Mongolian, or Manchurian backgrounds. One easily forgets that China consists of many races, divided into five large groups: the Han people, the Manchus, the Mongols, the Moslems, and the Tibetans and other minority groups. Ninety-five percent of the Chinese are Han people. But the Mongols and the Manchus once ruled China in Peking; and the Moslems have a substantial population spread through the north and the west of China. Many of these peoples do not eat pork, but rather beef and lamb. The Han people have adopted Moslem cooking and changed it into their own. The Peking Fire Pot, Beef in Vinegar Sauce, Peking Style, the Empress Dowager's Lamb, and many others are heavily flavored by Mongolian, Moslem, and Manchurian cooking.

For most Chinese, beef and lamb are eaten much less often than pork or poultry. It is not that the Chinese do not like beef and lamb, but rather because they are low in quality and quantity. Unlike America, there is not enough land in China for crops and grazing too. Chinese yellow cows and water buffaloes are lean and tough. And lamb is rare. The imported Australian beef is so strong that very few Chinese are willing to swallow it.

To me, American beef is the best. It did not take long for me—like many Asians—to love it. When my uncle and aunt made their first visit to America from Hong Kong, they were eager to taste the famous American T-bone steak which they had heard so much about. My dining table was like a Texas spread. Surprisingly, they even soaked up and ate the bloody sauce. Pictures were snapped of the diners for them to take home to show and tell about the famous American steaks and roasts.

For stir-frying, flank steak and leg of lamb are best. Never use more meat than the recipe calls for; it will alter the recipe and diminish the taste.

For red cooking (slow cooking), any kind of roast will do.

五香牛肉

AROMATIC SPICED BEEF

6 to 8 servings

PREPARATION OF INGREDIENTS

4 pounds beef roast (eye round, top round, or cross-cut rib)
2 tablespoons oil
1 chunk (big as a walunt) fresh ginger root: crush
3 cloves garlic: crush and peel
2 dried whole chili peppers

SAUCE MIXTURE (MIX IN A BOWL)*

   ⅓ cup black soy sauce
   2 tablespoons brown sugar
   ⅓ cup pale dry sherry

3 cups water
2 teaspoons five-fragrance powder
3 whole star anise
1 cinnamon stick, about 3 inches long

DIRECTIONS FOR COOKING

1. Bring a big pot of water to a boil. Put in beef and let it boil for 2 minutes. Remove beef and pat dry with towel. Discard water.

2. Heat a Dutch oven and put in oil. When it is hot, slightly brown ginger, garlic, and chili peppers. Add sauce mixture, then beef. Turn beef all over to coat with sauce. Add 3 cups water, five-fragrance powder, star anise, and cinnamon stick. Cover and simmer over low heat for about 3 hours, or until beef is tender. Check beef from time to time while it is cooking; add more water if it is needed. There should be about 2 cups of sauce left in pot.

3. Discard ginger, chili peppers, garlic, cinnamon stick, and anise. Slice beef and put on platter. Pour sauce over beef slices and serve hot or serve cold without the sauce.

軟炸牛肉片

CRISP BEEF SLICES
4 to 6 servings

PREPARATION OF INGREDIENTS

BEEF MIXTURE (MIX IN A BOWL. MARINATE STEAK AT LEAST 30 MINUTES)*

> *1 pound flank steak: cut against grain into thin slices 2 inches long*
> *2 beaten eggs*
> *1 tablespoon sesame seed oil*
> *1 tablespoon thin soy sauce*
> *¼ teaspoon ground pepper*
> *¼ teaspoon sugar*
> *½ teaspoon salt*
> *2 teaspoons finely minced fresh ginger root*
> *1 teaspoon pale dry sherry*

about ½ cup cornstarch
about 3 cups oil
double recipe Soy-Vinegar Dip (see recipe)

DIRECTIONS FOR COOKING

1. Dredge marinated beef slices in cornstarch until they are dry and not sticky.

2. Heat oil to deep-fry temperature. Deep-fry beef slices until golden brown. Drain. Put on platter and serve with dip.

橘香牛肉

ORANGE-FLAVORED BEEF
4 to 8 servings

PREPARATION OF INGREDIENTS

2 to 3 cups oil

BEEF MIXTURE (MIX AND MARINATE IN A BOWL)*

> *1 pound flank steak: cut against grain into pieces ⅛ inch thick*
> *and 2 inches long*
> *2 teaspoons black soy sauce*
> *1½ teaspoons Szechwan sweet bean sauce or ground bean sauce*
> *2 teaspoons brown sugar*
> *2 teaspoons pale dry sherry*
> *1 tablespoon cornstarch*

peel from 1 orange: peel by hand and break into about 8 pieces
1 teaspoon minced fresh ginger root
2 teaspoons minced garlic
3 scallions: cut into 1½-inch lengths, including green part
2 teaspoons pale dry sherry

SAUCE MIXTURE (MIX IN A BOWL)*

> *1 teaspoon black soy sauce*
> *2 teaspoons Chinese red vinegar*
> *1 teaspoon brown sugar*
> *½ teaspoon cornstarch*
> *1 teaspoon water*

¼ teaspoon orange extract

DIRECTIONS FOR COOKING

1. Heat oil in wok over high heat until almost smoking. Add beef mixture; stir to separate pieces. Blanch briskly until beef loses its red color. Remove with a drainer and put in a bowl.

2. Remove all but 3 tablespoons of oil from wok. Heat oil, then add orange peel and cook until golden brown. Add ginger, garlic, and scallions, and stir-fry them quickly. Be sure not to burn the garlic. Return beef to wok. Splash in sherry. Mix well. Stir in sauce mixture. Stir-fry until sauce is thickened. Add orange extract. Mix well. Put on plate and serve hot.

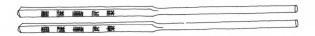

京葱牛肉

PEKING BEEF WITH SCALLIONS IN GARLIC SAUCE
4 to 8 servings

PREPARATION OF INGREDIENTS

about 2 cups oil

BEEF MIXTURE (MIX AND MARINATE STEAK IN A BOWL FOR ABOUT 30 MINUTES)

> *1 pound flank steak: cut against grain into slices ⅛ inch thick and 1½ inches long*
> *2 teaspoons black soy sauce*
> *½ teaspoon sugar*
> *1 tablespoon cornstarch*
> *2 teaspoons ground bean sauce*

8 ounces scallions: cut into 1½-inch lengths, including green part
1 tablespoon minced garlic

continued

SAUCE MIXTURE (MIX IN A BOWL)*

> 2 teaspoons ground bean sauce
> 1 tablespoon black soy sauce
> 3 tablespoons pale dry sherry
> ½ teaspoon sugar
> 2 teaspoons Chinese red vinegar

1 teaspoon sesame seed oil

DIRECTIONS FOR COOKING

1. Heat oil in wok to deep-fry temperature. Add beef mixture. Quickly stir to separate pieces. Remove with a drainer as soon as beef loses its redness; be sure not to overcook. Press beef to drain. Set aside.

2. Remove all but 3 tablespoons of oil from wok. Heat oil over medium heat, then add scallions and stir-fry for about 30 seconds. Remove with a drainer to a bowl.

3. Keep wok hot over medium-high heat. Add garlic and cook briskly until golden. Stir and swirl in sauce mixture. Cook and stir until sauce begins to bubble. Return beef and scallions to wok. Swirl in sesame seed oil. Mix well. Put on serving platter. Serve hot.

醋溜牛·肉

BEEF IN VINEGAR SAUCE, PEKING STYLE
2 to 6 servings

PREPARATION OF INGREDIENTS

2 cups oil

BEEF MIXTURE (MIX IN A BOWL)*

> 12 ounces flank steak: cut against grain into pieces ⅛ inch thick
> and 2 inches long
> 1 tablespoon cornstarch
> 1 egg white

1 teaspoon finely minced fresh ginger root
2 scallions: cut into pea-sized pieces, including green part

SAUCE MIXTURE (MIX IN A BOWL)*

> 4 teaspoons black soy sauce
> 4 teaspoons Chinese red vinegar or cider vinegar
> 2 teaspoons pale dry sherry
> 1 teaspoon sugar
> ¼ teaspoon salt

½ teaspoon sesame seed oil

DIRECTIONS FOR COOKING

1. Heat oil in wok to deep-fry temperature. Add beef mixture and stir to separate pieces. Blanch briskly until beef just loses red color. (It takes less than a minute.) Remove with drainer or slotted spoon to a bowl.

2. Remove all but 3 tablespoons of oil from wok. Heat oil over high heat, then drop in ginger and scallions. Stir-fry until ginger becomes golden. Stir in sauce mixture. Return beef to wok and stir-fry for about 15 seconds. Add sesame seed oil. Mix well. Put on a serving platter. Serve hot.

湘江牛肉

SPICED BEEF SHREDS, HUNAN STYLE
4 servings

PREPARATION OF INGREDIENTS

2 cups oil

BEEF MIXTURE (MIX AND MARINATE IN A BOWL)*

> *1 pound flank steak: slice paper-thin against grain, shred slices*
> *into matchstick strips*
> *1 egg white*
> *¼ teaspoon salt*
> *¼ teaspoon sugar*
> *1 tablespoon cornstarch*

1 teaspoon minced fresh ginger root
2 teaspoons minced garlic
3 scallions: cut into pea-sized pieces, including green part

SAUCE MIXTURE (MIX IN A BOWL)*

> *1 tablespoon ground bean sauce*
> *1 tablespoon Chinese Shaohsing wine or pale dry sherry*
> *1 tablespoon black soy sauce*
> *2 teaspoons Chinese red vinegar or cider vinegar*
> *1½ teaspoons sugar*
> *¼ teaspoon cayenne pepper*
> *1 to 2 teaspoons Chili Oil (see recipe)*

6 water chestnuts: chop coarsely
2 tablespoons cloud ears: soak in hot water until soft, discard
tough parts, tear each in half
½ cup water or clear chicken broth (not condensed)
2 teaspoons cornstarch mixed with 1 tablespoon water
1 teaspoon sesame seed oil

DIRECTIONS FOR COOKING

1. Heat 2 cups oil in wok to deep-fry temperature. Add beef mixture and stir to separate pieces. Blanch briskly until beef just loses its redness. Remove beef with a drainer to a bowl.

2. Remove all but 3 tablespoons of oil from wok. Heat oil, then add ginger, garlic, and scallions, and stir-fry for about 10 seconds. Stir in sauce mixture and cook until it bubbles gently. Add water chestnuts and cloud ears. Return beef to wok. Mix well. Pour in water or broth. When it begins to boil, stir in cornstarch water. Stir until sauce thickens. Add sesame seed oil. Mix and put on a serving platter. Serve hot.

四川麻辣牛·肉絲

SZECHWAN SPICED BEEF SHREDS ON FRIED NOODLES
about 2 servings

PREPARATION OF INGREDIENTS

2 to 3 cups oil
1 ounce bean thread noodles

BEEF MIXTURE (MIX IN A BOWL)*

    *12 ounces flank steak: slice paper-thin against grain, shred slices
        into matchstick strips*
    ¼ teaspoon salt
    about ⅓ egg white
    1 teaspoon pale dry sherry
    2 teaspoons cornstarch

1 teaspoon finely minced fresh ginger root
1 teaspoon minced garlic
2 scallions: cut into 1½-inch strips, including green part
½ cup bamboo shoots: cut into matchstick strips
½ green or red bell pepper: cut into ¼-inch strips
2 dried chili peppers: tear into small pieces, do not discard seeds

continued

SAUCE MIXTURE (MIX IN A BOWL)*

> ½ teaspoon sugar
> 2 teaspoons pale dry sherry
> 1 tablespoon Chinese red vinegar or cider vinegar
> 1 to 2 teaspoons Chili Oil (see recipe)
> 1 tablespoon black soy sauce

1 teaspoon sesame seed oil
¼ teaspoon flower peppercorn powder (optional; see recipe)

DIRECTIONS FOR COOKING

1. Heat oil in wok to deep-fry temperature. Meanwhile, loosen noodles by pulling them apart. Test oil by dropping in a piece of noodle; if it pops up and turns white, the oil is right. Deep-fry noodles on both sides. (This takes less than a minute.) Drain on paper towels; put on serving platter.

2. Keep oil hot. Add beef mixture and stir to separate pieces. Blanch briskly until beef just loses its redness. Remove with a drainer to a bowl.

3. Remove all but 2 tablespoons oil from wok. Heat oil, then add ginger, garlic, scallions, bamboo shoots, bell pepper, and chili peppers. Stir-fry for about 15 seconds. Stir in sauce mixture; cook and stir for several seconds. Return beef to wok. Mix well. Add sesame seed oil and flower peppercorn powder. Transfer entire contents of wok onto fried noodles. Serve hot.

乾炒牛肉絲

SZECHWAN DRY-FRIED BEEF SHREDS
4 to 6 servings

PREPARATION OF INGREDIENTS

1 cup oil

BEEF MIXTURE (MIX IN A BOWL AND MARINATE STEAK NO MORE THAN 30 MINUTES)

> 1 pound flank steak: cut against grain into matchstick strips
> 2 tablespoons black soy sauce
> ½ teaspoon sugar
> 2 teaspoons pale dry sherry
> 2 tablespoons cornstarch
> 2 teaspoons ground bean sauce

3 scallions: shred into 1½-inch lengths, including green part
1 teaspoon minced garlic
½ teaspoon finely minced fresh ginger root
2 dried chili peppers: tear into small pieces, do not discard seeds

DIRECTIONS FOR COOKING

1. Heat oil in wok to deep-fry temperature. Add beef mixture. Fry, stirring from time to time, over medium heat for 20 minutes or until beef is dry. If you prefer softer beef, fry for about 15 minutes. Remove with drainer or slotted spoon. Put in a bowl.

2. Remove all but 1 tablespoon oil from wok. Heat oil, then drop in scallions, garlic, ginger, and chili peppers. Brown them slightly. Put beef shreds back into wok. Mix well. Put on serving platter. Serve hot.

紅燒辣牛肉

SZECHWAN SPICED BEEF STEW
6 to 8 servings

PREPARATION OF INGREDIENTS

6 tablespoons oil
1 tablespoon minced fresh ginger root
1 tablespoon minced garlic
¼ cup chopped scallions, including green part

BEEF MIXTURE (MIX IN A BOWL)*

> 2 pounds stew beef: cut chunks into ¼-inch-thick pieces
> 5 teaspoons Szechwan chili bean sauce
> 2½ tablespoons ground bean sauce or Szechwan sweet bean
> sauce

SAUCE MIXTURE (MIX IN A BOWL)*

> 4 tablespoons pale dry sherry
> 4 tablespoons black soy sauce
> 2 teaspoons sugar
> 4 whole star anise
> ½ teaspoon flower peppercorn powder (see recipe)

about 3 cups water

DIRECTIONS FOR COOKING

Heat oil in a 4- to 6-quart pot. Add ginger, garlic, and scallions, and cook for a few seconds. Add beef mixture, and cook until meat loses its red color. Stir in sauce mixture and mix well. Add 2 cups water, cover, and simmer for an hour. Add remaining water and cook over low heat until beef is tender—about another hour. There should be 1½ cups of sauce left in the pot when beef is done. Serve hot.

NOTE: *This dish can be frozen and reheated in a pot over low heat.*

青椒牛肉

BEEF WITH PEPPERS
4 to 8 servings

PREPARATION OF INGREDIENTS

2 cups oil

BEEF MIXTURE (MIX AND MARINATE STEAK IN A BOWL)*

> *1 pound flank steak: cut against grain into slices ⅛ inch thick,*
> *2 inches long*
> *1 tablespoon black soy sauce*
> *2 teaspoons brown sugar*
> *1 pinch ground pepper*
> *2 teaspoons sesame seed oil*
> *1 tablespoon cornstarch*

½ pound green or red bell peppers: discard seeds and ribs, cut
lengthwise into ½-inch strips (to add more color, use both
green and red peppers)
1 teaspoon minced fresh ginger root
1 teaspoon minced garlic
2 scallions: cut into 1½-inch lengths, including green part

SAUCE MIXTURE (MIX IN A BOWL)*

> *2 tablespoons black soy sauce*
> *2 teaspoons brown sugar*
> *2 tablespoons pale dry sherry*
> *1 teaspoon cornstarch*
> *1 tablespoon water*

DIRECTIONS FOR COOKING

1. Heat oil in wok over high heat until it is hot but not smoking. Add
beef mixture. Stir quickly to separate pieces, and blanch briskly until meat

loses its redness. Remove beef from wok with a drainer or a slotted spoon and put in a bowl.

2. Remove all but 3 tablespoons oil from wok. Heat oil, then add peppers and stir-fry for about a minute. Remove peppers with a drainer or a slotted spoon to a bowl.

3. Keep wok hot over high heat. Add ginger, garlic, and scallions and lightly brown them. Return beef and peppers to wok and stir-fry for about 20 seconds to reheat. Stir in sauce mixture and cook until sauce is thickened. Put on a serving platter. Serve hot.

豉汁牛·肉炒玉筍

BEEF WITH BABY CORN AND CHINESE MUSHROOMS IN BLACK BEAN SAUCE
4 to 8 servings

Baby corn is light yellow miniature ears of corn, 1½ to 2 inches long. Originally imported from Thailand, corn was quite rare and a delicacy. But for the last several years, baby corn has been widely grown in Taiwan and canned in water. The ears are tender and juicy, and are served now not only at banquets and in restaurants but also at home, a great new addition to the vegetable catalog. But do not confuse this baby corn with the pickled variety sold in gourmet food stores.

PREPARATION OF INGREDIENTS

2 to 3 cups oil

BEEF MIXTURE (MIX IN A BOWL. MARINATE STEAK NO LONGER THAN 30 MINUTES)

> *1 pound flank steak: cut against grain into pieces ⅛ inch thick*
> *and 2 inches long*
> *1 tablespoon thin soy sauce*
> *1 tablespoon black soy sauce*
> *1 teaspoon sugar*
> *1 teaspoon pale dry sherry*
> *1 tablespoon cornstarch*

20-ounce can baby corn: rinse in cold water, drain

SEASONINGS (MIX IN A SMALL BOWL)*

> 1 teaspoon finely minced fresh ginger root
>
> 2 teaspoons minced garlic
>
> ½ teaspoon salt
>
> ½ teaspoon sugar
>
> 2 tablespoons salted black beans: rinse in hot water, drain and
> mash into paste
>
> 1 scallion: cut into pea-sized pieces, including green part

6 Chinese dried mushrooms: soak in hot water until spongy,
discard stems, leave caps whole

1 cup chicken broth (not condensed) mixed with 1 tablespoon
cornstarch

DIRECTIONS FOR COOKING

1. Heat oil in wok to deep-fry temperature. Add beef mixture, and stir to separate pieces. Blanch briskly until beef loses its redness. Remove with a drainer to a bowl.

2. Keep oil hot over medium heat. Add baby corn, and blanch for a few seconds. Remove with a drainer to a bowl.

3. Remove all but 2 tablespoons oil from wok. Heat oil over high heat, then add the seasonings and mushrooms. Stir-fry until ginger and garlic turn golden. Stir in broth and cornstarch mixture. Cook and stir until sauce is thickened. Return beef and baby corn to wok. Stir-fry for about 10 seconds. Put on serving platter. Serve hot.

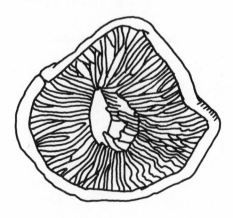

蠔油牛肉

BEEF IN OYSTER SAUCE
4 to 8 servings

PREPARATION OF INGREDIENTS

about 2 cups oil

BEEF MIXTURE (MIX AND MARINATE STEAK IN A BOWL)*

> 1 pound flank steak: cut against grain into pieces ⅛ inch thick
>   and 2 inches long
> 1 tablespoon black soy sauce
> 1 tablespoon cornstarch
> ¼ teaspoon sugar

1 teaspoon finely minced fresh ginger root
1 teaspoon minced garlic
4 scallions: cut into 1½-inch lengths, including green part

SAUCE MIXTURE (MIX IN A BOWL)*

> 4 tablespoons oyster-flavored sauce
> ½ teaspoon sugar
> 2 tablespoons Chinese Shaohsing wine or pale dry sherry

¼ pound snow peas: break off ends, blanch in water

DIRECTIONS FOR COOKING

1. Heat oil in wok to deep-fry temperature. Add beef mixture, and stir to separate pieces. Blanch briskly until meat just loses its redness. Remove with drainer or slotted spoon to bowl.

2. Remove all but 2 tablespoons oil from wok. Heat oil over high heat, then add ginger, garlic, and scallions and brown them slightly. Stir in sauce mixture; cook and stir until it begins to bubble. Add blanched snow peas and beef. Stir-fry for several seconds. Put on a serving plate. Serve hot.

牛肉炒椰菜花

STIR-FRIED BEEF WITH CAULIFLOWER
4 to 8 servings

PREPARATION OF INGREDIENTS

8 cups water
2 cups cauliflower cut into bite-sized pieces
2 cups oil

BEEF MIXTURE (MIX IN A BOWL. KEEP REFRIGERATED BEFORE USE)*

> *1 pound flank steak: cut against grain into pieces ⅛ inch thick
>   and 2 inches long*
> *¼ teaspoon sugar*
> *1 tablespoon thin soy sauce*
> *2 teaspoons cornstarch*
> *1 teaspoon pale dry sherry*

1 teaspoon finely minced fresh ginger root
1 teaspoon minced garlic
2 scallions: cut into 1½-inch lengths, including green part
*5 Chinese dried mushrooms: soak in hot water until spongy,
  discard stems, leave caps whole*

SAUCE MIXTURE (MIX IN A BOWL)*

> *2 tablespoons black soy sauce*
> *2 tablespoons thin soy sauce*
> *¼ teaspoon salt*
> *¼ cup Chinese Shaohsing wine or pale dry sherry*
> *1 tablespoon sugar*
> *¼ cup water*
> *2 teaspoons cornstarch*

1 teaspoon sesame seed oil

DIRECTIONS FOR COOKING

1. Bring water to a boil. Add cauliflower, and simmer over medium heat for 3 minutes. Pour cauliflower into a colander. Drain.

2. Heat oil in wok to deep-fry temperature. Add beef mixture. Stir to separate pieces. Blanch beef briskly until meat just loses its redness. Remove with a drainer to a bowl.

3. Remove all but 2 tablespoons oil from wok. Heat oil. Drop in ginger, garlic, scallions, and mushrooms. Stir-fry for about 15 seconds. Add cauliflower. Swirl in the sauce mixture. Cook and stir over medium heat until sauce thickens and cauliflower is hot. Return beef to wok. Stir-fry for about 15 seconds to reheat. Add sesame seed oil. Put on serving platter. Serve hot.

蘿蔔炆牛·腩

STEW BEEF WITH WHITE TURNIP, CANTONESE STYLE
8 to 12 servings

This dish will solve my brother Albert's entertainment problem, at least for a while. He wants to serve Chinese food without cooking it, or cooking it as little as possible. He likes something that tastes excellent, requires practically no work, can be cooked in advance and all in one pot.

I am sure that his guests will have this dish, in one big pot, served twenty times—Albert style.

PREPARATION OF INGREDIENTS

3 tablespoons oil

*2 chunks (each as big as a pecan) fresh ginger root: crack with
 flat side of cleaver*

*3 pounds stew beef or beef belly (the Chinese prefer the latter):
 leave stew beef in chunks; ask butcher to cut belly into 1-inch
 chunks*

SAUCE MIXTURE (MIX IN A BOWL)*

> *¼ cup black soy sauce*
> *2 tablespoons Chinese Shaohsing wine or pale dry sherry*
> *½ teaspoon sugar*
> *1 cup water*

2 to 3 cups water
1½ pounds Chinese white giant turnip: peel, cut into chunks
  slightly bigger than beef chunks

DIRECTIONS FOR COOKING

1. Heat a Dutch oven over medium heat. When it is hot, add oil and spread it around to cover bottom of pot. Add ginger and beef. Brown beef slightly and evenly. Pour in sauce mixture. Cover and cook over medium-low heat, adding water from time to time, for 1 hour.

2. Add turnips. Cover and continue to cook, adding water if needed, until beef and turnips are tender. It takes about another hour. There should be about 1 cup of sauce left in the pot at the end of cooking. Discard ginger. Serve hot.

NOTE: *This dish can be cooked one or two days in advance. Reheat on stove over medium heat.*

牠似蜜

THE EMPRESS DOWAGER'S LAMB
2 to 4 servings

It is said that this dish was created by one of the empress dowager's chefs during the Ching Dynasty. The new dish was presented to the old dowager, and she was pleased by its sweetness and delicacy. She reordered it soon after, but did not know what to call it. "It tastes like honey," she said. Thus for the last 200 years this dish has been called Tah Sze Mi, which means "It tastes like honey."

PREPARATION OF INGREDIENTS

5 tablespoons sesame seed oil

LAMB MIXTURE (MIX IN A BOWL AND MARINATE LAMB 30 MINUTES)

12 ounces leg of lamb: slice into thin pieces
2 tablespoons Szechwan sweet bean sauce or ground bean paste
1 teaspoon cornstarch

4 teaspoons sugar

SAUCE MIXTURE (MIX IN A BOWL)*

4 teaspoons Chinese red vinegar
1 tablespoon black soy sauce
1 tablespoon Chinese Shaohsing wine or pale dry sherry
1 teaspoon minced fresh ginger root
½ teaspoon cornstarch

DIRECTIONS FOR COOKING

1. Heat wok over high heat. Swirl in 4 tablespoons of the sesame seed oil. When oil is hot (not smoking), add lamb mixture and stir-fry for about 2 minutes. Remove lamb with drainer or slotted spoon and put in a bowl.

2. Clean wok and dry it thoroughly. Reheat wok over high heat. Swirl in remaining sesame seed oil. Add sugar and stir-fry briskly. Pour in sauce mixture, and stir-fry for about 10 seconds. Return lamb to wok, and stir-fry for another several seconds. Put on plate and serve hot.

湖南羊肉

SLICED LEG OF LAMB, HUNAN STYLE
4 to 6 servings

PREPARATION OF INGREDIENTS

1 cup oil

LAMB MIXTURE (MIX IN A BOWL)*

    12 ounces leg of lamb: slice paper-thin
    2 teaspoons black soy sauce
    ¼ teaspoon sugar
    2 teaspoons cornstarch
    1 teaspoon sesame seed oil

2 dried chili peppers: tear in half, do not discard seeds
1 teaspoon finely minced fresh ginger root
1 teaspoon minced garlic
4 ounces scallions (about 1 bunch): cut into 1½-inch lengths,
    including green part

SAUCE MIXTURE (MIX IN A BOWL)*

    2 tablespoons ground bean sauce
    2 tablespoons Chinese Shaohsing wine or pale dry sherry
    2 teaspoons Chili Oil (see recipe)
    ½ teaspoon sugar
    1 tablespoon black soy sauce

DIRECTIONS FOR COOKING

1. Heat wok, then swirl in oil. When oil is hot, add lamb mixture. Stir briskly until it is just done. Drain and put in a bowl.

2. Remove all but 3 tablespoons oil from wok. Heat oil, and drop in chili peppers, ginger, garlic, and scallions. Stir-fry until scallions just become soft. Remove from wok and put aside.

3. Keep wok hot over high heat. Swirl in sauce mixture. Stir and cook until sauce bubbles gently. Return lamb and scallions to wok. Mix well and stir to reheat. Put on a serving platter. Serve hot.

糟溜牛胸腺

FRIED SWEETBREADS IN SWEET WINE SAUCE
4 to 6 servings

PREPARATION OF INGREDIENTS

4 cups water
2 tablespoons pale dry sherry
2 slices fresh ginger root, each as big and thick as a quarter
1 pound sweetbreads: rinse in cold water
2 tablespoons cornstarch
3 cups oil
1 tablespoon minced garlic
2 scallions: cut into pea-sized pieces, including green part

SAUCE MIXTURE (MIX IN A BOWL)*

3 tablespoons Sweet Wine Sauce (sauce only, see recipe) or liqueur
1 tablespoon tomato ketchup
1 teaspoon Chinese red vinegar
5 teaspoons black soy sauce
3 tablespoons Chinese Shaohsing wine or pale dry sherry
½ teaspoon sugar

1 teaspoon cornstarch mixed with 4 teaspoons water

DIRECTIONS FOR COOKING

1. Pour water into a 3-quart pot, add sherry and ginger, and bring to a boil. Immerse sweetbreads in water. Cover and cook over low heat for 5 minutes. Drain sweetbreads. Discard ginger and water.

2. Remove membrane and vein from sweetbreads as much as possible. Cut sweetbreads into ½-inch pieces.*

3. Dredge sweetbreads in cornstarch.

4. Heat oil to deep-fry temperature. Deep-fry half the sweetbreads at a time until they just turn light gold. Remove with a drainer to a bowl.

5. Remove all but 2 tablespoons oil from wok. Heat oil, and drop in garlic and scallions. When garlic turns golden, swirl in sauce mixture. Stir and cook sauce until it begins to bubble. Stir in cornstarch water. When sauce thickens, return sweetbreads to wok. Stir-fry for about 15 seconds. Put on a serving platter. Serve hot.

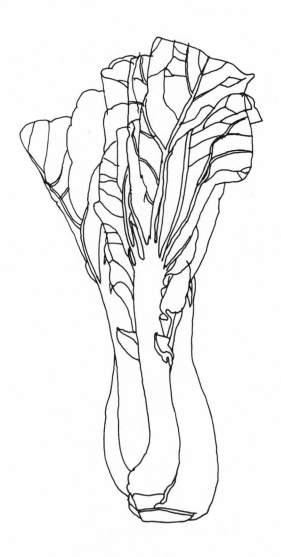

Seafood

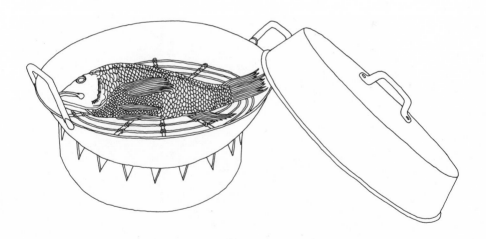

SEAFOOD

Fish are plentiful in many parts of China. From the rivers, ponds, and lakes, we had fresh-water shrimp, yellow perch, meaty crabs, and the king of Chinese fish, the plump and juicy carp. From the ocean we took the flounder, the red snapper, and the unbelievably expensive mouse garoupa, as well as many others.

Fish packed in ice or frozen were unheard of in China. They were sold while they were swimming in buckets filled with water. You just pointed to the one you desired, and the fish seller would tie a long piece of straw around the fish's belly. Dangling from your finger, the shiny, lively creature would wriggle all the way home with you.

Fish were also sold in parts, especially the big ones. Fish heads, bellies, and tails could be bought separately. The Chinese have a great passion for fish heads, and red-cooked fish heads was a well-loved dish.

For many Chinese, one of the great pleasures of life was to have a banquet in a seafood restaurant. Most of these restaurants were located near a fish market by the water. Some of them were floating restaurants. Usually they did not carry a great amount of seafood. It was expected that the customers would pick up their own in the nearby fish stalls: there shrimp of all sizes swam in the water tanks; crabs rolled their eyes in baskets; lobsters timidly moved their feelers and stretched their claws; mounds of oysters in their shells were piled on the ground. Fish of all kinds swam with luxurious grace while the buyers and the sellers bargained their fate. The restaurants would cook whatever the customers brought and prepare it the way they wanted.

At such a banquet many kinds of fish and shellfish were included. Usually oysters were deep-fried in batter. Medium-sized fresh-water shrimp were steamed or blanched in the shells, dipped in sauce, then eaten with one's fingers. Lobsters were stir-fried with black bean sauce. Crabs were deep-fried, then stir-fried in ginger, garlic, and soy sauce. Some fish were steamed whole, while others were filleted and stir-fried. The fish head and backbones, augmented by fresh bean curd, made a big bowl of delicious soup. But always the very expensive fish were steamed whole with few seasonings added so that the true flavor of the fish would be retained.

The banquet could go on and on, for as long as the diners' pockets could provide. Usually it concluded with a dish of noodles or fried rice. Then, full and happy, everybody stretched and sighed, "That was good."

Growing up near the sea, we were taught early how to choose a fresh fish, and were given these few practical rules, which you can easily follow: When a fish is fresh, the eyes are clear, the scales are shiny, the body is firm, and the gills are bright red. A bad fish has sunken dull eyes; its scales are loose and have no shine; the body is limp and smells bad too.

TO CLEAN AND WASH SHRIMP

Shrimp, after they are cooked, should be crisp, firm, and resilient—not dull, hard, or tough. Rinsing fresh shrimp in the following method will help to achieve this result.

Shell and devein the shrimp. Put them in a bowl and wash them by gently massaging under cold running water for about half a minute. Then put shrimp in a colander and rinse them under fast-running cold water for about 3 minutes. (The cold water freshens and expands the shrimp, and the force of the running water stiffens them so that when they are cooked they become crisp and almost crunchy.)

Drain and dry shrimp thoroughly with paper towels. Cut or leave them whole according to the recipe. Keep refrigerated before use.

TO BUTTERFLY SHRIMP OR PRAWNS

Peel shell off shrimp or prawn, except for the last section and the tail. Remove the back vein, then cut the shrimp or prawn from the underside (the stomach) almost through to the back (do not cut through!). Rinse the shrimp or prawn with cold water, and pat dry with paper towels. Arrange them split side up on a plate. Keep refrigerated before use.

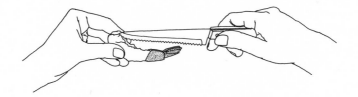

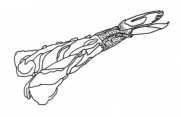

清蒸魚

STEAMED FISH
4 to 6 servings

PREPARATION OF INGREDIENTS

1 fresh fish, 1½ pounds (pike, sea bass, or striped bass): ask
   your fishman to scale, clean, and leave the fish whole; slash
   several cuts, about ½ inch deep, on both sides of fish
1 tablespoon pale dry sherry: use it to rub fish inside and out
   just before steaming
4 tablespoons oil
2 teaspoons minced garlic
4 slices fresh ginger root, each as big and thick as a quarter:
   shred into very thin strips
6 Chinese dried mushrooms: soak in hot water until spongy,
   discard stems

continued

SAUCE MIXTURE (MIX IN A BOWL)*

> *2 tablespoons pale dry sherry*
> *2 tablespoons black soy sauce*
> *2 tablespoons thin soy sauce*
> *½ teaspoon sugar*

1 tablespoon sesame seed oil
2 scallions: cut into 1½-inch lengths, including green part

DIRECTIONS FOR COOKING

1. Heat a few cups of water in wok over high heat. When water comes to a rapid boil, put in a steamer or rack. Be sure that the rack or steamer is at least an inch above the boiling water.

2. Place fish in steamer or rack. Cover and steam over high heat for about 12 minutes. Insert a fork into the thickest part of the fish. If the fork goes in easily, then the fish is done. Cover and keep fish hot.

3. Two minutes before the fish is done, heat a small saucepan over medium heat. Add 4 tablespoons oil. When oil is hot, slightly brown garlic, ginger, and mushrooms. Remove mushrooms and arrange them around a serving platter.

4. Reheat oil. Stir in sauce mixture. Cook over low heat until sauce begins to foam. Add sesame seed oil. Turn heat to very low to keep sauce hot.

5. Quickly remove fish from wok, put it on the serving platter and decorate with scallions. Pour hot sauce evenly over fish. Serve hot at once.

NOTE: *It is very important to eat the fish immediately.*

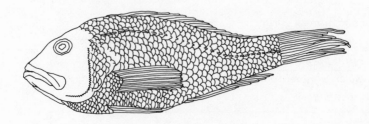

蒸金針全魚

STEAMED FLOUNDER WITH LILY BUDS
4 to 6 servings

PREPARATION OF INGREDIENTS

1 fresh flounder, 1½ pounds: scale, clean, and leave whole
15 dried lily buds: soak in hot water until soft, pinch off hard ends,
    tear buds in half lengthwise
1 tablespoon cloud ears: soak in hot water until soft, pinch off tough parts
6 Chinese dried mushrooms: soak in hot water until spongy, discard stems
3 pieces fresh ginger root, each as big and thick as a quarter:
    shred into thin strips
¼ cup shredded fresh pork fat or bacon, in strips 1½ inches long
4 tablespoons oil
2 scallions: cut into pea-sized pieces, including green part

SAUCE MIXTURE (MIX IN A BOWL)*

> *2 tablespoons thin soy sauce*
> *1½ tablespoons black soy sauce*
> *¼ teaspoon sugar*
> *1 tablespoon pale dry sherry*

1 tablespoon sesame seed oil

DIRECTIONS FOR COOKING

1. Place fish on a heatproof plate. Arrange lily buds, cloud ears, mushrooms, ginger, and pork fat or bacon on fish.

2. Cover and steam fish over boiling water for about 12 minutes. (See recipe for steamed fish.)

3. Meanwhile, heat a small saucepan. Add 4 tablespoons oil. When oil is hot, add scallions, sauce mixture, and sesame seed oil. Turn heat to low and cook until the sauce just comes to a boil. Pour hot sauce over fish. Serve hot at once.

香葱果皮煎魚

PAN-FRIED RED SNAPPER OR FLOUNDER WITH GINGER, GARLIC, AND TANGERINE SAUCE
2 to 4 servings

PREPARATION OF INGREDIENTS

1 fresh red snapper or flounder, 1½ pounds: scale, clean, leave whole

MARINADE (RUB SHERRY, GINGER, AND SALT INSIDE AND OUTSIDE FISH. REFRIGERATE FOR 30 MINUTES)

2 teaspoons pale dry sherry
1 tablespoon finely minced fresh ginger root
¼ teaspoon salt

2 tablespoons flour
4 tablespoons oil
2 scallions: chop into pea-sized pieces, including green part
2 teaspoons finely minced fresh ginger root
1 tablespoon minced garlic
*1 piece dried tangerine peel: soak in hot water 15 minutes or
    until soft, mince (to make about 1 tablespoon)*

SAUCE MIXTURE (MIX IN A BOWL)*

3 tablespoons thin soy sauce
1½ tablespoons black soy sauce
3 tablespoons pale dry sherry
¾ teaspoon sugar
4 tablespoons water

DIRECTIONS FOR COOKING

1. Sprinkle seasoned fish with flour.
2. Heat wok over high heat. Swirl in oil. When oil is hot, put fish in wok. Fry over medium-low heat until both sides are golden brown (about

12 minutes each side). Remove fish and put into a warm oven to keep hot.

3. Reheat oil left in wok. Slightly brown scallions, ginger, garlic, and tangerine peel. Stir in sauce mixture and heat to boil. Return fish to wok. Spoon sauce over fish. Put on an oval platter. Serve hot at once.

紅燒鯉魚

CARP IN BROWN SAUCE
about 4 servings

PREPARATION OF INGREDIENTS

1 fresh carp, 1½ pounds (whole or section): slash several cuts,
  about ½ inch deep, on both sides of fish, rinse, pat dry thoroughly
1 tablespoon cornstarch
about 3 cups oil
2 tablespoons rendered chicken fat or oil
1 tablespoon minced fresh ginger root
1 tablespoon minced garlic
2 scallions: cut into 1½-inch lengths, including green part

SAUCE MIXTURE (MIX IN A BOWL)*

  4 tablespoons ground bean sauce
  2 tablespoons black soy sauce
  4 teaspoons sugar
  4 tablespoons Chinese Shaohsing wine or pale dry sherry
  1 tablespoon Chinese red vinegar

about ⅔ cup clear chicken broth (not condensed)

DIRECTIONS FOR COOKING

1. Dust carp inside and outside with cornstarch.

2. Heat oil in wok over high heat. Gently slide in fish. Deep-fry each side for 8 minutes. The fish should be nicely browned, but not yet thoroughly cooked. Remove fish carefully with the help of two spatulas. Put on plate. Remove all the oil from wok. (Save oil for frying fish in the future; keep refrigerated.)

3. Heat wok over high heat. Add chicken fat or oil. When hot, drop in ginger, garlic, and scallions. When garlic turns light gold, add sauce mixture. Cook and stir until sauce becomes thick and pasty. Return fish to wok. Pour in half the chicken broth. Cover and simmer fish for about 8 minutes. Turn fish over, and add remaining broth if sauce seems to be drying out. Cover and simmer for another 8 minutes. Remove entire contents to a serving platter. Discard scallions. Serve piping hot at once.

糖醋全魚

WHOLE FISH IN SWEET AND SOUR SAUCE
about 6 servings

PREPARATION OF INGREDIENTS

1 fresh sea bass, 1½ to 2 pounds: scale, clean, and leave fish
whole, rinse in cold water, pat dry, cut deeply from stomach to
back, but not splitting fish in half, score both sides about
½ inch deep into diamond design

MARINADE (MIX IN A BOWL)*

1 teaspoon finely minced fresh ginger root
1 scallion: mince, including green part
½ teaspoon salt
⅛ teaspoon ground pepper
1 teaspoon pale dry sherry

2 to 3 tablespoons cornstarch to dust fish

BATTER (COMBINE EGG, WATER, OIL, AND SOY SAUCE. ADD CORNSTARCH, FLOUR, AND BAKING POWDER. MIX WITH SPOON UNTIL SMOOTH)

1 beaten egg
3 tablespoons cold water
2 tablespoons oil
1 teaspoon thin soy sauce
3 tablespoons cornstarch
6 tablespoons all-purpose flour
2 teaspoons baking powder

5 to 6 cups oil for deep-frying
2 tablespoons oil
¼ cup frozen green peas, defrosted
½ red or green bell pepper: cut into thin slices
4 water chestnuts: cut into quarter-sized pieces
2 scallions: cut into pea-sized pieces, including green parts

SWEET AND SOUR SAUCE (MIX IN A BOWL)*

2 ounces shan jah beng or 3 tablespoons tomato ketchup
1 tablespoon black soy sauce
1 tablespoon thin soy sauce
2 cloves garlic: mince
½ teaspoon salt
⅓ cup cider vinegar
7 tablespoons brown sugar
1 cup clear chicken broth (not condensed) or water

2 tablespoons cornstarch mixed with 2 tablespoons water

DIRECTIONS FOR COOKING

1. Rub fish inside and out with marinade, then dust with cornstarch. Dip fish in batter and thoroughly coat inside and outside.

2. Heat 5 to 6 cups oil in wok over medium heat to deep-fry temperature. Immerse fish in oil and deep-fry each side about 8 minutes or until crisp and golden brown.

3. Meanwhile, in a medium-sized pot, heat 2 tablespoons oil. Add peas, pepper, water chestnuts, and scallions. Pour in sweet and sour sauce. Cook over medium heat until it almost comes to a boil. Stir in cornstarch water. Stir and cook until sauce is thickened. Cover and keep warm over very low heat.

4. When fish is done, drain and put on a serving platter with stomach side down. Pour sauce over fish. Serve hot at once.

NOTE: *The fish should be eaten immediately while it is hot and crisp. Be sure to gather your family or guests around the table to wait for the fish. Never let the fish wait for you!*

長沙脆魚

HUNAN CHANGSHA CRISP WHOLE SEA BASS
about 6 servings

Hunan Province is the birthplace of Chairman Mao Tse-tung, and Changsha is the capital of Hunan where he received his education and from which he began the revolution. Hunan is like her neighbor, Szechwan, where the summer is hot and humid; her people like peppery food.

PREPARATION OF INGREDIENTS

1 fresh whole sea bass, 1½ to 2 pounds: scale, clean, and leave whole, score both sides about ½ inch deep into diamond design, split fish along belly almost to bone, pat dry with towels

MARINADE (MIX IN A SMALL BOWL)*

> *1 teaspoon finely minced fresh ginger root*
> *1 teaspoon finely minced scallion*
> *½ teaspoon salt*
> *¼ teaspoon ground pepper*
> *1 teaspoon pale dry sherry*

about 2 tablespoons cornstarch to dust fish
2 teaspoons oil
2 ounces ground pork
2 scallions: cut into pea-sized pieces, including green part
¼ cup coarsely chopped red or green bell pepper

SAUCE MIXTURE (MIX IN A BOWL)*

> *2 tablespoons tomato ketchup*
> *2 tablespoons black soy sauce*
> *2 tablespoons pale dry sherry*
> *5 tablespoons sugar*
> *2 tablespoons white vinegar*
> *1 cup water*

½ teaspoon cayenne pepper
¼ teaspoon salt
1 teaspoon chili oil (see recipe)
2 teaspoons minced fresh ginger root
2 teaspoons minced garlic

1 tablespoon cornstarch mixed with 1 tablespoon water
5 to 6 cups oil for deep-frying

BATTER (BEAT EGG, WATER, OIL, AND SOY SAUCE TOGETHER. ADD FLOUR,
CORNSTARCH, AND BAKING POWDER. MIX WITH A SPOON UNTIL SMOOTH)*

1 egg
3 tablespoons cold water
2 tablespoons oil
1 teaspoon thin soy sauce
6 tablespoons all-purpose flour
3 tablespoons cornstarch
2 teaspoons baking powder

DIRECTIONS FOR COOKING

1. Rub fish inside and outside with marinade.

2. Dust fish with cornstarch inside and out. Put it on a tray, stomach down.

3. Heat 2 teaspoons oil in a medium-sized saucepan. Add ground pork, and stir to separate pieces. Cook until meat is no longer pink. Drop in scallions and bell pepper. Pour in sauce mixture and cook over low heat until it bubbles gently. Stir in the cornstarch water. Cook, stirring constantly, until sauce is thickened. Cover to keep hot.

4. Heat 5 to 6 cups oil in wok to deep-fry temperature. Meanwhile, pour batter over and inside fish. Carefully put fish, stomach side down, in the very hot oil. Deep-fry over medium heat for 8 minutes; then turn fish over and deep-fry for another 10 minutes. Remove fish gently with the help of 2 spatulas and place it on a big serving platter with its stomach down.

5. Pour sauce over fish. Serve hot at once.

NOTE: *The fish should be eaten immediately while it is hot and crisp. Be sure to gather your family or guests around the table to wait for the fish.*

醋溜瓦塊魚

FISH SLICES IN HOT VINEGAR SAUCE, PEKING STYLE
4 to 6 servings

PREPARATION OF INGREDIENTS

1 pound fillets (flounder, sole, or bass): cut into pieces 1 by 2 inches

MARINADE (MIX AND MARINATE FISH IN A BOWL. REFRIGERATE BEFORE USE)*

> *½ teaspoon salt*
> *⅛ teaspoon white pepper*
> *¼ teaspoon sugar*
> *2 teaspoons pale dry sherry*
> *1 teaspoon finely minced fresh ginger root*
> *1 beaten egg*

about ½ cup cornstarch for dredging fish
about 4 cups oil for deep-frying
4 dried chili peppers (or 2 if you do not like it so hot): tear into
*   small pieces, do not discard seeds*
1 thin slice ginger: mince finely
2 cloves garlic: peel and mince
2 scallions: cut into 1½-inch lengths, including green part
3 Chinese dried mushrooms: soak in hot water until spongy,
*   discard stems, shred caps*
4 ounces ground pork

SAUCE MIXTURE (MIX IN A BOWL)*

> *1 tablespoon white vinegar*
> *4 teaspoons sugar*
> *3 tablespoons black soy sauce*
> *2 tablespoons Chinese Shaohsing wine or pale dry sherry*
> *1 cup clear chicken broth (not condensed)*

2 tablespoons cornstarch mixed with 3 tablespoons water
2 teaspoons sesame seed oil

DIRECTIONS FOR COOKING

1. Dredge marinated fish slices in cornstarch.

2. Heat oil in wok to deep-fry temperature. Fry fish slices until they are light gold. Drain on paper towels. Put in warm oven to keep hot.

3. Remove all but 2 tablespoons oil from wok. Heat oil, then slightly brown chili peppers, ginger, garlic, and scallions. Add mushrooms and pork. Stir-fry until pork loses its pink color. Stir in sauce mixture and cook until it almost comes to a boil. Stir in cornstarch water and cook until sauce is thickened. Return fish slices to wok. Swirl in sesame seed oil. Put on a serving platter. Serve hot.

豉汁魚片

FISH SLICES IN GARLIC AND BLACK BEAN SAUCE
4 to 6 servings

PREPARATION OF INGREDIENTS

1 pound fillets (sole or flounder): cut into 1-by-2-inch pieces

MARINADE (MIX AND MARINATE FISH IN A BOWL)*

½ teaspoon salt
⅛ teaspoon white pepper
¼ teaspoon sugar
2 teaspoons pale dry sherry
1 teaspoon finely minced fresh ginger root
1 beaten egg

about ½ cup cornstarch
about 4 cups oil for deep-frying
3 tablespoons oil for stir-frying

continued

SEASONINGS (PUT IN A BOWL)*

> 1 tablespoon salted black beans: rinse in hot water, drain, mash
>   into paste
> 1 teaspoon finely minced garlic
> 2 scallions: cut into pea-sized pieces, including green part
> 1 piece dried tangerine peel: soak in hot water to soften,
>   chop into rice-sized pieces to make 1 teaspoon
> 1 teaspoon finely minced fresh ginger root

SAUCE MIXTURE (MIX IN A BOWL)*

> 2 tablespoons thin soy sauce
> 2 tablespoons pale dry sherry
> ½ teaspoon sugar
> 6 tablespoons water
> ¼ teaspoon salt

1 teaspoon cornstarch mixed with 1 teaspoon water

DIRECTIONS FOR COOKING

1. Roll marinated fish in cornstarch. Coat fish slices twice until they are not sticky.

2. Heat 4 cups oil in a medium-sized pot to deep-fry temperature. Fry half the fish slices at a time to golden brown. Drain on paper towels.

3. Heat wok over high heat. Swirl in 3 tablespoons oil. When oil is hot, slightly brown the seasonings. Pour in sauce mixture and cook to boil. Stir in cornstarch water and cook until sauce is thickened. Put fish slices into wok. Mix with sauce and cook for about 20 seconds. Put on a serving platter. Serve hot.

假梅子

FRIED MOCK PLUMS
about 6 servings

For this dish, shrimp paste is rolled up in bean curd skin to form a long cylinder. At 1-inch intervals, string is tied tightly around the cylinder, pinching it somewhat.

Tied in this fashion, the cylinder is said to resemble a string of plums. After it is fried, the skin is crisp and the shrimp paste is almost crunchy.

PREPARATION OF INGREDIENTS

2 pieces dried bean curd skin, each 5 by 10 inches

SHRIMP MIXTURE (MIX IN A BOWL. REFRIGERATE BEFORE USE)*

> *1 pound fresh shrimp: shell, devein, rinse in cold running water,*
> *pat dry, mince into paste*
> *4 slices cooked, crisp bacon: mince*
> *2 teaspoons sesame seed oil*
> *⅛ teaspoon white pepper*
> *2 teaspoons pale dry sherry*
> *2 teaspoons thin soy sauce*
> *½ teaspoon sugar*

3 to 4 cups oil
Flower Peppercorn and Salt Dip (see recipe) or Soy-Vinegar Dip
　(see recipe)

DIRECTIONS FOR COOKING

1. Run hot tap water on bean curd skins for several seconds to soften them. Pat dry with paper towels and put on a flat surface.

2. Put half the shrimp mixture, approximately 1 inch in diameter, on the bean curd skin lengthwise near the edge of the skin. Roll it into a long cylinder. Tie string tightly around cylinder at 1-inch intervals, leaving the ends open. Put aside. Repeat process for second bean curd skin.

3. Heat oil to deep-fry temperature. Deep-fry cylinders until they are golden brown. Drain.

4. Cut cylinders at the strings into plum-sized pieces. Put on a serving platter. Serve hot with dip.

炸蝦球

DEEP-FRIED SHRIMP BALLS
about 6 servings

PREPARATION OF INGREDIENTS

4 cups oil for deep-frying
1 small bowl of cold oil

SHRIMP MIXTURE (MIX IN A BOWL)*

> 1 pound fresh shrimp: shell, devein, rinse in running cold water,
>   drain and dry, mince into paste
> 3 tablespoons minced pork fat or bacon fat
> ¼ teaspoon fresh ginger root juice (use garlic press)
> ⅓ cup minced water chestnuts
> 1 pinch white pepper
> ½ teaspoon salt
> 1 teaspoon sesame seed oil
> 1 teaspoon cornstarch
> 1 egg white: beat until slightly foamy

Five-Fragrance Dip (see recipe)

DIRECTIONS FOR COOKING

1. Preheat oven to low (only a warm oven is needed).

2. Heat oil in wok to deep-fry temperature. Have the small bowl of cold oil and a soup spoon within reach.

3. Using your left hand, grasp a handful of the shrimp mixture and squeeze it between the base of your thumb and your index finger. When it forms a walnut-sized ball, scoop it with the spoon and put it into the heated oil. Dip the spoon into the bowl of cold oil before scooping another shrimp ball. The cold oil keeps the shrimp paste from sticking to the spoon. Repeat this until there are enough shrimp balls in the hot oil. Fry until they are golden. Drain and put them in the preheated oven until the others are done. Serve hot with dip.

醸大蝦

STUFFED PRAWNS
8 servings

PREPARATION OF INGREDIENTS

8 big fresh prawns: shell, devein, and butterfly as illustrated in
   this chapter
1 egg yolk

STUFFING (MIX IN A BOWL)*

   4 ounces ground pork
   4 ounces fresh small shrimp: shell, devein, and rinse in cold
      water, pat dry, mince into paste
   1/4 cup minced water chestnuts
   1 scallion: mince, including green part
   1/4 teaspoon salt
   1/4 teaspoon sugar
   1 big pinch ground pepper
   1 teaspoon thin soy sauce
   1 egg white: beat until slightly foamy

4 cups oil

BATTER (MIX IN A BOWL)

   1 egg: beat until slightly foamy
   2 tablespoons flour
   1/4 teaspoon five-fragrance powder
   1 tablespoon water
   1/8 teaspoon salt
   2 teaspoons cornstarch
   1/2 teaspoon baking powder

Soy-Vinegar Dip (see recipe)

DIRECTIONS FOR COOKING

1. Brush split side of prawns with egg yolk. Then spread stuffing generously on egg-yolked side of prawns.

2. Heat oil in wok to deep-fry temperature. Gently dip stuffed prawns into batter. Deep-fry until golden brown. Drain on paper towels. Serve hot with dip.

酥炸虫胡蝶蝦

PUFFED BUTTERFLY SHRIMP
about 6 servings

PREPARATION OF INGREDIENTS

1 pound (15 to 20) fresh shrimp: shell, devein, and butterfly as
illustrated in this chapter

GINGER JUICE MIXTURE (MIX IN A SMALL BOWL)*

¼ teaspoon fresh ginger root juice (use garlic press)
1 teaspoon minced garlic
¼ teaspoon salt
1 teaspoon pale dry sherry

1 cup all-purpose flour, unsifted
1 tablespoon baking powder
¼ teaspoon salt
5 tablespoons oil
⅔ cup cold water
4 teaspoons white sesame seeds
3 tablespoons minced scallions, including green part
about 4 cups oil for deep-frying

DIRECTIONS FOR COOKING

1. Brush ginger juice mixture only on split side of shrimp.

2. Mix flour, baking powder, and salt in a bowl. Add 5 tablespoons of oil gradually while stirring. Mix well. The dough should look like pie dough. Stir in water, a little at a time, until mixture becomes a thick batter. Add sesame seeds and scallions. Mix well. (To test whether consistency of the batter is right, hold a shrimp by the tail, dip it into the batter, then hold it over the bowl. The batter should drip down slowly from the shrimp.)

3. Heat oil to deep-fry temperature. Take each shrimp by the tail, dip it into the batter, then put directly into the hot oil. The shrimp should puff up and swim to the surface immediately. If it stays on the bottom, the oil is not hot enough. (Deep-fry a few at a time; too many will cool down the oil temperature too much.) Turn the shrimp when the batter is set. Fry until light gold. Place on paper towels to drain. Serve hot or warm.

NOTE: *You can put the shrimp in a warm oven. They will keep hot and crisp for half an hour or longer.*

清炒蝦仁

PEKING PURE SHRIMP
2 to 4 servings

In China this is a very popular and famous dish. The shrimp presents itself with very little make-up, but is delicate and crunchy. It is a great art to cook shrimp in such a simple style.

PREPARATION OF INGREDIENTS

5 tablespoons oil
¼ cup chopped scallions, in pea-sized pieces, including green part

SHRIMP MIXTURE (MIX IN A BOWL AND REFRIGERATE FOR AT LEAST AN HOUR)*

> *1 pound fresh shrimp: shell, devein, rinse in cold water, drain, dry*
> *about ½ egg white*
> *1 pinch white pepper*
> *1 teaspoon salt*
> *½ teaspoon baking soda*
> *1 teaspoon sesame seed oil*
> *2 teaspoons cornstarch*
> *¼ teaspoon sugar*
> *2 teaspoons pale dry sherry*

1 teaspoon sesame seed oil
Soy-Sesame Dip (see recipe) or Soy-Chili Dip (see recipe)

DIRECTIONS FOR COOKING

Heat wok over high heat until it almost begins to smoke. Swirl in oil and spread it evenly with a spatula. Drop in scallions and stir-fry for about 10 seconds. Add shrimp mixture. Stir-fry until shrimp turn white-pink. (It takes about a minute.) Add sesame seed oil. Put on a serving platter. Serve hot at once with dip.

四川燒燒蝦仁

SZECHWAN SPICED SHRIMP
2 to 4 servings

PREPARATION OF INGREDIENTS

about 2 cups oil for deep-frying

SHRIMP MIXTURE (MIX AND KEEP REFRIGERATED FOR AT LEAST AN HOUR BEFORE USE)*

> *1 pound fresh shrimp: shell, devein, cut into halves lengthwise, rinse in cold running water for a minute, drain, pat dry*
> *¼ teaspoon salt*
> *1 teaspoon Chinese Shaohsing wine or pale dry sherry*
> *1 teaspoon thin soy sauce*
> *2 tablespoons flour*
> *1 tablespoon cornstarch*
> *1 egg, slightly beaten*
> *¼ teaspoon baking soda*

SEASONINGS (PUT IN A BOWL)*

> *1 teaspoon finely minced fresh ginger root*
> *2 teaspoons minced garlic*
> *2 scallions: cut into pea-sized pieces, including green part*
> *2 to 3 dried chili peppers: tear into small pieces, do not discard seeds*

SAUCE MIXTURE (MIX IN A BOWL)*

1 tablespoon sugar
5 teaspoons black soy sauce
3 tablespoons tomato ketchup
2 teaspoons pale dry sherry
1 teaspoon white vinegar
1 tablespoon water

1 teaspoon sesame seed oil

DIRECTIONS FOR COOKING

1. Heat oil in wok over medium heat to deep-fry temperature. Add shrimp mixture, half at a time, and stir briskly until shrimp turn whitish-pink (less than 10 seconds). Remove with a drainer to a bowl.

2. Remove all but 2 tablespoons oil from wok. Heat oil, then slightly brown seasonings. Stir in sauce mixture. Stir and cook until it begins to bubble. Return shrimp to wok. Stir-fry for several seconds. Swirl in sesame seed oil. Put on a serving platter. Serve hot.

鼓汁蝦球

SHRIMP CANTONESE
6 to 8 servings

PREPARATION OF INGREDIENTS

6 tablespoons oil

SHRIMP MIXTURE (MIX IN A BOWL. REFRIGERATE FOR AT LEAST AN HOUR)*

> *1 pound fresh shrimp: shell, devein, wash under running cold*
> *water, drain, dry*
> *½ teaspoon pale dry sherry*
> *1 egg white*
> *¼ teaspoon salt*
> *½ teaspoon baking soda*
> *½ teaspoon sesame seed oil*
> *⅛ teaspoon ground pepper*

SEASONINGS (PUT IN A BOWL)*

> *2 scallions: cut into pea-sized pieces, including green part*
> *1 teaspoon finely minced fresh ginger root*
> *2 teaspoons minced garlic*
> *1 tablespoon salted black beans: rinse in hot water, drain, mash*
> *into paste*

4 ounces minced pork
½ green or red bell pepper: cut into 1-inch squares

SAUCE MIXTURE (MIX IN A BOWL)*

> *¼ teaspoon sugar*
> *2 teaspoons cornstarch*
> *1 tablespoon black soy sauce*
> *2 teaspoons thin soy sauce*

½ teaspoon sesame seed oil

½ cup clear chicken broth (not condensed) or water

2 tablespoons Chinese Shaohsing wine or pale dry sherry

2 eggs: beat until slightly foamy

DIRECTIONS FOR COOKING

1. Heat wok over high heat. Swirl in 4 tablespoons of the oil. When hot, add shrimp mixture. Stir-fry until shrimp just turn white-pink (less than a minute). Remove with drainer or slotted spoon to a bowl. Clean and dry wok.

2. Heat wok over high heat until it is hot. Swirl in the remaining 2 tablespoons oil. When oil is hot, add seasonings. Stir-fry over high heat until garlic turns golden. Add pork. When pork loses its pink color, add bell pepper. Mix well. Stir in sauce mixture. Stir constantly. When sauce begins to bubble, return shrimp to wok. Mix well.

3. Pour eggs evenly over shrimp. Do not stir. Cover and cook over medium heat for 2 minutes or until eggs are slightly set around the edge. Stir to mix well. Put on a serving platter. Serve hot.

白灼蝦

EASY WATERFRONT SHRIMP
2 to 4 servings

These shrimp are mostly served in seafood restaurants by the water or on floating restaurants, where shrimp is always fresh. The shrimp is blanched in water for less than a minute when it is just cooked. Thus, it is sweet and crunchy, unlike the always overcooked shrimp here, tasteless and dull.

When this dish arrives at the table, all manners can be disregarded temporarily. One can roll up the sleeves and eat with fingers. Using chopsticks is not considered proper for this dish. After the shell is removed, the shrimp is eaten with the sauce. Slow eaters simply get fewer shrimp because everyone is eating from the same pile. Those with the biggest pile of shells will be only slightly embarrassed, if at all.

Then a big bowl of warm tea will be placed in front of you. Do not drink it though. It is for you to wash your fingers, for tea takes away the odor.

PREPARATION OF INGREDIENTS

4 cups water
2 slices fresh ginger root, each as big and thick as a quarter
2 tablespoons pale dry sherry
1 pound fresh medium-sized shrimp: just before cooking, rinse in
cold running water, drain in colander
Fresh Chili-Soy Dip (see recipe): prepare in advance

DIRECTIONS FOR COOKING

Pour water into a 5- or 6-quart pot, add ginger, and bring to a rapid boil. Add sherry. Immediately drop in the shrimp, cover and count 35 seconds. Turn off heat. Remove shrimp with a drainer and put on a serving platter. Serve hot at once with dip.

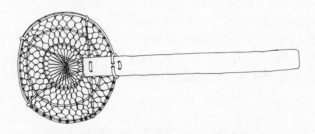

蘇梅蝦

MAI'S SHRIMP IN PLUM SAUCE
4 to 6 servings

PREPARATION OF INGREDIENTS

6 tablespoons oil

SHRIMP MIXTURE (MIX IN A BOWL. REFRIGERATE FOR 1 TO 2 HOURS)*

1 pound fresh shrimp: shell, devein, rinse in cold water, pat dry
1 teaspoon pale dry sherry
⅛ teaspoon white pepper
about ½ egg white
¼ teaspoon sugar
½ teaspoon baking soda

2 teaspoons minced garlic
2 scallions: cut into pea-sized pieces, including green part
4 ounces ground pork
¼ cup coarsely chopped water chestnuts

SAUCE MIXTURE (MIX IN A BOWL)*

    4 tablespoons plum sauce
    1 tablespoon pale dry sherry
    1 tablespoon black soy sauce

DIRECTIONS FOR COOKING

1. Heat wok over high heat until it just begins to smoke. Swirl in oil. Add shrimp mixture, and cook until shrimp turn whitish-pink (less than a minute). Drain and put on a plate.

2. Remove all but 1 tablespoon oil from wok. Heat oil, add garlic, scallions, and ground pork. Stir-fry until pork loses its pink color. Add water chestnuts. Stir in sauce mixture. Cook and stir for about 15 seconds. Return shrimp to wok. Stir-fry for 10 seconds. Put on a platter. Serve hot.

腰果蝦球

SHRIMP WITH CASHEW NUTS
about 6 servings

PREPARATION OF INGREDIENTS

5 tablespoons oil
⅓ cup uncooked cashew nuts
¼ cup Chinese dried mushrooms: soak in hot water until
    spongy, discard stems, cut caps into squares
⅓ cup quartered water chestnuts

SHRIMP MIXTURE (MIX IN A BOWL AND REFRIGERATE FOR AT LEAST 30 MINUTES)*

    1 pound fresh shrimp: shell, devein, rinse, drain, pat dry
    ⅛ teaspoon salt
    ½ teaspoon pale dry sherry
    about ½ egg white

continued

SAUCE MIXTURE (MIX IN A BOWL)*

> 1 tablespoon thin soy sauce
> ½ teaspoon black soy sauce
> 1 teaspoon pale dry sherry
> ¼ teaspoon sugar

1 scallion: chop into pea-sized pieces, including green part
1 teaspoon sesame seed oil

DIRECTIONS FOR COOKING

1. Heat oil in wok to deep-fry temperature. Add cashew nuts, and turn heat to low. Deep-fry cashews slowly until they are golden brown. Drain on paper towels.

2. Reheat oil in wok over medium heat. Brown mushrooms slightly. Add water chestnuts, then shrimp mixture. Stir-fry until shrimp turn whitish-pink (about 1 minute). Stir in sauce mixture, and drop in scallion. Stir-fry for about 15 seconds. Add sesame seed oil. Throw in cashew nuts. Mix and serve hot.

豉汁龍蝦

LOBSTER CANTONESE
about 8 servings

PREPARATION OF INGREDIENTS

3 pounds live lobster (3 1-pound lobsters)
2 tablespoons cornstarch
about 4 cups oil for deep-frying

SEASONINGS (PUT IN A BOWL)*

> 3 tablespoons salted black beans: rinse in hot water, drain, mash
>   into paste
> ¼ cup chopped scallions, including green part
> 1 teaspoon finely minced fresh ginger root
> 1 tablespoon minced garlic

4 ounces ground pork

SAUCE MIXTURE (MIX IN A BOWL)*

1 tablespoon black soy sauce
2 tablespoons thin soy sauce
4 tablespoons Chinese Shaohsing wine or pale dry sherry
1 teaspoon sugar
¼ teaspoon salt
1 cup clear chicken broth (not condensed)
1 tablespoon cornstarch

¼ cup red or green bell peppers, in ½-inch squares
2 eggs: beat until slightly foamy
1 tablespoon sesame seed oil

DIRECTIONS FOR COOKING

1. Chop off each lobster's tail, and section it into desired pieces. Cut off claws, crack them, then chop them into big pieces. Cut off and discard feet. Split heads into halves, and cut halves crosswise. Discard gill and mouth area. Put lobster pieces in a colander to drain.

2. Mix lobster pieces and 2 tablespoons cornstarch in a bowl.

3. Heat oil in wok to deep-fry temperature. Add lobster pieces and deep-fry for about 10 minutes or until they are just done. Remove with a drainer or slotted spoon to a bowl.*

4. Skim off residue from oil. Remove all but 2 tablespoons oil from wok. Heat remaining oil in wok over high heat, then add seasonings. Stir-fry until garlic turns golden. Add pork, break it into small pieces, and stir-fry until no longer pink. Stir in sauce mixture. Add peppers and lobster pieces. Stir and cook until sauce bubbles gently.

5. Turn heat to medium. Swirl eggs evenly over lobster. Cover and cook over low heat for about 3 minutes. When eggs are slightly set around the edge, stir to mix well. Cover and cook for another minute. Add sesame seed oil. Put on a serving platter. Serve hot.

NOTE: *There is a lot of sauce in this dish. You might like to prepare more rice than usual.*

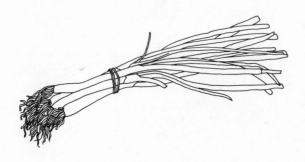

煎蠔餅

OYSTER PANCAKES WITH SOY-VINEGAR DIP
2 to 4 servings

The sign "Eat oysters, love longer" is seen here and there in fish stores in this country. I assume that some Westerners have the same idea as the Chinese—oysters enhance sexuality, especially in women. "It nourishes the Yin (female)," my grandmother used to say. Sea slugs were supposed to have the same effect.

In old China, the emperor had 3,000 women at his disposal in the palace, and his male subjects could have as many wives as their purses could afford; therefore sexual potency has always been a common concern among the Chinese. For thousands of years, the search for remedies to promote potency was perpetual. Ginseng was found, the rare Manchurian plant whose root resembles a man's figure. This manlike root, believed to restore health and to strengthen any body weakness, was revered as the root of life and happiness. But ginseng was too scarce and too expensive for most people. Therefore, they turned to more ordinary substances and created their own folk prescriptions for sexuality. Dog meat (not the pet, but a special kind of Chinese dog) cooked with wine, mutton cooked with herbs, snake meat cooked with pork, mushrooms, ginger, and a special kind of dark chicken meat called Chu Sui Chi were prescriptions believed to heat one's body and reinvigorate the spirit of Yang.

My two grandfathers had ten wives between them; sometimes they got together with friends and held snake banquets at which dozens of snake dishes were prepared in many ways. It was said that the diners were stimulated for many days afterward.

Customarily, eating snake meat and dog meat occurred in the fall and winter, when one's body was cool and the spirit calm. In Hong Kong, dog eating was illegal, yet there were plenty of places away from the city where one could easily find a dog dinner. Once during my college years, I planned to join a dog-eating evening adventure, but dropped out when I imagined myself in jail, the headlines blaring: "College Girl Arrested for Eating Dog." I was told afterward by my fellow adventurers that all of them ate standing up, ready to run if the police came!

PREPARATION OF INGREDIENTS

½ pint fresh oysters
1 tablespoon salt

BATTER (MIX WELL IN A BOWL)*

> *2 beaten eggs*
> *⅓ cup flour*
> *½ teaspoon baking powder*
> *½ teaspoon salt*
> *⅛ teaspoon white pepper*
> *1 tablespoon oil*
> *¼ cup chopped scallions, in pea-sized pieces, including green part*

4 to 5 tablespoons oil
double recipe Soy-Vinegar Dip (see recipe)

DIRECTIONS FOR COOKING

1. Add salt to oysters and squeeze them gently for about half a minute. Rinse in cold water and drain. Bring a small pot of water to a boil. Add oysters and blanch for 10 seconds. Drain in colander.*

2. Add oysters to batter and mix well.

3. Heat a skillet. Add 2 tablespoons of the oil. When oil is hot, spoon about 1 tablespoon batter with an oyster into skillet to make 1 pancake. You may pan-fry 4 to 5 pancakes at a time. Turn heat to medium-low. Fry pancakes until both sides are golden brown, then place in a warm oven. Serve hot with dip.

洞庭干貝

LAKE TUNG TING SCALLOPS
2 to 4 servings

Tung Ting Lake, the largest lake of China, is in the northern part of Hunan. The tranquil water of the lake, surrounded by green valleys, gentle hills, and stretches of densely forested mountains, portrays the beauty of the region.

This method of cooking scallops was taught by Lee, an old Hunanese friend. The scallops are enhanced by the delicious sauce, which is slightly sweet and spiced with chili peppers and garlic.

PREPARATION OF INGREDIENTS

2 cups oil

1 pound fresh scallops: if big, cut each crosswise into ¼-inch-thick pieces

1 tablespoon cornstarch: mix cornstarch and scallops in a bowl. Refrigerate before use.*

SEASONINGS (PUT ON A PLATE)*

1 piece dried tangerine peel: soak in hot water for about 15 minutes or until soft, mince (to make about 1 tablespoon)

2 to 3 dried chili peppers: tear into small pieces, do not discard seeds

1 teaspoon finely minced fresh ginger root

1 tablespoon minced garlic

3 scallions: cut into pea-sized pieces, including green part

¼ cup green or red bell pepper (optional), in ½-inch squares

SAUCE MIXTURE (MIX IN A BOWL)*

3 tablespoons tomato ketchup
5 teaspoons black soy sauce
1 tablespoon sugar
1 teaspoon white vinegar
2 teaspoons pale dry sherry
1 tablespoon water

DIRECTIONS FOR COOKING

1. Heat oil in wok to deep-fry temperature. Add scallops. Stir to separate them, and blanch in oil for about 30 seconds or until they are just done. Remove with a drainer to a bowl.

2. Remove all but 2 tablespoons oil from wok. Heat oil over medium heat, then drop in seasonings. When garlic and ginger turn golden, swirl in sauce mixture. Return scallops to wok. Mix well. Cook and stir gently until sauce begins to bubble. Put on a serving platter. Serve hot at once.

豉椒炒蟹

SOFT-SHELL CRABS IN BLACK BEAN AND CHILI SAUCE
2 to 4 servings

When you buy soft-shell crabs, be sure that they are still alive. Usually they look quite dead, weak and limp. Touch their legs, eyes, or mouth. Even if they respond only slightly and slowly, they are still alive. Refrigerate them as soon as you get home.

Cleaning them is quite simple. Clip off the eyes and mouth. Lift the top shell and remove the soft featherlike gills and discard them. Turn the crab bottom up. Tear off and discard the cartilage (the shape of the female's is half oval, the male's is a narrow triangle).

PREPARATION OF INGREDIENTS

1 cup oil for deep-frying
4 soft-shell crabs (about 1 pound)
2 tablespoons oil for stir-frying

SEASONINGS (PUT IN A BOWL)*

2 tablespoons salted black beans: rinse in hot water, drain, mash into paste
4 cloves garlic: mince
½ teaspoon finely minced fresh ginger root
2 dried red chili peppers: tear into small pieces, do not discard seeds
1 scallion: cut into pea-sized pieces, including green part

½ cup chopped green or red bell pepper

SAUCE MIXTURE (MIX IN A BOWL)*

1½ tablespoons Chinese Shaohsing wine or pale dry sherry
½ teaspoon sugar

2 tablespoons thin soy sauce
¼ cup clear chicken broth (not condensed)

1 teaspoon cornstarch mixed with 2 tablespoons water

DIRECTIONS FOR COOKING

1. Heat 1 cup oil in wok to deep-fry temperature. Add crabs and deep-fry until they turn orange. Drain crabs and discard oil. Clean and dry wok.

2. Heat wok over high heat. Swirl in 2 tablespoons oil. When oil is hot, add seasonings. Stir-fry for about 30 seconds. Add bell pepper and stir-fry for about 10 seconds. Stir in sauce mixture. Put cooked crabs back into wok. Cover, turn heat to low, and cook until sauce comes to a boil. Stir in cornstarch water. Stir and cook until sauce is thickened. Put on a serving platter. Serve hot.

Note: *For a less pungent hot dish, use 1 tablespoon salted black beans and 1 dried chili pepper.*

❁❁❁❁

Vegetables and Bean Curd

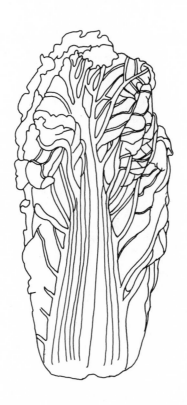

VEGETABLES AND BEAN CURD

I do not understand why so many Westerners cook their vegetables as if they were cooking potatoes. The peas, the beans, the broccoli, even the luscious asparagus are cooked so much that they all taste the same, like cooked potatoes—dull, mushy, and lifeless.

The Chinese prefer to cook vegetables briefly in oil to bring out a most beautiful green color that is even brighter and shinier than it was in the field. Short cooking preserves natural sweetness, crispness, and vitamins. My father maintains that vegetables made the Chinese strong in spirit and endurance; that was why we won the war. (Do not argue with my father. He argues with his heart, not his mind.)

Vegetables are plentiful here, even the Chinese variety. They look fresh and healthy. And taste as good as in their mother soil. But I have found that many people in this land do not know how to buy vegetables, and cannot tell the good from the bad. The suggestions in the following pages might help on your next shopping trip.

Fresh bean curd is made of soybeans puréed then pressed into bricklike cakes 1 inch thick and 2 to 4 inches square. Smooth, fragile, custardlike, and ivory-colored, bean curd itself is bland in taste, but it quickly absorbs flavor from other ingredients with which it is cooked. As it is inexpensive and high in protein, bean curd serves the purpose of meat and milk for many Chinese in addition to being used as a vegetable. Bean curd is a nutritious and well-loved food. My grandmother used to say, "Eat bean curd every day and your eyes will shine like the autumn moon, your skin will be smooth, and your hair soft and black." Generally available in Oriental grocery stores, bean curd is carried in relatively few supermarkets. The canned variety is not acceptable as a substitute for fresh bean curd. Store in a jar, cover with water, and change water daily. It will keep for a week or more.

HOW TO CHOOSE VEGETABLES

Asparagus: Choose stalks that are firm and green and moist-looking, with closed tips. Avoid those that have long white bases and droopy tips.

Bean Sprouts: Fresh bean sprouts are white, firm, and dry. Bad bean sprouts are brownish, limp, and watery because they are fermenting. Do not use them. And never, never use canned bean sprouts, for they will not enhance your dishes but diminish them instead.

Bok Choy: Pick the ones with stalks that are soft and not stiff. Discard the discolored leaves. The inner stalks are more tender and sweeter; therefore it is better to buy two smaller heads than one big one.

Broccoli: Good broccoli has the fresh smell of the green. The flowers are perky and green. Old broccoli smells. Its flowers are yellowish and droopy.

Chinese Celery Cabbage: Choose the cabbage with tight white or pale green leaves. Avoid the green leafy cabbage.

Chinese Giant White Turnip: A good white turnip is solid, heavy, and firm. Inside it is moist, clear, and without lines. An undesirable turnip is light, and the inside is dry and full of fancy designs. The Chinese describe an untrue mate as "Flower heart turnip," for he or she is light in heart and full of fancy desires.

Eggplant: A good eggplant has a firm body, shiny and smooth. An old one has a spongy body with discolored and wrinkled skin.

Ginger Root (Fresh): Always choose the one that is plump and smooth. Do not pick ginger that is dry and wrinkled. Its body will be dry and stringy.

Lettuce: "Lettuce" in Chinese sounds like the word for "thriving"; therefore, it is often included in Chinese New Year dinners, as a symbol of prosperity. Because waste matter is often used as fertilizer in China, we seldom eat lettuce raw; rather, we stir-fry it briefly (see recipe). My first choice is iceberg lettuce, my second is romaine, for their crispness after being cooked. Choose a head that is tight and pale green.

Snow Peas: Choose pods that are soft and thin. These are young pods in which the peas have not yet matured. They are juicy, crisp, and sweet. Those that have thick pods and large peas with yellowish color are old.

String Beans: The young ones have beans that have not yet matured. When you break off the tips from both ends, the break should be easy and have a crisp snappy sound, revealing moisture if the beans are young. If the tips pull off small strings, the beans are old.

HOW TO GROW BEAN SPROUTS
makes about 4 cups

The Chinese prefer bean sprouts that have white, plump bodies and yellow heads. To obtain this result, bean sprouts should be grown without too much light. Otherwise, the heads turn green and the bodies are skinny. There are many easy ways of growing bean sprouts. Here is one of them.

½ cup mung beans
2 quart plastic bowl (a lettuce crisper)
piece of cheesecloth

Soak beans overnight in plenty of cold water until they are plump. Put soaked beans into colander and shake off water. Transfer beans to container and cover it with a layer of cheesecloth. Secure the cheesecloth around the container with a rubber band. Place the container upside down on a dish rack. This is to give good drainage, to prevent the beans from rotting in water, and to protect them from excessive light.

At least 4 times daily, remove cheesecloth and generously spray the young sprouts with cold water. Each time cover the container again with the cheesecloth and return it to the dish rack upside down.

After 2 to 3 days, when the bean sprouts have grown 1 to 1½ inches long, immerse them in a big bowl of water so that the green hoods float to the top. Skim off as many hoods as possible, leaving only the yellow heads and white bodies. Drain. The bean sprouts are now ready for eating.

HOW TO MAKE SCALLION BRUSHES

Take a 2-inch-long piece from the white of the scallion. If convenient, slip a green ring from the stalk around it. Slice ends to form a brush. Put in ice water to curl brushes.

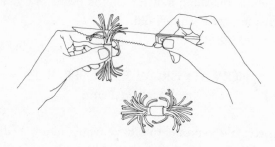

蟹肉扒露筍

ASPARAGUS IN CRABMEAT SAUCE
6 to 8 servings

Asparagus is a delicacy in China, and is uncommon among the people. It is usually served at banquets for it is scarce and expensive.

This dish is formal and elegant—a vegetable for special occasions.

PREPARATION OF INGREDIENTS

water or chicken broth to cover asparagus
5 tablespoons lard or oil
1½ pounds asparagus: break off tough ends

SAUCE MIXTURE (MIX IN A BOWL)*

    1 cup clear chicken broth (not condensed)
    1 tablespoon cornstarch

¼ *teaspoon salt*
¼ *teaspoon sugar*

1 *teaspoon Chinese Shaohsing wine or pale dry sherry*
6 *ounces fresh or frozen crabmeat: thaw and drain on paper towels*
2 *egg whites,* ⅛ *teaspoon salt: beat together until foamy*

DIRECTIONS FOR COOKING

1. Bring water or broth to rolling boil, put in 3 tablespoons lard or oil, and add the asparagus. Cook over medium heat for 2 minutes. Turn off heat. Let asparagus remain in the water while you are preparing the sauce.

2. Heat wok over high heat until hot. Add remaining lard or oil. Stir in sauce mixture and turn the heat to medium. Cook and stir sauce constantly until it is clear. Swirl in the wine. Add the crabmeat and then the egg whites. Stir gently over low heat until sauce is thickened. Turn off heat.

3. Drain asparagus. Arrange on a serving platter and top with the crabmeat sauce. Serve hot.

蠔油露筍

CRISP ASPARAGUS IN OYSTER SAUCE
6 to 8 servings

PREPARATION OF INGREDIENTS

6 *cups clear chicken broth or 2 chicken bouillon cubes dissolved*
   in 6 cups water
2 *tablespoons oil*
1 *to 1½ pounds asparagus: break off tough ends*
2 *tablespoons rendered chicken fat or duck fat*

SAUCE MIXTURE (MIX IN A BOWL)*

   3½ *tablespoons oyster-flavored sauce*
   1 *tablespoon water*
   1 *tablespoon pale dry sherry*

2 *teaspoons sesame seed oil*

DIRECTIONS FOR COOKING

1. Bring chicken broth to a rapid boil. Add oil and asparagus. Cook in broth for 2 minutes. Turn off heat. Let asparagus remain in the broth while you are preparing the sauce.

2. Heat chicken or duck fat in a small saucepan. Stir in sauce mixture and cook over low heat until it foams. Add sesame seed oil. Turn off heat.

3. Drain asparagus and arrange on a serving platter. Pour sauce over asparagus. Serve hot.

NOTE: *Asparagus may be cut into 1½- to 2-inch lengths.*

鷄油生菜

STIR-FRIED LETTUCE OR BEAN SPROUTS
4 to 6 servings

PREPARATION OF INGREDIENTS

2 tablespoons rendered chicken fat or duck fat
1 head iceberg lettuce (or 1 pound fresh bean sprouts): detach
   leaves, tear big ones in half, keep others whole

SAUCE MIXTURE (MIX IN A BOWL)*

   1 tablespoon black soy sauce
   ¼ teaspoon sugar
   2 teaspoons pale dry sherry
   1 teaspoon cornstarch

2 slices bacon: fry until crisp, chop into small pieces

DIRECTIONS FOR COOKING

Heat wok over high heat. Add chicken or duck fat and spread it around. When it is hot, add lettuce or bean sprouts. Stir-fry over medium heat for about 1 minute. Swirl in sauce mixture. Mix well. Stir-fry for about 30 seconds or until sauce bubbles. Top with chopped bacon. Serve hot.

銀芽炒鶏絲

BEAN SPROUTS WITH CHICKEN SHREDS AND ALMONDS

PREPARATION OF INGREDIENTS

4 tablespoons oil
⅓ cup uncooked sliced almonds
¼ cup shredded scallions
4 Chinese dried mushrooms: soak in hot water until spongy,
  discard stem, shred caps

CHICKEN MIXTURE (MIX IN A BOWL)*

> *1½ boned, skinless chicken breasts: shred*
>   *into matchstick strips*
> *¼ teaspoon salt*
> *about ⅓ egg white*
> *1 pinch white pepper*
> *1 pinch sugar*
> *1 teaspoon cornstarch*

8 ounces fresh bean sprouts: wash in cold water, drain
¼ cup shredded red or green bell pepper

SAUCE MIXTURE (MIX IN A BOWL)*

> *4 teaspoons thin soy sauce*
> *2 teaspoons pale dry sherry*
> *1 teaspoon sesame seed oil*
> *¼ teaspoon sugar*
> *1 teaspoon black soy sauce*
> *¼ teaspoon salt*
> *1 teaspoon cornstarch*
> *2 tablespoons water*

DIRECTIONS FOR COOKING

1. Heat 4 tablespoons oil in wok. Deep-fry almonds until they are a light gold color. Drain.

2. Reheat oil in wok over high heat. Slightly brown scallions and mushrooms. Add chicken mixture and stir-fry until it is just cooked. Add bean sprouts and pepper. Stir-fry briefly to heat them. Swirl in sauce mixture and stir to cook until sauce is thickened. Put on a serving platter. Top with almonds. Serve hot.

薑酒炒玉蘭

JADE GREEN BROCCOLI IN GINGER AND WINE SAUCE
6 to 8 servings

Chinese broccoli looks a little bit different from its American cousin. It is slimmer, taller, and has more leaves with fewer flowers. But its taste is not much different. Don't shy away from the amount of sugar and wine in this recipe, for broccoli loves the company of sugar and wine.

In this dish the broccoli is very green and crunchy, and there is plenty of sauce for the rice.

PREPARATION OF INGREDIENTS

3 tablespoons oil
2 slices fresh ginger root, each as big and thick as a quarter
3 cloves garlic: crush and peel
1 pound broccoli: cut into finger-sized pieces, blanch in water

SAUCE MIXTURE (MIX IN A BOWL)*

    2 tablespoons thin soy sauce
    1 tablespoon black soy sauce
    2 tablespoons brown sugar
    1 teaspoon sesame seed oil
    ¼ cup Chinese Shaohsing wine or pale dry sherry

1 teaspoon cornstarch mixed with 2 tablespoons water

DIRECTIONS FOR COOKING

Heat wok over high heat and add oil. When oil is hot, brown ginger and garlic and discard. Add blanched broccoli. Stir in sauce mixture and mix well. Cover and cook for about 20 seconds. Stir in cornstarch water and cook for about 15 seconds. Put on a serving platter. Serve hot.

蠔油玉筍炒時菜

BABY CORN AND BROCCOLI IN OYSTER SAUCE
6 to 8 servings

PREPARATION OF INGREDIENTS

½ pound fresh broccoli: cut into finger-sized pieces
15-ounce can baby corn: drain
3 tablespoons oil for stir-frying
6 Chinese dried mushrooms: soak in hot water until spongy,
    discard stems, leave caps whole

SAUCE MIXTURE (MIX IN A BOWL)*

   3 tablespoons oyster-flavored sauce
   ½ teaspoon sugar
   2 teaspoons pale dry sherry
   1 tablespoon thin soy sauce
   1 tablespoon water

1 teaspoon sesame seed oil

DIRECTIONS FOR COOKING

   1. Blanch broccoli and baby corn in water (see Cooking Techniques). Drain.*
   2. Heat wok over high heat. Swirl in oil. When oil is hot, add mushrooms and brown lightly. Add broccoli and baby corn and cook for about 30 seconds. Stir in sauce mixture. Stir and cook for about 20 seconds. Swirl in sesame seed oil. Put on a serving platter. Serve hot.

炒素什錦

STIR-FRIED FRESH SNOW PEAS, WATER CHESTNUTS, AND BAMBOO SHOOTS
4 servings

PREPARATION OF INGREDIENTS

2 tablespoons oil for stir-frying
2 scallions: cut into 1-inch lengths, including green part
4 Chinese dried mushrooms: soak in hot water until spongy,
   discard stems
½ pound fresh snow peas: pinch off tips and ends
¼ cup sliced bamboo shoots
¼ cup water chestnuts: cut in half crosswise

SAUCE MIXTURE (MIX IN A BOWL)*

   1 tablespoon thin soy sauce
   1 tablespoon oyster-flavored sauce
   1 teaspoon pale dry sherry
   ¼ teaspoon sugar
   ¼ teaspoon salt

1 teaspoon sesame seed oil

DIRECTIONS FOR COOKING

Heat wok over high heat. Swirl in oil for stir-frying. When oil is hot, drop in scallions, then mushrooms. Stir-fry for 10 seconds. Add snow peas, bamboo shoots, and water chestnuts. Stir-fry until snow peas turn bright green. Stir in sauce mixture and stir-fry for about 20 seconds. Swirl in sesame seed oil. Mix well. Put on a serving platter. Serve hot.

醸茄夾

STUFFED EGGPLANT
4 servings

PREPARATION OF INGREDIENTS

*1 to 1½ pounds eggplant: cut crosswise into ½-inch-thick circles,
cut each circle in half; slit straight edge, but not all the way
through, to make pocket for stuffing*

STUFFING (MIX AND BLEND FOR ABOUT 1 MINUTE OR UNTIL STUFFING BECOMES A
STICKY PASTE)*

> *½ pound ground pork*
> *2 tablespoons Chinese dried shrimp (**optional**): soak in hot water to
>   soften, mince*
> *2 scallions: mince, including green part*
> *½ teaspoon sugar*
> *¼ teaspoon five-fragrance powder*
> *4 teaspoons thin soy sauce*
> *1 big pinch pepper*
> *1 teaspoon pale dry sherry*

2 eggs
½ teaspoon salt
⅔ cup cornstarch
½ cup oil
Soy-Vinegar Dip (see recipe)

DIRECTIONS FOR COOKING

1. Fill pockets of eggplant half-circles with stuffing.

2. Beat eggs with salt. Dip stuffed eggplant into egg batter, then dredge it with cornstarch. Put aside.

3. Heat a skillet and pour in 4 tablespoons oil or enough to cover bottom of skillet. Heat oil, then arrange some of the eggplant pieces in skillet and pan-fry them over medium-low heat for about 10 minutes or until both sides are golden brown. Drain and put in warm oven to keep hot while the others cook. Add more oil to skillet as necessary. Serve hot with dip.

魚香茄子

SZECHWAN EGGPLANT IN CHILI GARLIC SAUCE
4 servings

PREPARATION OF INGREDIENTS

2 pounds eggplant
3 tablespoons oil for frying
2 whole dried chili peppers
6 cloves garlic: mince
2 scallions: chop into pea-sized pieces, including green part

SAUCE MIXTURE (MIX IN A BOWL)*

    1 tablespoon Szechwan sweet bean sauce or ground bean sauce

    2 tablespoons black soy sauce

    2 teaspoons brown sugar

    1 tablespoon pale dry sherry

    1 teaspoon chili oil (see recipe)

1 teaspoon sesame seed oil

DIRECTIONS FOR COOKING

1. Make 4 slashes around eggplant, about 1 inch deep. Steam eggplant over water until soft. Cool slightly. Tear eggplant into thin strips lengthwise. Discard part of the seeds.

2. Heat oil for frying in wok over high heat. Fry chili peppers until dark brown, then discard. Add garlic and scallions and brown them slightly. Stir in sauce mixture and cook until it begins to bubble. Add eggplant strips. Stir-fry gently until eggplant is heated through. Add sesame seed oil. Serve hot.

NOTE: *Chili oil and dried chili peppers can be omitted if you do not like peppery food, or add the amount according to taste.*

乾燒四季豆

PEKING CRISP STRING BEANS WITH GARLIC
4 servings

The success of this dish depends on fresh young string beans.

PREPARATION OF INGREDIENTS

about 4 cups oil
1 pound fresh string beans: wash, pat dry, break off tips and ends
2 tablespoons ground pork

SEASONINGS (MIX IN A BOWL)*

> *1 tablespoon Szechwan jah choy (optional): rinse, cut into rice-sized pieces*
> *2 scallions: cut into pea-sized pieces, including green part*
> *5 cloves garlic: mince*
> *1 teaspoon salt*
> *½ teaspoon sugar*

2 teaspoons Chinese Shaohsing wine or pale dry sherry

DIRECTIONS FOR COOKING

1. Heat oil in wok over high heat until almost smoking. Add string beans. Deep-fry, stirring from time to time, until beans begin to wrinkle (about 2 minutes). Remove with a drainer or a slotted spoon to a bowl.

2. Remove all but 2 tablespoons oil from wok. Heat oil over high heat and add fat or pork and stir-fry until golden. Add seasonings. Stir-fry for about 1 minute. Splash in wine. Add cooked string beans immediately. Mix thoroughly. Put on a serving platter. Serve hot.

鷄油津白

CHINESE CELERY CABBAGE WITH CHICKEN FAT

6 to 8 servings

PREPARATION OF INGREDIENTS

2 tablespoons oil
1 pound Chinese celery cabbage: cut leaves lengthwise into about
  1-inch-wide strips: use tender part or heart

BROTH I (MIX IN A BOWL)*

  1 chicken bouillon cube dissolved in ½ cup water
  ½ teaspoon salt

2½ tablespoons rendered chicken fat
5 Chinese dried mushrooms: soak in hot water until spongy,
  discard stems
2 tablespoons pale dry sherry

BROTH II (MIX IN A BOWL)*

  ½ cup clear chicken broth (not condensed)
  ½ teaspoon salt
  ½ teaspoon sugar

2 teaspoons cornstarch mixed with 2 teaspoons water
¼ cup chopped Smithfield ham or crisp cooked bacon

DIRECTIONS FOR COOKING

1. Heat wok over high heat. Swirl in oil. Add celery cabbage and mix well. Add Broth I. Cook for about 2 minutes or until cabbage is tender. Drain cabbage and discard Broth I. Clean and dry wok.

2. Heat wok hot. Add 2 tablespoons chicken fat. When fat is hot, stir-fry mushrooms for 30 seconds. Splash in sherry, add cooked cabbage, and stir-fry briskly. Add Broth II and cook until it begins to boil. Stir in cornstarch water. Stir and cook until it is thickened. Add remaining chicken fat. Mix well. Put on a serving platter. Garnish with ham or bacon. Serve hot.

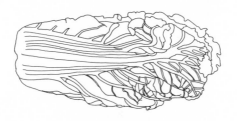

义燒炒豆角

LONG BEANS WITH BARBECUED PORK
about 6 servings

Long beans are really long—12 to 14 inches in length and thin like pencils. There are two varieties. I prefer the deep-green beans to the pale-green ones. The former are firmer and crispier. They are sold in a bundle in Chinese grocery stores.

PREPARATION OF INGREDIENTS

2 tablespoons oil
2 teaspoons minced garlic
4 ounces Cantonese barbecued pork: cut into thin slices
12 ounces long beans: discard ends and tips, cut into 1½-inch
lengths, blanch in water (see Cooking Techniques), drain*
½ cup canned straw mushrooms: rinse, drain

continued

SAUCE MIXTURE (MIX IN A BOWL)*

> 2 tablespoons black soy sauce
> 2 tablespoons pale dry sherry
> ½ teaspoon sugar
> 2 tablespoons water

1 teaspoon cornstarch mixed with 1 teaspoon water
2 teaspoons sesame seed oil

DIRECTIONS FOR COOKING

Heat wok over high heat. Swirl in oil. When oil is hot, brown garlic slightly. Add barbecued pork and stir-fry for about 1 minute. Add long beans and mushrooms. Stir-fry for another minute. Swirl in sauce mixture and thicken it with the cornstarch water. Add sesame seed oil. Mix well. Put on a serving platter. Serve hot.

雞油白菜

STIR-FRIED BOK CHOY WITH CHICKEN FAT
6 to 8 servings

PREPARATION OF INGREDIENTS

3 tablespoons rendered chicken fat
¼ teaspoon salt
1 slice of fresh ginger root, as big and thick as a quarter
1 pound bok choy: detach stalks, cut into bite-sized pieces*

SAUCE MIXTURE (MIX IN A BOWL)*

> ¼ cup clear chicken broth (not condensed)
> ¼ teaspoon sugar
> 2 teaspoons thin soy sauce

1 teaspoon cornstarch mixed with 1 teaspoon water

DIRECTIONS FOR COOKING

Heat wok over high heat. Add chicken fat and spread it with a spatula. When fat is hot, drop in salt and ginger. Discard ginger when it turns golden brown. Add bok choy. Stir-fry over medium heat for 30 seconds. Swirl in sauce mixture. Stir and cook until sauce begins to bubble. Stir in cornstarch water. Stir constantly until sauce is slightly thickened. Put on a serving platter. Serve hot.

肉片炒涼瓜

STIR-FRIED BITTER MELON WITH PORK SLICES
about 6 servings

When we were children, we made faces and called this dish "the grownups' dish." The melon *was* bitter—it made our tongues quiver, even more so because our tastes were uncultivated. Then we were told that one day, after we had had a few sorrows, some tears, and a little wisdom, the melon would seem mild.

Now that we have all aged and are somewhat seasoned by life, the bitterness of this melon has indeed become pleasant and mellow.

Yet, no Chinese would like to be called "a bitter melon," which means one is weepy and bitter. We would rather be called "a winter melon," big and clumsy—that we don't mind.

PREPARATION OF INGREDIENTS

6 cups water
½ teaspoon baking soda
1 pound fresh bitter melon: cut lengthwise, scoop out seeds and
*   soft center, cut melon crosswise into thin slices**
3 teaspoons oil
2 teaspoons minced garlic
2 scallions: cut into pea-sized pieces, including green part

continued

PORK MIXTURE (MIX IN A BOWL)*

> *8 ounces lean pork: cut into very thin slices (to make 1 cup)*
> *1 tablespoon cornstarch*
> *2 teaspoons black soy sauce*
> *½ teaspoon sugar*

SAUCE MIXTURE (MIX IN A BOWL)*

> *1 tablespoon black soy sauce*
> *4 tablespoons water*
> *½ teaspoon sugar*
> *2 tablespoons Chinese Shaohsing wine or pale dry sherry*
> *1 teaspoon cornstarch*

DIRECTIONS FOR COOKING

1. Bring water to a boil. Add baking soda and melon. Simmer over medium-low heat for about 4 minutes (reduces the bitterness of the melon). Remove from pot and quickly rinse thoroughly in cold water. Drain in colander.*

2. Heat wok over medium-high heat. Swirl in oil. When oil is hot, add garlic and scallions. Stir-fry until garlic turns golden. Put in pork mixture. Stir and cook until pork loses its pink color. Remove from wok with a drainer or a slotted spoon. Press to let oil drip back into wok. Put pork aside.

3. Keep wok hot over high heat. Swirl in sauce mixture. Cook and stir over medium-high heat until sauce bubbles gently. Add melon, then pork. Stir-fry for about 30 seconds to reheat. Put on a serving platter. Serve hot.

羅漢齋

BUDDHIST DELIGHT
6 to 8 servings

PREPARATION OF INGREDIENTS

2 tablespoons oil for frying

6 Chinese dried mushrooms: soak in hot water until spongy, discard stems

½ pound Chinese celery cabbage: cut crosswise into 1-inch-wide pieces

⅓ cup thinly sliced bamboo shoots

2 tablespoons cloud ears: soak in hot water for about 15 minutes or until soft, tear each in half

⅓ cup water chestnuts sliced as thick as a quarter

4 fried bean curd puffs: cut each into 4 pieces

1 ounce bean thread noodles: soak in hot water, shorten with scissors

10 ginkgo nuts (optional): shell and peel off skins, or use canned ones

2 cups clear chicken broth (not condensed)

SAUCE MIXTURE (MIX IN A BOWL)*

 ½ teaspoon sugar
 2 teaspoons thin soy sauce
 ½ teaspoon salt, or to taste

1 teaspoon sesame seed oil

DIRECTIONS FOR COOKING

1. Heat 3- to 4-quart pot over high heat. Swirl in oil for frying. When oil is hot, add mushrooms and brown them slightly. Add celery cabbage and stir until it is coated with oil. Put in the rest of the solid ingredients. Pour in the broth. Cover and cook over medium heat for about 15 minutes or until cabbage is soft, stirring from time to time.

2. Stir in sauce mixture. Cook for another 2 minutes. Swirl in sesame seed oil. Mix well. Put on a serving platter. Serve hot.

NOTE: *This dish can be cooked one or two days in advance. Reheat over low heat.*

龍鳳炒鮑魚菇

MAI'S SURPRISE
6 to 8 servings

The star in this dish is the abalone mushroom, a new ingredient which arrived in New York's Chinatown from Taiwan very recently. It looks like a small fan rather than the usual round mushroom. It is thick, tender, very savory, and tastes quite like abalone. So far, it is still unknown to most Chinese except the grocers. I am sure it will become popular in the Chinese menu.

Recently, my grocer asked me to make some dishes out of these delicious mushrooms. Here is one of the recipes which my family and my cooking classes love. One of my classes suggested two names for this new dish: "Yum Yum" and "Mai's Surprise." We decided to leave "Yum Yum" for the *Mikado.*

PREPARATION OF INGREDIENTS

2 cups oil

CHICKEN MIXTURE (MIX IN A BOWL AND REFRIGERATE BEFORE USE)*

> *1 whole small boned, skinless chicken breast: cut into paper-thin pieces when half-frozen*
> *1 teaspoon pale dry sherry*
> *⅓ egg white*
> *2 teaspoons cornstarch*

SHRIMP MIXTURE (MIX IN A BOWL AND REFRIGERATE BEFORE USE)*

> *½ pound fresh shrimp: shell, devein, slit back, flatten each shrimp, rinse in cold running water, pat dry*

1 teaspoon pale dry sherry
1/4 teaspoon baking soda
1/2 egg white
2 teaspoons cornstarch

2 scallions: cut into 1 1/2-inch lengths, including green part
1 teaspoon minced fresh ginger root
1 teaspoon minced garlic
half a 15-ounce can straw mushrooms: drain
10-ounce can abalone mushrooms
10 snow peas (optional): break off tips and ends

SAUCE MIXTURE (MIX IN A BOWL)*

2 teaspoons oyster-flavored sauce
1 tablespoon thin soy sauce
1 tablespoon black soy sauce
1/2 teaspoon sugar
2 tablespoons pale dry sherry

1/2 teaspoon cornstarch mixed with 2 tablespoons water
1 teaspoon sesame seed oil

DIRECTIONS FOR COOKING

1. Heat oil in wok to deep-fry temperature. Blanch chicken mixture (see Cooking Techniques). Drain and put into bowl. Reheat oil, blanch shrimp mixture, drain, and add to chicken.

2. Remove all but 2 tablespoons oil from wok. Heat oil over high heat. When hot, slightly brown scallions, ginger, and garlic. Add mushrooms and snow peas. Stir-fry for about 20 seconds. Stir in sauce mixture. Cook and stir until it begins to bubble. Return chicken and shrimp to wok. Stir-fry for about 15 seconds. Add cornstarch water. Cook and stir until sauce is thickened. Swirl in sesame seed oil. Mix well. Put on a serving platter. Serve hot.

麻婆豆腐

POCKMARKED WOMAN'S SPICED BEAN CURD
6 to 8 servings

I have not made up the name of this popular dish! It is said that the wife of a cook named Chan, who lived in Szechwan more than a century ago, created this bean curd recipe. Mrs. Chan's face was pockmarked. So, the Chinese have always called this Pockmarked Woman's Spiced Bean Curd.

This famous dish is hot, spicy, and extraordinarily smooth, and it makes one perspire. The emphasis is on the smoothness of the bean curd. The key to success is to cook the bean curd over low heat.

PREPARATION OF INGREDIENTS

3 tablespoons oil
1 teaspoon finely minced fresh ginger root
4 ounces ground pork

SAUCE MIXTURE (MIX IN A BOWL)*

> *¼ teaspoon cayenne pepper*
> *2 teaspoons ground bean sauce*
> *1 tablespoon Szechwan chili bean sauce*
> *1 tablespoon black soy sauce*
> *½ teaspoon salt*
> *½ teaspoon sugar*
> *1 tablespoon Chinese Shaohsing wine or pale dry sherry*

1 pound fresh bean curd: rinse in cold water, cut into ½-inch cubes
½ cup clear chicken broth (not condensed)
1 teaspoon cornstarch mixed with 1 teaspoon water
2 scallions: cut into pea-sized pieces, including green part

¼ teaspoon flower peppercorn powder
1 teaspoon sesame seed oil

DIRECTIONS FOR COOKING

1. Heat wok over high heat. Swirl in oil. When oil is hot, slightly brown ginger. Add pork and stir-fry until it is no longer red. Stir in sauce mixture. Cook and stir constantly for 10 seconds. Add bean curd. Mix well. *Turn heat to low.* Pour in broth, cover, and cook over low heat for 3 to 4 minutes. Stir in cornstarch water. Cook and stir constantly until sauce is thickened.

2. Add scallions, peppercorn powder, and sesame seed oil. Mix well. Put on a serving platter. Serve hot.

客家釀豆腐

HAKKA STUFFED BEAN CURD
about 6 servings

A small minority of people in the south of China are called Hakka or K'o Chia, meaning "stranger and visiting family." They originated in the north and migrated to the south and southwest as early as the Chin Dynasty, 249–209 B.C. They still speak a language which is closer to the northern dialects than to those of the south. The women can be distinguished from the native women because they wear big broad hats with black ruffles hanging down around the rim, and they perform most of the manual labor in the fields. The men seem more inclined to domestic affairs. Hakka cooking is well-known for its bean curd dishes. This stuffed bean curd is one of the most popular and well-loved among the Chinese.

PREPARATION OF INGREDIENTS

3 pieces fresh bean curd, each about 3 inches square: pat dry
  with paper towels, cut each square into 4 triangles, slice some
  bean curd out of middle of one side of triangle to make pocket
  for stuffing

STUFFING (MIX AND BLEND IN A BOWL FOR ABOUT 1 MINUTE)*

> 4 ounces ground pork
> 1 scallion: mince, including green part
> 4 Chinese dried mushrooms: soak in hot water until spongy,
>   discard stems, mince
> 1 tablespoon Chinese dried shrimp: soak in very hot water for
>   about 20 minutes or until soft, peel off shells (if any), drain, mince
> 2 teaspoons thin soy sauce
> 1 teaspoon sesame seed oil
> ¼ teaspoon sugar
> ¼ teaspoon salt

4 tablespoons oil
2 scallions: cut into 1½-inch strips, including green part
4 Chinese dried mushrooms: soak in hot water until spongy,
    discard stems, cut caps into thin strips
4 ounces lean pork: cut into matchstick strips

SAUCE MIXTURE (MIX IN A BOWL)*

> 4 teaspoons thin soy sauce
> ¼ teaspoon sugar
> 2 teaspoons pale dry sherry
> ½ teaspoon cornstarch
> ½ cup clear chicken broth (not condensed)

Soy-Chili Dip (optional; see recipe)

DIRECTIONS FOR COOKING

1. Stuff bean curd triangles with stuffing mixture.

2. Heat a skillet over medium heat. Swirl in 4 tablespoons oil. When oil is hot, arrange bean curd triangles, meat side down, in skillet and pan-fry until meat sides are golden brown. Brown other sides. Remove from skillet.

3. Keep skillet hot. Slightly brown scallions, mushrooms, and pork strips. Pour in sauce mixture. Cook until sauce comes to a boil. Return bean curd pieces to skillet and reheat them. Put on a serving platter and pour sauce over them. Serve hot with or without dip.

肉絲豆腐

STIR-FRIED BEAN CURD WITH PORK SHREDS
about 6 servings

PREPARATION OF INGREDIENTS

about 2 cups oil
1 pound fresh bean curd: slice ⅓ inch thick and size of pea pod
2 scallions: cut into 1½-inch lengths, including green part
4 Chinese dried mushrooms: soak in hot water until spongy,
    discard stems, cut into thin strips
4 ounces lean pork: cut into matchstick pieces

SAUCE MIXTURE (MIX IN A BOWL)*

   2 teaspoons black soy sauce
   2 teaspoons thin soy sauce
   ¼ teaspoon sugar
   2 teaspoons pale dry sherry
   ½ cup clear chicken broth (not condensed)

1 teaspoon cornstarch mixed with 1 teaspoon water
¼ cup coarsely chopped fresh coriander (optional)

DIRECTIONS FOR COOKING

1. Heat oil in wok to deep-fry temperature. Deep-fry bean curd until golden. Remove from wok with a drainer to a bowl.

2. Remove all but 2 tablespoons oil from wok. Heat oil, add scallions, mushrooms, and pork. Stir-fry over high heat until pork loses its pink color. Stir in sauce mixture. Stir and cook until sauce begins to bubble. Thicken sauce slightly with cornstarch water. Add coriander. Return bean curd to wok. Stir-fry gently for about 15 seconds. Put on a serving platter. Serve hot.

Soups and Fire Pots

SOUP

The presence of a big bowl of soup on a Chinese dinner table was as indispensable as water and milk to a Western table. The soup was neither the first course nor the last. It was there to stay from the beginning of the meal until the end. "Finish your soup!"—as children we were urged constantly to drink soup at every dinner.

The Chinese drink soups not only for nourishment and pleasure but also for medicinal purposes. Soups are supposed to aid circulation, to help digestion, to induce *liang* (cool) air and clear excessive *yeh* (hot) air out of the system. Many Chinese believe that the balance of *yeh* (heat) and *liang* (coolness) in one's body is the key to good health. Lots of foods are considered either *yeh* or *liang*, and to keep a good balance of both, one eats food that equalizes the body's heat and coolness.

For example, watercress soup purifies the lungs; mustard green soup cools down the overheated faculties; shark's fin soup and bird's nest soup strengthen potency; mung bean with seaweed soup clears up pimples. The terribly bitter-tasting soup of the lotus seed cones is supposed to be good for sour-tempered children. It certainly made us more docile, since we became exhausted from crying and screaming at being forced to drink such hair-raising stuff.

Chinese soups come in many varieties, from thin to thick, sweet to sour, and hot to mild. A sample of each appears in the following pages. Some are easy to prepare, others have to be slaved over. But they are all good for your health in some way. If it does not soothe your cranky child or calm your nerves, soup at least moistens your throat.

濃鷄湯

RICH CHICKEN BROTH
makes about 6 cups

PREPARATION OF INGREDIENTS

3½ pounds fresh chicken: leave whole
1½ pounds lean pork: leave whole

DIRECTIONS FOR COOKING

1. Bring 10 cups of water, chicken, and pork to a rapid boil. Turn off heat. Remove pork and chicken and rinse in cold water. Discard water in pot.

2. Bring another 10 cups of fresh water to a boil. Return chicken and pork to pot. Cover and cook over medium-low heat for 3 hours. Turn off heat and remove chicken.

3. Tear drumsticks and wings from chicken, and put chicken and parts back into the pot. Cover and cook over medium heat for 30 minutes. Turn off heat. There should be about 6 cups of broth left in the pot at the end of cooking.

4. Remove pork and chicken to a bowl. By now they are quite taste-less; discard them or eat them with a dish of Soy-Sesame Dip (see recipe).

5. Pour broth into a bowl. Refrigerate it overnight. Skim off fat and discard residue. The broth is ready to be used in required recipe(s).

Note: *The broth can be frozen or refrigerated for about 5 days.*

清鷄湯

CLEAR CHICKEN BROTH
makes about 4 cups

PREPARATION OF INGREDIENTS

*1 fresh chicken, 3½ pounds: leave whole, discard fat from
cavity, rinse, pat dry*

DIRECTIONS FOR COOKING

1. Put chicken and 4 cups of water into a covered casserole. Place casserole into a wok. Pour water into wok to come halfway up the side of the casserole. Dry-steam (see Dry Steaming) the chicken for 2 hours, adding boiling water to wok from time to time to maintain water level.

2. Pour broth from casserole into a serving bowl, but be careful not to disturb the chicken. If the chicken falls apart, the broth will not be very clear! Cover broth and refrigerate it overnight. Skim off fat. The broth is now ready for use.

3. Serve the steamed chicken—whole—with a dish of Soy-Sesame Dip (see recipe). The chicken should be so tender that the meat can be plucked off with chopsticks.

NOTE: *The broth can be frozen or refrigerated for about 5 days.*

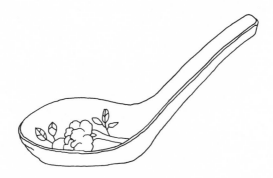

蛋花湯

EGG FLOWER SOUP
(EGG DROP SOUP)
about 4 servings

In order to have the beautiful cloudlike egg flowers floating in the soup, do not stir when you swirl in the eggs.

PREPARATION OF INGREDIENTS

¼ teaspoon sugar
¾ teaspoon salt
5 cups clear chicken broth (not condensed)
1 tablespoon cornstarch mixed with ¼ cup cold water
2 eggs: beat until slightly foamy
2 scallions: cut into pea-sized pieces, including green part
2 teaspoons sesame seed oil

DIRECTIONS FOR COOKING

1. In a 3-quart pot, add sugar, and salt to broth. Bring broth to a rapid boil. Stir in cornstarch water. Stir and cook until soup is no longer cloudy. Slowly swirl in beaten eggs. Do not stir! Turn off heat at once.

2. Drop in scallions and sesame seed oil. Now you can stir—gently. Pour into a serving bowl. Serve hot.

鷄絲西洋菜湯

CHICKEN AND WATERCRESS SOUP
4 servings

PREPARATION OF INGREDIENTS

BROTH (MIX IN A 3-QUART POT)*

2½ cups clear chicken broth (not condensed)
2½ cups water
¼ teaspoon sugar
1 teaspoon salt

4 ounces watercress: discard hard stalks, wash, rinse

CHICKEN MIXTURE (MIX IN A BOWL)*

1 boned, skinless chicken breast: cut into matchstick strips
½ teaspoon thin soy sauce
2 teaspoons cornstarch

1 teaspoon sesame seed oil (optional)

DIRECTIONS FOR COOKING

1. Bring broth mixture to a boil. Add watercress. Cook over medium heat for a minute or until watercress just turns bright green.

2. Add chicken strips. Stir to separate pieces. Cook briskly until chicken just turns white (about 30 seconds). Turn off heat immediately. Swirl in sesame seed oil if you wish. Serve hot.

粟米芙蓉羹

CHICKEN FU YUNG SOUP
6 to 8 servings

PREPARATION OF INGREDIENTS

3 cups clear chicken broth (not condensed)
1½ teaspoons salt
½ teaspoon sugar
2 tablespoons cornstarch mixed with 2 tablespoons water

CHICKEN AND CORN MIXTURE (MIX IN A BOWL)*

> *½ boned, skinless chicken breast: mince into fine paste*
> *1 egg white: beat slightly, but do not create bubbles*
> *17-ounce can cream-style corn*

2 egg whites: beat slightly, but not until foamy

DIRECTIONS FOR COOKING

1. Bring broth to a boil; add salt and sugar. Stir in cornstarch water. Stir and cook over medium heat until broth is clear and not cloudy.

2. Pour in chicken and corn mixture. Cook and stir until it bubbles gently. Slowly swirl in beaten egg whites. Do not stir! Allow a few seconds for egg whites to form a mass of white clouds in the soup. Turn off heat at once. Stir. Serve hot.

什錦湯

SUBGUM SOUP
6 to 8 servings

PREPARATION OF INGREDIENTS

4 cups clear chicken broth (not condensed)
⅔ cup canned straw mushrooms: rinse, drain in colander
½ pound bok choy: rinse well, cut into bite-sized pieces

CHICKEN MIXTURE (MIX IN A BOWL. REFRIGERATE BEFORE USE)*

*½ boned, skinless chicken breast: cut into paper-thin slices
    while half-frozen*
⅓ egg white
⅛ teaspoon salt
1 teaspoon cornstarch
½ teaspoon sesame seed oil

SHRIMP MIXTURE (MIX IN A BOWL. REFRIGERATE BEFORE USE)*

*6 ounces fresh shrimp: shell, devein, rinse in running cold water,
    pat dry, cut into halves lengthwise*
⅓ egg white
⅛ teaspoon salt
½ teaspoon pale dry sherry
1 teaspoon cornstarch
½ teaspoon sesame seed oil
⅛ teaspoon white pepper

½ teaspoon salt
¼ teaspoon sugar
1 teaspoon sesame seed oil

DIRECTIONS FOR COOKING

1. Pour chicken broth into a 3-quart pot and bring it to a rapid boil. Add straw mushrooms and bok choy. Cook uncovered over medium heat for 2 minutes.

2. Keep broth boiling. Stir in chicken mixture. Immediately turn off heat. Stir to separate chicken pieces. (The chicken should be cooked in 10 seconds.)

3. Turn heat to medium. As soon as broth begins to bubble, stir in shrimp mixture. Immediately turn off heat (so that shrimp will not be overcooked). Stir to separate shrimp. Add salt and sugar. Swirl in sesame seed oil. Serve hot.

蝦丸草菇湯

SHRIMP BALLS AND STRAW MUSHROOM SOUP
6 to 8 servings

PREPARATION OF INGREDIENTS

⅔ cup canned straw mushrooms: rinse, drain
½ cup canned button mushrooms: rinse, drain
12 fresh snow peas: break off tips and ends

BROTH (MIX IN A 3-QUART POT)*

> *4 cups clear chicken broth (not condensed)*
> *¾ teaspoon salt*
> *¼ teaspoon sugar*

1 small bowl cold water

SHRIMP MIXTURE (MIX IN A BOWL. KEEP REFRIGERATED BEFORE USE)*

> *1 pound fresh shrimp: shell, devein, rinse in cold water, pat dry,*
>   *mince into paste*
> *2 tablespoons minced pork fat or bacon fat*
> *1 egg white: beat until slightly foamy*
> *½ teaspoon salt*
> *1 teaspoon sesame seed oil*
> *1 teaspoon cornstarch*
> *1 tablespoon minced scallion, white part only*

2 teaspoons sesame seed oil

DIRECTIONS FOR COOKING

1. Combine straw mushrooms, button mushrooms, and snow peas with broth mixture.

2. Have small bowl of cold water and a soup spoon within reach. Using your left hand, grasp a handful of the shrimp mixture and squeeze it between the base of your thumb and your index finger. When it forms a walnut-sized ball, scoop it with the spoon and put it into the broth. Dip the spoon into the bowl of cold water before you scoop another shrimp ball (this keeps the shrimp mixture from sticking to the spoon). Repeat until shrimp mixture is used up.

3. Bring broth to a gentle boil over medium heat. When all the shrimp balls float to the top, they are done. Turn off heat. Add sesame seed oil. Pour into a big serving bowl. Serve hot.

八宝冬瓜盅

EIGHT PRECIOUS JEWELS WHOLE WINTER MELON SOUP
8 to 12 servings

This soup is a summer event. The whole melon comes to the table, looking like a green pumpkin, soft from cooking and piping hot. It is filled with soup containing eight delicious ingredients: mushrooms, barbecued pork, shrimp, lotus seeds, chicken, straw mushrooms, abalone, pork. These are called jewels.

The soup should be clear, tasty, and not rich because winter melon is believed to cool and clear out summer heat. After the soup is finished, the soft and tender melon pulp is scooped out and eaten.

With this soup, I first experienced the power that comes with the ability to cook. I was twelve years old then. In China in those days, the role of a father was to be strict. Kindness and tenderness came only from the mother. My father accurately played his role, which he had learned from his father. We used to be in awe when he spoke, silently retreating from a room when he entered. He was such a handsome man, flamboyant, fun, always joking with his friends. But to his children, he was distant, aloof, and restricted by his role.

It was his birthday. I requested that the family cook permit me the honor of surprising my father with this winter melon soup. With help from the cook, I did the preparing and the cooking. Carving the melon, however, was my chore alone. It was not a piece of stunning art, but on it were cut all the good words that a Chinese cherishes—happiness, prosperity, good health, and longevity—and that a child could carve.

I can still see the shine of those many pairs of eyes when the cook announced and presented my majestic soup. My father's face quivered and his eyes grew moist. I did not get a pat on my shoulder, but rather several generous nods. For many days, though, I did not have to practice my fifteen minutes' straight walk for my pigeon toes.

Time has carried away many old memories. But neither my father nor I have forgotten this winter melon soup.

PREPARATION OF INGREDIENTS

10-pound good-looking winter melon (that will fit into a big pot)

BROTH (MIX IN A BOWL)*

>*5 cups clear chicken broth (not condensed)*
>*½ teaspoon sugar*
>*¾ teaspoon salt*

15 dried skinless lotus seeds: boil in water until tender, drain
4 Chinese dried mushrooms: soak until spongy, discard stems,
*   cut caps into ¼-inch squares*
⅓ cup diced Cantonese barbecued pork or Cantonese roast duck

CHICKEN AND PORK MIXTURE (MIX IN A BOWL)*

1 boned, skinless chicken breast: cut into ¼-inch cubes
⅓ cup lean pork cubes: cut like chicken
2 teaspoons pale dry sherry
1 teaspoon cornstarch
¼ teaspoon salt

SHRIMP MIXTURE (MIX IN A BOWL)*

6 ounces fresh shrimp: shell, devein, rinse in running cold water,
  drain, pat dry, cut into peanut-sized pieces
½ teaspoon pale dry sherry
1 big pinch white pepper
½ teaspoon cornstarch

½ cup canned straw mushrooms: rinse in cold water, drain in
  colander
⅓ cup canned abalone: cut into ¼-inch cubes
chrysanthemum flowers or greens for garnishing

DIRECTIONS FOR COOKING

1. Cut about a quarter of the melon off the top. Scoop out seeds and soft center. Cut edge into a zigzag pattern. Carve words or designs on the melon's skin if you wish.

2. Rinse inside of melon with a pot of boiling water. Discard water and dry melon with a towel.

3. Place a big piece of cheesecloth under melon. Put broth, lotus seeds, and dried mushrooms into melon. Loosely tie corners of the cheesecloth on top of melon. (This is to help lift it out of the pot after it is cooked.) Place melon in pot big enough to allow steam to circulate. Fill pot with water one-third of the way up the melon. (If melon begins to float, remove some water.) Cover and cook over medium heat for about 1 hour. Add barbecued pork or duck to broth in melon. Cover and cook for another 15 minutes.

4. Add chicken and pork mixture to piping hot broth in melon. Stir to separate pieces. They should be cooked almost instantly. Add shrimp mixture, straw mushrooms, and abalone. Turn off heat.

5. Grasp cheesecloth and lift melon out gently. Place it on a big round serving platter or in a big bowl. Remove cheesecloth carefully. Decorate around the melon with flowers or greens. Bring melon to the table. Serve hot.

Note: *Eat melon pulp only after finishing the soup because the shell is needed to hold the soup.*

蝦仁鷄粒鍋巴湯

SIZZLING RICE SOUP WITH SHRIMP AND CHICKEN
4 to 6 servings

Serving this soup is a pleasure. It always creates excitement when the piping hot rice crusts sizzle noisily at the table, catching the guests by surprise. The main ingredient is the rice crusts. Formerly, you had to make them yourself, but now you can purchase them in Chinese grocery stores.

PREPARATION OF INGREDIENTS

1 cup rice crusts, about half-dollar size (see recipe)

BROTH (MIX IN A MEDIUM-SIZED POT)*

    4 cups clear chicken broth (not condensed)
    ¾ teaspoon salt
    ¼ teaspoon sugar

1½ tablespoons cornstarch mixed with 3 tablespoons water

CHICKEN MIXTURE (MIX IN A BOWL. KEEP REFRIGERATED BEFORE USE)*

    ½ boned, skinless chicken breast: cut into very thin strips
    ⅓ egg white
    1 teaspoon cornstarch
    ⅛ tablespoon salt

SHRIMP MIXTURE (MIX IN A BOWL. KEEP REFRIGERATED BEFORE USE)*

> 6 ounces fresh shrimp: shell, devein, rinse in running cold water,
>   drain, pat dry, cut into peanut-sized pieces
> ½ teaspoon pale dry sherry
> 1 teaspoon cornstarch
> ⅛ teaspoon salt

⅓ cup canned baby corn: cut crosswise into thin round pieces
2 tablespoons green peas (frozen will do)
¼ cup canned straw mushrooms
1 scallion: cut into pea-sized pieces, including green part
1 teaspoon sesame seed oil
4 cups oil for deep-frying

DIRECTIONS FOR COOKING

1. Bring broth mixture to a gentle boil over medium heat. Stir in cornstarch water. Cook, stirring constantly, until broth is clear.

2. Keep broth bubbling gently. Add chicken and shrimp mixtures. Quickly stir to separate pieces. Add corn, peas, and mushrooms. Immediately turn the heat to very, very low to wait for the rice crusts.

3. Put scallions and sesame seed oil in a big serving bowl which will hold the soup.

4. While the soup is cooking, heat oil for deep-frying in wok over high heat until very hot. Test by dropping in a small piece of rice crust; it should pop and float to the top immediately. Add rice crusts and deep-fry until they are golden color. Remove with a drainer or a slotted spoon to a small serving plate.

5. Quickly pour the hot soup into the serving bowl. Immediately bring soup and rice crusts to the table. Immerse rice crusts in soup at once. Be proud of the sizzling sound. Stir and serve hot.

鴨骨津白湯

CHINESE CELERY CABBAGE IN DUCK BONE SOUP
about 6 servings

This recipe makes especially good use of the carcass left by cooking Peking duck. The duck's carcass gives a smooth white broth, then it is sweetened gently by the celery cabbage. The soup, almost creamy, is rich in good natural flavor.

PREPARATION OF INGREDIENTS

1 duck carcass left over from Peking duck
1 slice fresh ginger root, as big and thick as a quarter
1 pound Chinese celery cabbage: cut crosswise into 1-inch pieces
½ teaspoon sugar
salt

DIRECTIONS FOR COOKING

1. Break duck carcass into pieces and put in a big pot. Pour in 10 cups of water and add ginger. Half-cover the pot and cook over medium-high heat for about 2 hours, adding boiling water if necessary to maintain about 5 cups of broth. Discard bones and ginger and strain broth through cheese-cloth or a colander.

2. Pour duck broth into a medium-sized pot and bring it to a boil. Add celery cabbage and sugar. Half-cover the pot and cook over medium-low heat for about an hour, leaving about 3 cups of soup. Salt to taste. Serve hot.

酸辣湯

HOT AND SOUR SOUP
6 to 8 servings

This is an excellent soup for a cold winter day. It warms your body and clears your nose. It is an offering from Szechwan. Where else?

Who else would think of pouring vinegar and ladling pepper into the soup? The cook who invented this must be mad! However, we love it.

PREPARATION OF INGREDIENTS

10 dried lily buds: soak in hot water for 15 minutes
2 tablespoons cloud ears: soak in plenty of hot water for 15
*   minutes*
4 cups clear chicken broth (not condensed)
6 ounces lean pork (or chicken breast): cut into matchstick strips
½ cup fresh bean curd: cut into thin strips
¼ cup bamboo shoots: cut into matchstick strips
6 Chinese dried mushrooms: soak in hot water until spongy,
*   discard stems, cut caps into thin strips*

SAUCE MIXTURE (MIX IN A BOWL)*

*   1 tablespoon thin soy sauce*
*   ¼ teaspoon sugar*
*   ¾ teaspoon salt*

2 tablespoons cornstarch mixed with 3 tablespoons water
1 egg: beat until slightly foamy

VINEGAR AND PEPPER MIXTURE (PUT IN A BIG SERVING BOWL WHICH WILL HOLD
THE SOUP)*

*   3 tablespoons Chinese red vinegar*
*   ½ teaspoon ground white pepper*
*   2 teaspoons sesame seed oil*

2 scallions: cut into pea-sized pieces, including green part

DIRECTIONS FOR COOKING

1. Pinch off tough parts of soaked lily buds and cloud ears. Tear cloud ears and lily buds into halves lengthwise. Put aside.

2. In a 3-quart pot, bring chicken broth to a boil. Add pork (or chicken), bean curd, bamboo shoots, lily buds, cloud ears, and mushrooms, and cook for a few minutes. Stir in sauce mixture and cornstarch water. Stir and cook until soup boils gently. Slowly swirl in the beaten egg. Turn off heat immediately. Do not stir! (This allows the egg to set slightly. It will resemble a mass of yellow clouds.) After the egg sets slightly, stir to mix. Pour soup into serving bowl containing vinegar and pepper mixture. Add scallions. Stir gently to bring up vinegar and pepper mixture from the bottom. Serve hot.

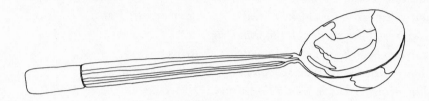

酸辣魚羹

HOT AND SOUR FISH SOUP
8 to 10 servings

PREPARATION OF INGREDIENTS

1 pound fish fillets (sole or flounder): marinate in 1 tablespoon
  pale dry sherry not more than 20 minutes
⅓ cup cornstarch to coat fish
4 cups oil
5 cups clear chicken broth (not condensed)
4 Chinese dried mushrooms: soak in hot water until spongy,
  discard stems, shred caps
1 tablespoon cloud ears: soak in hot water until soft, tear into
  small pieces
½ cup fresh bean curd: cut into small strips

SAUCE MIXTURE (MIX IN A BOWL)*

  4 teaspoons thin soy sauce
  ½ teaspoon sugar
  ¾ teaspoon salt
  1 teaspoon black soy sauce

4 tablespoons cornstarch mixed with ¼ cup water
1 egg: beat until slightly foamy

VINEGAR AND PEPPER MIXTURE (PUT IN A BIG SERVING BOWL WHICH WILL HOLD
THE SOUP)*

> *3 tablespoons Chinese red vinegar*
> *½ to ¾ teaspoon ground white pepper*
> *1 tablespoon sesame seed oil*

2 scallions: cut into pea-sized pieces, including green part
1 tablespoon coarsely chopped fresh coriander (optional)

DIRECTIONS FOR COOKING

1. Coat fish slightly in cornstarch. Put aside.
2. Heat oil in wok to deep-fry temperature. Deep-fry fillets until they are just golden brown. Gently remove from wok. Drain.
3. Heat broth in a 3-quart pot to a boil. Add mushrooms, cloud ears, and bean curd. Stir in sauce mixture, then cornstarch water. Stir and cook over medium heat until broth is clear and thickened. Add fish. Stir gently. As soon as broth bubbles again, slowly swirl in the egg. Turn off heat immediately. Do not stir! (This allows the egg to set slightly. It will resemble a mass of yellow clouds.) Allow egg to set for several seconds, then stir to mix.
4. Pour soup into serving bowl containing vinegar and pepper mixture. Add scallions and coriander. Stir gently to bring up vinegar and pepper from the bottom. Break fillets into big chunks. Serve hot at once.

芙蓉燕窩湯

FU YUNG BIRD'S NEST SOUP
6 to 8 servings

These are no ordinary birds' nests! They are the nests of sea swallows of Southern Asia. Instead of using grass and twigs, the swallows digest seaweeds and sea plants and turn them into a gelatinous fluid which they spit out to build their nests.

The sea swallows build their nests on high cliffs along the coast. Monkeys were trained to fetch these precious nests in the olden days.

The nests of top quality are free from feathers, shaped like small petals of the water lily, hard and wax-colored. Less expensive nests are darker in color, with some tiny feathers attached. The most popular kinds served in restaurants are pieces of broken nests or crumbs of ground-up nests that are made into balls or patties.

In spite of its preciousness, the nest is almost odorless and tasteless. Its flavor depends solely on being cooked in good broth, borrowing flavor from the other ingredients. Like its celebrated sister, the shark's fin, the swallow's nest is the rich man's whim, the poor people's dream, and a formal banquet's necessity.

PREPARATION OF INGREDIENTS

2 ounces dried bird's nest: soak in plenty of hot water for at least
  3 to 4 hours (makes about 2 cups after soaking), drain before
  cooking
2 scallions: leave whole
4 slices fresh ginger root, each as big and thick as a quarter
2 tablespoons pale dry sherry
4 cups clear chicken broth (not condensed)
½ teaspoon sugar
1½ tablespoons cornstarch mixed with 2 tablespoons water

CHICKEN MIXTURE (MIX IN A BOWL. REFRIGERATE BEFORE USE)*

  1 whole boned, skinless chicken breast: cut into matchstick
    strips (to make about 1 cup)
  1 egg white
  2 teaspoons cornstarch

2 eggs: beat until just slightly foamy
salt to taste (1–1½ teaspoons)

DIRECTIONS FOR COOKING

1. Pour enough water into a 3-quart pot to reach two-thirds up the sides. Add soaked bird's nest and boil over medium-low heat for 30 minutes. Drain in colander.

2. Heat dry wok over high heat, then throw in 1 whole scallion, 2 slices of ginger, and 1 tablespoon of sherry. Quickly add 4 cups of water and the bird's nest. Cook over medium heat for 10 minutes. Drain in colander. Discard scallion and ginger. Repeat this entire process with remaining scallion, ginger, and sherry. Then put bird's nest in a bowl. Cover until use.

3. Heat chicken broth and sugar in a 3-quart pot and bring to a boil. Add bird's nest and cornstarch water. Stir and cook until broth is clear and thickened. Add chicken mixture, stir to separate pieces, and cook briskly for several seconds. As soon as broth bubbles again, slowly swirl in beaten eggs. Turn heat off immediately. Do not stir in order to allow the eggs to form a mass of clouds. (It takes only several seconds.) Salt to taste. Stir to mix well. Pour into a serving bowl. Serve hot.

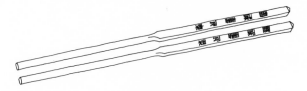

魚翅鷄絲湯

SHARK'S FIN CHICKEN SOUP
about 8 servings

PREPARATION OF INGREDIENTS

4 ounces dried shark's fin: soak in 6 cups of hot water at least 8 hours or overnight, drain just before use
2 scallions: leave whole

continued

4 slices fresh ginger root, each as big and thick as a quarter
2 tablespoons pale dry sherry

BROTH (PUT IN A 3-QUART POT)*

    4 cups Rich Chicken Broth (see recipe) or clear chicken broth
       (not condensed)
    ½ teaspoon sugar
    ¼ teaspoon white pepper

2 tablespoons cornstarch mixed with 2 tablespoons water

CHICKEN MIXTURE (MIX IN A BOWL. REFRIGERATE BEFORE USE)*

    8 ounces boned, skinless chicken breast: cut into matchstick
       strips (to make about 1 cup)
    ⅓ egg white
    1 teaspoon cornstarch

1 teaspoon thin soy sauce
1 tablespoon lard
½ teaspoon salt or to taste

DIRECTIONS FOR COOKING

1. Bring 6 cups water to a rapid boil. Add shark's fin. Cook over medium heat for 30 minutes. Drain shark's fin in a colander.

2. Bring another 6 cups water to a rapid boil. Add shark's fin. Cook over medium heat for another 30 minutes. Drain in a colander.

3. Heat dry wok over high heat, then throw in 1 scallion, 2 slices of ginger, and 1 tablespoon of sherry. Quickly add 2 cups water and shark's fin. Cook over medium heat for 10 minutes. Drain in colander. Discard scallion and ginger. Repeat entire process with remaining scallion, ginger, and sherry. Put shark's fin in a bowl. Cover until use.

4. Bring broth mixture to a rapid boil. Add shark's fin and cornstarch water. Stir and cook until broth is clear and thickened. Add chicken mixture, stir to separate pieces, and cook briskly for several seconds. Add soy sauce, lard, and salt. Mix well. Pour into a serving bowl. Serve hot.

FIRE POTS

The cooking of northern China has been very much influenced by Mongolian cooking, for the Mongols conquered China and ruled in Peking for eighty-eight years. It was they who planned and built a large part of Peking. It was their ascendancy that Marco Polo so lavishly described. Most of the Mongols lived in tents and cooked and ate around the fire. Their cooking was distinguished by barbecued ducks and meat, sliced lamb and beef cooked in hot broth, then dipped in spiced sauces. The famous Peking duck and the Peking fire pot still have much of the Mongolian flavor even though these dishes have long since been refined by the Chinese.

In the north, when winter fell and the wind from inner Mongolia started to blow, fire pots were a familiar sight on the tables of families and restaurants. Chinese homes did not have central heating; therefore gathering and eating around a blazing fire pot and dipping food into piping hot broth was not only fun but sometimes a necessity for keeping warm.

In the Peking fire pot (which is also called Mongolian fire pot or Mongolian rinsed lamb), the chief ingredient is the thinly sliced lamb, which is accompanied by celery cabbage, bean curd, bean thread noodles, shao-bings (sesame seed rolls), and sauces. The fire pot looks like a giant bowl with a big chimney rising high in the middle. Charcoal burns in the base under the chimney, and the broth is held around the chimney. The intense heat keeps the broth bubbling. Each person immerses one or two slices of lamb in the piping hot broth, which cooks the lamb in a matter of seconds (it is cooked as fast as if one just rinsed the lamb in broth). Then the lamb is dipped and eaten with sauces. In order not to lose the food that is put into the broth, little wire drainers with long handles are provided for everybody to immerse his own food. Otherwise, argument between brother and sister would not be uncommon during the meal, at least in my household.

The fire pot is not exclusively a northern spread. It is also very popular in the south, where winter is not bitter but damp and chill. The southerners prefer the chrysanthemum pot, in which everything delicious can go into the pot: shrimp, fried shrimp balls, oysters, sliced chicken, liver, lettuce, bean thread noodles, fish fillet, and so on.

If you do not have a fire pot, a chafing dish or an enamel pot placed on an electric stove or a hibachi will do. Many Chinese are not equipped with fire pots either; they use a clay pot on a portable charcoal stove.

Eating around a fire pot is always a joyful event, and it often lasts for hours. Somehow one seems unable to stop eating until the last drop of soup is gone. Then stomachs are full, bodies are warm, eyes begin to feel heavy, and no one seems to mind the north wind raging.

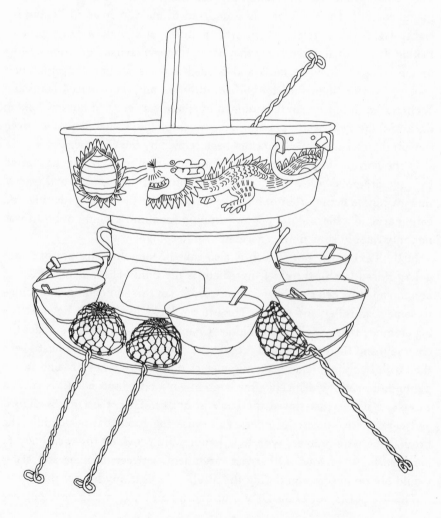

涮羊肉

PEKING FIRE POT
serves 8 to 12 persons

PREPARATION OF INGREDIENTS*

*6 pounds boned leg of lamb (save the bone): slice paper-thin
when half-frozen, arrange slices slightly overlapping on two
serving plates, brush lightly with sesame seed oil, garnish
plates with scallion brushes, cover and refrigerate before use*

*6 to 8 pieces fresh bean curd: slice into ⅓-inch-thick pieces,
arrange on two serving plates, garnish plates with snow peas
or scallion brushes, cover and refrigerate before use*

*8 ounces bean thread noodles: soak in plenty of hot water for
about 10 minutes or until soft, drain in colander, cut with
scissors 3 or 4 strokes to shorten a little, put in two serving
bowls, cover*

*2 pounds Chinese celery cabbage: cut off stem, separate stalks,
cut into bite-sized pieces, put in a serving bowl*

*⅓ pound snow peas (optional): break off ends, wash, dry, put on
a plate, cover*

*1 head iceberg lettuce (optional): separate leaves, wash, dry,
break into big pieces, put in a big serving bowl*

12 Scallion Brushes (see recipe)

MASTER SAUCE (MIX IN A BOWL UNTIL SMOOTH. PUT IN A SERVING BOWL. COVER)*

¼ cup black soy sauce
⅓ cup sesame seed oil
½ cup Chinese Shaohsing wine or pale dry sherry
4 tablespoons brown sugar
⅔ cup smooth peanut butter mixed with ½ cup boiling water
2 tablespoons Chinese red vinegar
4 tablespoons Chinese red bean curd cheese: mash into paste
2 tablespoons Chili Oil (see recipe)

continued

SAUCE INGREDIENTS (PUT EACH ITEM IN AN INDIVIDUAL BOWL)*

½ cup black soy sauce
½ cup sesame seed oil
½ cup Chinese red vinegar
⅓ cup Chinese red bean curd cheese: mash into paste
½ cup smooth peanut butter mixed with ½ cup boiling water
½ cup Chinese Shaohsing wine or pale dry sherry
⅓ cup brown sugar
¼ cup Chili Oil (see recipe)
½ cup fish sauce (optional)
1 cup minced scallions, including green part
½ cup chopped fresh coriander

5 to 6 quarts water: cook lamb bone in water for an hour or until
about 4 quarts of broth are left in pot, discard bone and skim
off scum, keep broth in a cool place before use. Salt to taste.
Shao-Bings with Scallion and Ham Filling (see recipe)

DIRECTIONS FOR COOKING

1. Give each person a small drainer, specially made for a fire pot, a small bowl for dip, a bigger bowl for food and soup, a plate under the soup bowl, and spoons.

2. Arrange all the ingredients on table, except broth and shao-bings.

3. Bring broth to a boil on stove. Salt to taste, cover and simmer.

4. Put charcoal (about 15 pieces) on a shallow pan and place it under the broiler (as close as possible). Turn oven to broil until part of each piece of charcoal becomes red. Transfer charcoal to the base of the fire pot.

5. Pour broth into fire pot. Cover broth with lid. Carry the fire pot to the table before people gather around it. (The base of the fire pot will be very hot. Be sure you put a lot of heatproof material under it, otherwise the intense heat will burn your table.)

6. When the charcoal is burning happily and the broth is boiling, seat your family and guests. Everyone makes his own sauce mixture in a small bowl from his choice of sauce ingredients. The master sauce is at hand if individual sauces aren't successful.

7. If small drainers are provided, put one or two slices of lamb in a drainer and immerse it in the broth. Take it out in about 7 seconds. With chopsticks, dip lamb into the sauce and eat. (If small drainers are not available, hold on to the meat with chopsticks.) Dip vegetables, noodles, and bean curd in broth and eat in the same manner. Serve shao-bings (kept in warm oven) throughout the whole meal. Add more charcoal when the heat gets low; add more broth to the fire pot if it begins to cook down. Do not drink the broth at the beginning, but wait until the end of the meal. By then, the broth will be seasoned with the lamb and other ingredients. It is just wonderful and healthful.

NOTE: *Besides serving shao-bings, you might like to serve Scallion Bread (see recipe). During the meal, appetizers such as Kuo-Tiehs (see recipe) and Spring Rolls (see recipe) can also be served.*

菊花鍋

CHRYSANTHEMUM FIRE POT
serves 8 to 12 persons

PREPARATION OF INGREDIENTS*

3 whole boned, skinless chicken breasts: slice paper-thin while half-frozen, arrange slices slightly overlapping on serving plate, brush with a little sesame seed oil, garnish with scallion brushes, cover, refrigerate before use

1 pound (23 to 25) fresh shrimp: peel off shell except tails, devein, butterfly (see Seafood Chapter), rinse in cold running water, pat dry, arrange slightly overlapping on a serving plate, brush with sesame seed oil, cover, refrigerate before use

2 pints oysters: blanch in water (see Cooking Techniques), drain, put in a serving bowl, refrigerate before use

½ pound fresh chicken livers: slice thinly, mix with ½ teaspoon finely minced fresh ginger root and ½ teaspoon sesame seed oil, put in a covered bowl, refrigerate before use

½ pound fresh fish fillet (sole, striped bass, or sea bass): slice paper-thin, arrange slightly overlapping on plate, cover, refrigerate before use

1 pound lean pork or flank steak: slice paper-thin while half-frozen, brush with a little sesame seed oil, arrange slices slightly overlapping on a plate, cover, refrigerate before use

continued

*8 ounces bean thread noodles: soak in plenty of hot water for
about 10 minutes or until soft, drain in colander, cut with
scissors 3 or 4 strokes to shorten a little, put in a serving bowl,
cover*

*6 pieces fresh bean curd: slice into ⅓-inch-thick pieces, put on
a serving plate, garnish with snow peas or scallion brushes,
cover, refrigerate before use*

*⅓ pound snow peas: break off ends, wash, dry, put on a serving
plate, cover*

Scallion Brushes (see recipe)

*1 head iceberg lettuce: separate leaves, wash, dry, break into big
pieces, put in a serving bowl*

*½ pound watercress (optional): discard tough stalks, wash, dry,
put in a bowl*

2 big chrysanthemum flowers from the florist: leave them whole

SAUCE INGREDIENTS (PUT EACH ITEM IN AN INDIVIDUAL BOWL)

½ cup black soy sauce
½ cup thin soy sauce
½ cup Chinese red vinegar
⅔ cup hoisin sauce
½ cup sesame seed oil
¼ cup chili oil
3 to 4 eggs: beat to mix yolks and whites
¼ cup brown sugar
¼ cup Chinese Shaohsing wine or pale dry sherry
⅔ cup chopped scallions: in pea-sized pieces, including green part

5 to 6 quarts thin chicken broth or water: salt to taste
Plain Rice for 6 to 8 persons (see recipe)

DIRECTIONS FOR COOKING

1. Give each person a small drainer, specially made for a fire pot, a small bowl for dip, a bigger bowl for food, rice, and soup, a plate under the soup bowl, and spoons.

2. Arrange all the ingredients on table, except broth and rice.

3. Put broth or water on stove and bring it to a boil. Cover and simmer to wait for the charcoal.

4. Put charcoal (about 15 pieces) on a shallow pan and place it under the broiler (as close as possible). Turn oven to broil until part of each piece becomes red. Transfer charcoal to base of fire pot.

5. Pour broth into fire pot. Cover the broth with lid. Carry fire pot to table before people gather around it. (The base of the fire pot will be very hot. Be sure you put a lot of heatproof material under it, otherwise the intense heat will burn your table.)

6. When the charcoal is burning merrily and the broth is bubbling, seat your family and guests.

7. Begin the meal with this little opening ceremony: as host or hostess, uncover the lid of the fire pot. Pick up a chrysanthemum flower, detach a few petals, and drop them into the broth. Your family and guests can follow you in this procedure if they wish. The petals are edible.

8. Each guest makes his own sauce by mixing his choice of sauce ingredients in the small bowl.

9. If small drainers are provided, put one or two pieces of meat or seafood in a drainer and immerse it in broth. Take it out after several seconds. With a pair of chopsticks, dip meat or seafood in the sauce and eat. (If small drainers are not available, hold on to the meat with chopsticks.) Dip vegetables, noodles, and bean curd in broth and eat in the same manner. Serve rice during the meal. Add more charcoal when the heat gets low; add more broth to the fire pot if it begins to cook down. Drink broth at the end of the meal, not at the beginning.

NOTE: *Appetizers such as Kuo-Tiehs (see recipe), Spring Rolls (see recipe), and Scallion Bread (see recipe), or dishes such as Deep-Fried Shrimp Balls (see recipe) and Steamed Giant Pearls (see recipe) can also be served during the meal.*

Rice, Noodles, Wontons, Buns, and Congee

RICE

In southern China, rice is a must in our daily meals. Everything we eat without rice usually is considered a snack, not a real meal. I remember that when my uncle used to come home late from doing business, he always announced that he had not eaten for the whole day! A mutual understanding among the household was that he was far from starving, for he had eaten dumplings or noodles in the teahouses many times during the day. But he never considered that those were meals or that he had been eating at all. He was like many of the southern Chinese: a good healthy meal was plain rice, a bowl of soup, and a few dishes prepared at home.

There are many stories about rice. Here is one I remember. Thousands of years ago, before the Chinese had rice, their struggle for food was seen by the Goddess of Mercy, Kuan Yin. She reported this to the God of Heaven. Unfortunately, the All-Mighty was in a bad humor and refused to hear any bad news. But Kuan Yin could not bear to abandon the suffering. So she came down to earth seeking a way to help. Finding the fields full of rice plants, but without their ears filled, she squeezed her breasts and filled the ears of the rice plants with her milk. There were many ears of rice still to be filled. So she squeezed her breasts harder, so hard that blood mixed with milk flowed from her breasts and filled the rest of the rice plants. Therefore, in China we have not only white rice but also red rice.

Our ancestors were still starving, despite the Goddess's help and their hard work. They could feed themselves only one meal every four or five days. This matter was brought to the attention of the God of Heaven. This time the All-Mighty was moved. He sent his heavenly Ox star to tell our people that if they would work hard enough, they would be blessed with one meal every three days. The Ox star was a good fellow, but not particularly bright, especially with numbers. On his way down to earth, he was confused: one meal for every three days or three meals for every one day? He was not quite sure. The latter seemed right to him, and he told the people that they would eat three meals a day! The God of Heaven was furious because it was impossible for the people to provide three meals a day for themselves. Some help from the superpower was needed. Since it was the mistake of the Ox star, he was sent to earth to help our people plow.

Leaving his heavenly home, the majestic-looking Ox star became the water buffalo, and he has been working for our people ever since. His strength makes farming easier. A tireless and good-natured helper, he pulls the plow in the field as silently and patiently as man himself. He never complains, never cries, for his mission is to help men.

China has always been a farming country. Most Chinese are farmers. Both of my grandfathers owned farms. As children, my younger brother and I tagged along with Ah Lin, my grandmother's maid, when she delivered lunch to the hired hands. We slogged through the muddy paddy fields; we trapped the tiny crabs, scared the frogs, and teased the water snakes with sticks. Our feared enemy was the water leech. We would shriek and cry when they fed on our legs. Ah Lin spat on the leeches to loosen their grip, and tore them away from our legs. Frightened by seeing our own blood, we bawled and cried some more, while the workers burst with laughter.

Before our tears were dried, the workers, bending down with their bare hands and feet, which fed the water leeches all day, resumed nursing the rice plants under the brutal sun.

As children, not wasting a single grain of rice was one of the very important lessons we learned. My grandmother used to threaten us: every grain of rice left in our bowls meant a pockmark on the face of our future mate. We giggled, but we shined our bowls; nobody dared to risk having a pockmarked mate!

THE THREE KINDS OF RICE

Refined long-grain white rice is preferred by the Chinese. The short and stout variety is considered to be lower grade, though it is more nutritious. The pearly white glutinous rice, also called sweet rice, is used mainly in pastry and sweets or for stuffing. Red rice, because of its coarseness, is not commonly used in eating, but for brewing wine.

Rice cooked with salt or butter is foreign to the Chinese. We like to eat it plain to enjoy its natural sweetness.

白飯

PLAIN RICE
makes about 6 cups of rice

PREPARATION OF INGREDIENTS

2 cups long-grain rice: wash and rinse in cold water until water
* is not cloudy, drain*
3 cups cold water

DIRECTIONS FOR COOKING

1. Use a 3-quart pot with a tight lid. Put in the washed rice and add the water. Cook over medium heat without a cover. When it is boiling, you will see that the water is very foamy, almost obscuring the rice. Do not go away! Stand by and watch it closely. You will see the water evaporating to the point where many small holes (like craters) appear in the rice. The Chinese call them rice eyes.

2. Put lid on, turn heat to very low, and cook for 10 minutes. Then turn off heat, but do not remove the pot or uncover it. Let it stay covered for 15 minutes or more. (Do not peek during this 25 minutes! Otherwise the magic steam will escape; you will have half-cooked rice for not having faith!)

3. Remove the cover. Loosen the rice with a fork or chopsticks. Serve hot.

鍋巴

RICE CRUST
(FOR SIZZLING RICE SOUP)
makes about 2 cups of crusts

PREPARATION OF INGREDIENTS

4 cups long-grain rice: wash and rinse in cold water until water
* is not cloudy, drain*
4 cups cold water

DIRECTIONS FOR COOKING

1. Choose a heavy wide-bottomed pot with a tight lid; the best is a Dutch oven. Put in rice, add water, and cook over medium heat, watching closely until the appearance of "rice eyes," the small, craterlike holes that develop as water evaporates.

2. Put lid on, turn heat to medium, and cook for 10 minutes. Then turn heat to low and cook for 15 minutes. (Do not peek during these 25 minutes. You may hear a little cracking noise from the rice, or smell the aroma of the crust.) Turn heat off.

3. Loosen rice gently and remove it from pot, leaving the crust. Using a small spatula, work carefully under the crust, and try to remove it in big pieces. Leave them on a tray to dry overnight. Put crusts in plastic bag and keep refrigerated. Or they can be frozen indefinitely. Thaw before use.

揚州炒飯

YANGCHOW FRIED RICE
6 to 8 servings

PREPARATION OF INGREDIENTS

4 tablespoons oil for frying

EGG MIXTURE (BEAT TOGETHER UNTIL SLIGHTLY FOAMY)

4 eggs
¼ teaspoon salt

⅓ cup chopped scallions, in pea-sized pieces, including green part
6 Chinese dried mushrooms: soak in hot water until spongy,
   discard stems, cut caps into ¼-inch squares

*6 ounces Smithfield ham or Cantonese barbecued pork: cut into
¼-inch cubes*

SHRIMP MIXTURE (MIX IN A BOWL. REFRIGERATE BEFORE USE)*

*4 ounces fresh shrimp: shell, devein, rinse in running cold water,
    pat dry, cut into peanut-sized pieces
½ teaspoon cornstarch
½ teaspoon pale dry sherry*

⅓ cup fresh or frozen green peas

SAUCE MIXTURE (MIX IN A BOWL)*

*2 tablespoons thin soy sauce
2 teaspoons black soy sauce
¼ teaspoon salt
½ teaspoon sugar
⅛ teaspoon white pepper*

*4 cups cold cooked long-grain rice: cook a day in advance (see
    recipe)
1 teaspoon sesame seed oil*

DIRECTIONS FOR COOKING

1. Heat wok over high heat. Swirl in 2 tablespoons oil for frying.
When oil is hot, pour half the egg mixture into wok and swirl it around,
spreading it into a thin pancake. Turn pancake when it is set. Remove from
pan before it is golden brown. Cook remaining egg mixture in the same
manner. Cut pancakes into ⅓-inch squares. Set aside.

2. Heat wok over high heat. Add remaining 2 tablespoons oil for frying. When oil is hot, add scallions, mushrooms, and ham or pork. Stir-fry
for about 30 seconds. Add shrimp mixture. Stir-fry until shrimp turns
whitish (less than 20 seconds). Add peas. Stir in sauce mixture. Mix well.
Break up lumps in cooked rice, and add it along with egg squares. Stir-fry
for 3 to 5 minutes or until rice is thoroughly hot. Swirl in sesame seed oil.
Mix well. Put on a serving platter. Serve hot.

臘腸蝦仁炒飯

SHRIMP AND CHINESE SAUSAGE FRIED RICE
6 to 8 servings

PREPARATION OF INGREDIENTS

4 tablespoons oil for frying
3 eggs: beat until slightly foamy

SHRIMP MIXTURE (MIX IN A BOWL. REFRIGERATE BEFORE USE)*

> *8 ounces fresh shrimp: shell, devein, rinse in running cold water,*
> *pat dry, cut into peanut-sized pieces*
> *about ½ egg white*
> *½ teaspoon pale dry sherry*
> *1 teaspoon cornstarch*

3 Chinese pork sausages: cut into peanut-sized pieces
6 Chinese dried mushrooms: soak in hot water until spongy,
discard stems, cut into ¼-inch squares
⅓ cup chopped scallions, in pea-sized pieces, including green part
4 cups (8 ounces) fresh bean sprouts: rinse and drain well

SAUCE MIXTURE (MIX IN A BOWL)*

> *1 tablespoon black soy sauce*
> *1 tablespoon thin soy sauce*
> *¼ teaspoon sugar*
> *¾ teaspoon salt*

4 cups cold cooked long-grain rice: cook a day in advance (see
recipe)
2 teaspoons sesame seed oil

DIRECTIONS FOR COOKING

1. Heat wok over high heat. Swirl in 1 tablespoon oil for frying. When oil is hot, pour in eggs. Cook as you would an omelet. Remove from wok while eggs are still slightly moist. Cut eggs into chunks about the size of sugar cubes. Set aside.

2. Reheat wok over high heat. Swirl in remaining 3 tablespoons oil for frying. When oil is hot, add shrimp mixture. Stir-fry briefly until shrimp turns whitish. It takes less than 20 seconds. Remove shrimp with a drainer, and press to drain oil back into wok. Put shrimp in a bowl.

3. Reheat oil in wok over high heat. Add sausages, mushrooms, and scallions. Stir-fry for about 30 seconds. Drop in bean sprouts. Stir-fry for about 15 seconds. Swirl in sauce mixture. Mix well.

4. Break up lumps in rice, and add it to wok. Stir-fry over medium heat for about 5 minutes or until rice is heated thoroughly. Add cooked eggs. Stir and cook for another minute. Swirl in sesame seed oil. Mix well. Put on a serving platter. Serve hot.

素麵

PLAIN NOODLES, COLD OR HOT
about 4 cups

PREPARATION OF INGREDIENTS

4 quarts water
2 teaspoons salt
½ pound fresh egg noodles or 6 ounces dried noodles
1 tablespoon oil

DIRECTIONS FOR COOKING

1. Bring water to a rapid boil. Add salt, then noodles. Stir and cook until they are just done. Fresh noodles take less than a minute, and sometimes they are cooked even before the water returns to a boil. Dried noodles take a little longer. It is better to undercook them a little rather than overcook them.

2. For cold noodles, quickly pour noodles into a colander and immediately run cold tap water over them, tossing with chopsticks or a fork to prevent further cooking. When noodles are no longer warm to the touch, drain them in the colander for several seconds. Add oil. Toss to coat them evenly. The oil is to keep them from sticking to each other. Put in a bowl. The cold noodles are ready to be used in the required recipe(s).

3. For hot noodles, quickly pour noodles into colander. Shake to drain off water. Add oil, toss to coat noodles evenly. Put on a serving platter or in a serving bowl. Cover to keep noodles hot. The noodles are ready to be used in required recipe(s).

紅油涼麵

COLD SPICY NOODLES
4 to 6 servings

PREPARATION OF INGREDIENTS

½ pound fresh lo mein noodles or 6 ounces dried egg noodles:
cook as in Plain Cold Noodles (see recipe)
12 ounces fresh bean sprouts: blanch in water (see Cooking
Techniques), drain in colander
3 scallions: cut into 1½-inch lengths, including green part, shred
into thin strips

SAUCE MIXTURE (MIX INTO A SMOOTH SAUCE. COVER BEFORE USE)*

    3 tablespoons smooth peanut butter
    3 tablespoons black soy sauce
    1½ tablespoons Chinese red vinegar
    1½ tablespoons sesame seed oil
    1½ teaspoons sugar
    1 to 3 teaspoons Chili Oil (see recipe)

DIRECTIONS FOR COOKING

1. Toss cooked noodles and blanched bean sprouts together to mix well. Put on a serving platter and top with scallions.

2. Pour sauce mixture evenly over noodles. Toss before serving. Serve at room temperature.

長壽麵

NOODLES OF LONGEVITY
6 to 8 servings

There is nothing the Chinese desire more than longevity. Even if life is miserable, they prefer it to be long. To be old is to be respected; one has been blessed by heaven. The intention toward longevity starts very early; at the moment an infant is born, he is declared to be one year old. If an infant were born at 11:59 on New Year's Eve, when the clock struck twelve, the one-minute-old infant would legally be two years old.

Even when life's journey is ended, the bereaved make the last effort: they add a couple of years to the deceased's age in the obituary.

Unlike Christianity, the traditional Chinese religion has no heaven; rather, there are many hells. One of the religious traditions claimed that age had its privileges, even in hell.

Among the Chinese, birthday celebrations are for the old rather than for children. When we were young, our hearts did not "skip a beat" when our birthdays were near. We had no parties, no hats to wear, no horns to blow. We were merely reminded that we were one year older and that we should work harder, learn more, behave better, and listen to our elders. A hard-boiled egg was given to the birthday child. The egg represented birth; the yolk was orange, encouraging the child to become conscientious and vigorously earnest.

Some parents might give their children presents, but such a practice was uncommon. I was served my first birthday cake in America; I was twenty-six years old.

For the adult, a birthday was an event; the older the person, the bigger the celebration, depending on the purse. Big banquets were held. Long noodles, symbolizing long life, were always included. Nobody was allowed or dared to cut the noodles, even if they swung and spotted our clothes. Good wishes such as "May you, Old Master (or Old Mistress), live so long as the South Mountain; your happiness as vast and deep as the Eastern Sea," would be repeated throughout the feast. The birthday celebrant, very proud, would nod and smile.

The American feeling about old age is quite opposite to that of the Chinese. My American mother-in-law abruptly experienced the Chinese way when she visited my family in Hong Kong. A welcoming banquet was given on her arrival. Most of my family members' English was limited to "yes" or "no." Conversation would not be easy, so my father had rounded up his English-speaking friends to cheer the party.

Knowing English better than they knew the Western attitude toward growing old, they respectfully asked my mother-in-law her age. Swallowing her surprise, she said, "Sixty-five." Applause, toasts, approving nods, and cries of "Ah! Very old!" greeted her reply. My mother-in-law, eyes wide, barely regained her breath as my mother and grandmother formally congratulated her for being so very old.

Happiness was not always guaranteed by being old. In large households, one could easily hear the resentful mutterings of "Damned Old Ghost" against the old one. If one were poor, plodding and toil continued. If one were rich, the purse strings must be loose; otherwise, one was sure to be a "lonely old ghost"!

PREPARATION OF INGREDIENTS

about ½ cup oil
12 ounces fresh lo mein noodles or 8 ounces dried egg noodles:
  cook as in Plain Cold Noodles (see recipe)

SHRIMP MIXTURE (MIX IN A BOWL. REFRIGERATE BEFORE USE)*

> *4 ounces fresh shrimp: shell, devein, rinse in cold water, pat dry*
> *about ⅓ egg white*
> *½ teaspoon pale dry sherry*
> *1 teaspoon cornstarch*

3 scallions: shred into 1½-inch lengths, including green part
6 Chinese dried mushrooms: soak in hot water until spongy, shred caps

CHICKEN MIXTURE (MIX IN A BOWL. REFRIGERATE BEFORE USE)*

> *1½ boned, skinless chicken breasts: cut into matchstick*
>   *strips (to make 1 cup)*
> *about ½ egg white*

2 teaspoons cornstarch
¼ teaspoon salt

2 cups chopped celery cabbage cut crosswise into ¼-inch-wide
   pieces
½ cup canned straw mushrooms or button mushrooms

SAUCE MIXTURE (MIX IN A BOWL)*

1 tablespoon thin soy sauce
1 tablespoon black soy sauce
1 tablespoon pale dry sherry
½ teaspoon sugar
½ teaspoon salt
½ cup clear chicken broth (not condensed)
2 teaspoons cornstarch

DIRECTIONS FOR COOKING

1. Heat wok over high heat. Swirl in 4 tablespoons oil. When oil is hot, add cooked noodles and spread them evenly on bottom of wok. Pan-fry over medium heat until golden brown on bottom. Turn noodles; swirl in another tablespoon of oil if needed. Fry noodles until second side is golden brown. Remove from wok to an ovenproof plate. Place in a 300-degree oven to keep hot.

2. Heat wok over high heat. Swirl in 4 tablespoons oil. When oil is hot, add shrimp mixture. Stir-fry until shrimp turns whitish-pink (less than 10 seconds). Remove with a drainer to a bowl.

3. Heat remaining oil in wok over high heat. Add scallions, dried mushrooms, and chicken mixture. Stir-fry until chicken just turns white. Drop in celery cabbage and straw mushrooms. Mix well. Stir in sauce mixture. Stir and cook until sauce bubbles gently. Return shrimp to wok. Mix well. Turn off heat.

4. Put fried noodles on a big serving platter and top with the chicken, shrimp, and vegetable mixture. Serve hot at once.

滑鷄拌麵

VELVET CHICKEN LO MEIN
4 to 6 servings

In Cantonese, *lo* means "toss," *mein* means "noodles."

PREPARATION OF INGREDIENTS

3 tablespoons oil
2 teaspoons finely minced fresh ginger root
1 tablespoon minced garlic
6 Chinese dried mushrooms: soak in hot water until spongy,
　discard stems, shred caps

CHICKEN MIXTURE (MIX IN A BOWL. BLANCH IN WATER [SEE COOKING TECHNIQUES])*

　　1½ boned, skinless chicken breasts: cut into matchstick
　　　　strips (to make 1 cup)
　　⅛ teaspoon salt
　　½ teaspoon thin soy sauce
　　about ½ egg white
　　1 tablespoon cornstarch

2 cups fresh bean sprouts

SAUCE MIXTURE (MIX IN A BOWL)*

　　1 tablespoon thin soy sauce
　　1 tablespoon black soy sauce
　　2 tablespoons oyster-flavored sauce
　　½ teaspoon sugar
　　¼ teaspoon salt
　　2 teaspoons sesame seed oil
　　¼ cup chicken broth or water

½ pound fresh lo mein noodles or 6 ounces dried egg noodles:
  cook as in Plain Noodles (see recipe) just before use
4 scallions: cut into 1½-inch lengths, including green part
Soy-Chili Dip (optional; see recipe)

DIRECTIONS FOR COOKING

Heat wok over high heat, then swirl in oil. When oil is hot, drop in ginger, garlic, and mushrooms. Stir-fry until garlic turns golden. Add blanched chicken mixture and blanched bean sprouts. Mix well. Swirl in sauce mixture. Stir-fry for about 30 seconds. Add noodles and scallions. Turn heat to medium. Stir and toss for about 2 minutes. Put on a serving platter. Serve hot with or without dip.

牛肉炒河粉

STIR-FRIED FLAT RICE NOODLES WITH BEEF
4 servings

PREPARATION OF INGREDIENTS

5 tablespoons oil
⅔ teaspoon salt
2 scallions: cut into 1½-inch lengths, including green part
3 Chinese dried mushrooms: soak in hot water until spongy,
  discard stems, cut caps into thin strips

BEEF MIXTURE (MIX IN A BOWL)*

　　½ pound flank steak: cut against grain into thin narrow strips,
　　　　2 inches long
　　2 teaspoons thin soy sauce
　　1 teaspoon pale dry sherry
　　2 teaspoons cornstarch

½ pound fresh bean sprouts

continued

SAUCE MIXTURE (MIX IN A BOWL)*

> 4 teaspoons black soy sauce
> ¼ teaspoon sugar
> 1 teaspoon pale dry sherry
> 2 teaspoons Chinese red vinegar or cider vinegar

1 pound fresh flat rice noodles

DIRECTIONS FOR COOKING

1. Heat wok over high heat. Swirl in oil. When oil is hot, drop in salt and scallions and cook for about 10 seconds. Add mushrooms and brown them slightly. Add beef mixture. Stir-fry until meat loses its redness. Add bean sprouts, and stir in sauce mixture. Mix well.

2. Turn heat to medium. Add rice noodles. Toss and stir-fry gently until they are heated and evenly coated with sauce. Put on a platter. Serve hot.

際南米粉

STIR-FRIED RICE STICKS WITH PORK AND SHRIMP
4 servings

PREPARATION OF INGREDIENTS

5 tablespoons oil
3 eggs: beat until slightly foamy
1 teaspoon minced garlic
3 scallions: cut into 1½-inch lengths, shred, including green part

PORK MIXTURE (MIX IN A BOWL. REFRIGERATE BEFORE USE)*

> 8 ounces lean pork: cut into matchstick strips (to make 1 cup)
> 1 teaspoon cornstarch

SHRIMP MIXTURE (MIX IN A BOWL. REFRIGERATE BEFORE USE)*

> 6 ounces fresh medium-sized shrimp: shell, devein, rinse in cold
>> water, pat dry, cut into peanut-sized pieces
> 1 teaspoon pale dry sherry
> about ⅓ egg white

1 cup fresh bean sprouts or 1 cup matchstick-sized celery strips

SAUCE MIXTURE (MIX IN A BOWL)*

> ½ teaspoon salt
> 2 tablespoons thin soy sauce
> 1 tablespoon black soy sauce
> 1 tablespoon oyster-flavored sauce
> ½ teaspoon sugar

½ pound dried rice sticks: soak in hot water for 15 minutes or a little
longer, drain, cut through rice sticks once or twice with scissors

DIRECTIONS FOR COOKING

1. Heat wok over high heat. Swirl in 1 tablespoon oil. When oil is hot, pour in beaten eggs and spread into a thin pancake. Turn pancake when it is set. Do not brown. Remove from wok and cut pancake into strips ¼ inch wide and 3 inches long. Set aside.

2. Heat wok over high heat. Swirl in remaining 4 tablespoons oil. When oil is hot, slightly brown garlic. Add scallions and pork mixture. Stir-fry until pork loses its pink color. Add shrimp mixture and stir-fry until it just turns whitish. Drop in bean sprouts or celery. Mix well. Stir in sauce mixture. Turn heat to medium. Add rice sticks and shredded eggs. Mix well by constant tossing and stirring. Stir-fry for about 2 minutes or until rice sticks are thoroughly hot. Put on a serving platter. Serve hot.

蝦肉餛飩

WONTONS IN SOUP
6 to 8 servings

PREPARATION OF INGREDIENTS

40 wonton skins

FILLING (MIX IN A BOWL. REFRIGERATE BEFORE USE)*

> *½ pound ground pork (ask the butcher to grind it once only)*
> *6 ounces fresh shrimp: shell, devein, rinse in running cold water,*
> *pat dry, cut into peanut-sized pieces*
> *2 scallions: cut into pea-sized pieces, including green part*
> *1 beaten egg*
> *½ tablespoon sesame seed oil*
> *¼ teaspoon sugar*
> *2 teaspoons pale dry sherry*
> *1 tablespoon thin soy sauce*
> *1 big pinch ground pepper*

BROTH MIXTURE (MIX IN A 3-QUART POT)*

> *4 cups clear chicken broth (not condensed)*
> *¼ teaspoon sugar*
> *¾ teaspoon salt*

3 scallions: cut into pea-sized pieces, including green part
1 tablespoon sesame seed oil
4 ounces watercress: discard hard stalks, rinse, blanch in water
*(see Cooking Techniques)**
Soy-Sesame Dip (see recipe)

DIRECTIONS FOR COOKING

1. Cover wonton skins to keep them moist. Have a small bowl of water handy for sealing wontons.

2. Put about 1 tablespoon of filling in the middle of a wonton skin. Make wontons as illustrated in recipe for Fried Wontons with Shrimp or Pork Filling.

3. Bring the broth to a boil. Cover and simmer over very low heat.

4. Put chopped scallions and sesame seed oil in a big serving bowl.

5. Bring a big pot of water to a rapid boil. Drop wontons in water and boil over medium-high heat for about 7 minutes. Remove wontons with a drainer or a slotted spoon, and put them in the serving bowl with the scallions and sesame seed oil.

6. Pour piping hot broth over the wontons. Add watercress. Stir and serve hot in individual bowls, with dip served in individual bowls alongside.

7. Dip wontons as you eat them, for added flavor.

NOTE: *You may use 12 ounces of shrimp and omit the pork. You may do this ahead of time: Cook the wontons and put them in broth; refrigerate. Reheat wontons in broth over medium-low heat until they are just heated through. Be sure not to overcook them; otherwise the skins will come apart and the filling will be tough.*

鷄肉餛飩

CHICKEN WONTON SOUP
6 to 8 servings

PREPARATION OF INGREDIENTS

40 wonton skins

FILLING (MIX IN A BOWL. REFRIGERATE BEFORE USE)*

> *2½ boned, skinless chicken breasts: cut into pea-sized pieces, mince into paste*
> *2 ounces ground pork*

continued

½ teaspoon finely minced fresh ginger root
2 scallions: mince coarsely, including green part
2 teaspoons pale dry sherry
⅛ teaspoon white pepper
¼ teaspoon salt
1 tablespoon water
2 teaspoons sesame seed oil
1 teaspoon cornstarch
2 teaspoons thin soy sauce
1 egg white: beat until slightly foamy

BROTH MIXTURE (MIX IN A 3-QUART POT)*

4 cups clear chicken broth (not condensed)
¼ teaspoon sugar
¾ teaspoon salt

3 scallions: cut into pea-sized pieces, including green part
1 tablespoon sesame seed oil
4 ounces watercress: discard hard stalks, rinse, blanch in water
Soy-Chili Dip (see recipe) or Soy-Sesame Dip (see recipe)

DIRECTIONS FOR COOKING

1. Cover wonton skins to keep them moist. Have a small bowl of water handy for sealing wontons.

2. Put about 1 tablespoon of filling in middle of a wonton skin. Make wontons as illustrated in recipe for Fried Wontons with Shrimp or Pork Filling.

3. Bring broth to a boil. Cover and simmer over very low heat to wait for the wontons.

4. Put chopped scallions and sesame seed oil in a big serving bowl.

5. Bring a big pot of water to a rapid boil. Drop wontons into boiling water and boil over medium-high heat for about 5 minutes. Remove with a drainer or a slotted spoon, and put them in the serving bowl with the scallions and sesame seed oil.

6. Pour the piping hot broth over the wontons. Add watercress. Stir and serve hot in individual bowls. Serve dip in individual bowls alongside.

义燒飽

CANTONESE BARBECUED PORK BUNS
makes 16

PREPARATION OF INGREDIENTS

3 tablespoons lard for stir-frying
1 teaspoon minced garlic
10 to 12 ounces Cantonese barbecued pork: cut into peanut-sized
  pieces
1 tablespoon plus 2 teaspoons black soy sauce
2 tablespoons flour
1 tablespoon sugar
6 tablespoons water

WRAPPERS

  Step 1
    1 teaspoon active dry yeast
    4 tablespoons lukewarm water
    ½ cup cake flour, sifted
  Step 2
    2 cups cake flour, sifted
    ½ cup sugar
    ½ cup warm water
  Step 3
    1 cup cake flour, sifted
    2 teaspoons baking powder
    1 tablespoon lard
    ¼ cup slightly warm water

16 pieces wax paper, 1½ inches square

DIRECTIONS FOR COOKING

To prepare the filling, heat wok over high heat until it is hot. Add 1 tablespoon of the lard for stir-frying and spread it around. When lard is hot,
drop in garlic and stir for a few seconds. Add barbecued pork. Stir-fry for

about 15 seconds. Add 1 tablespoon black soy sauce. Stir and mix well. Remove pork to a bowl.

Keep wok hot over medium heat. Add remaining 2 tablespoons lard for stir-frying. When lard is hot, add the 2 tablespoons flour and 1 tablespoon sugar. Stir-fry quickly for a few seconds. Swirl in remaining 2 teaspoons black soy sauce and 6 tablespoons water. Mix and stir constantly until it becomes a paste. Return the pork to wok. Mix well. Put in a bowl and put in the refrigerator to cool.*

To prepare the wrappers, use ingredients as specified in steps in the ingredients list:

Step 1: Dissolve yeast in the lukewarm water in a bowl; then add the flour to the yeast water. Mix well. Cover, but do not let the cover touch the dough. Keep in a warm place (an unheated oven) for 15 minutes.

Step 2: In the mixing bowl, thoroughly mix the Step 2 ingredients with the yeast dough from Step 1. Cover, but do not let the cover touch the dough. Keep in a warm place for 2 hours or until the dough doubles in size.

Step 3: In a big mixing bowl, thoroughly mix the 1 cup flour and 2 teaspoons baking powder; then knead with the dough from Step 2. Gradually add lard and ¼ cup slightly warm water. Mix to form dough. Turn dough out onto a slightly floured surface and knead until homogenized. Put dough in a bowl and cover, but do not allow the cover to touch the dough. Keep in a warm place for about 2 hours or until double in size. Punch dough down and roll it into a sausage 1½ inches in diameter. Cut sausage into 16 equal sections and roll them into round balls. Cover with a towel to prevent drying.

To assemble the buns, roll a piece of round dough into a circle about 2½ inches in diameter, but not less than ¼ inch thick. Pinch the outer edges of the circle to make them slightly thinner than the center. Put about a tablespoon of filling in the center of the circle. Pull and gather together the edges, then twist the pleated edges to seal. Put the flat bottom on a piece of wax paper (to keep the bun from sticking to steamer or other surfaces) and cover with a towel. Repeat with the others in the same manner. Let covered buns rise for 15 minutes in a warm place before steaming.

Arrange buns in a bamboo steamer or on a rack lined with one layer of cheesecloth. Cover and steam over high heat for 15 minutes. Peel off wax paper, and serve buns hot.

NOTE: *Steamed buns can be frozen; resteam after thawing.*

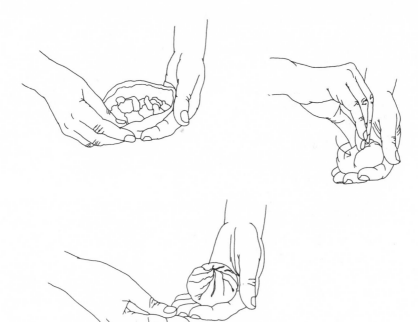

牛肉粥

BEEF CONGEE WITH CONDIMENTS
8 to 12 servings

In Chinese, congee is called "jook." It is served as breakfast, an informal meal, or a late evening snack. But it is never served on a formal occasion.

PREPARATION OF INGREDIENTS

3 cups oil for deep-frying
½ cup uncooked skinless peanuts
1 ounce bean thread noodles or rice sticks
20 wonton skins: cut into ¼-inch-wide strips
10 cups water
1 cup rice: soak in water for 2 hours or more, drain before cooking

continued

BEEF MIXTURE (MIX IN A BOWL. REFRIGERATE BEFORE USE)*

> 1 pound flank steak: cut against grain into pieces ⅛ inch thick
>   and 2 inches long
> 1 tablespoon black soy sauce
> 1 tablespoon thin soy sauce
> ½ teaspoon sugar
> 2 teaspoons sesame seed oil
> 1 teaspoon finely minced fresh ginger root
> 2 teaspoons cornstarch

SAUCE MIXTURE (MIX IN A BOWL)*

> 1 tablespoon thin soy sauce
> ½ teaspoon sugar

1 to 1½ teaspoons salt
⅓ cup chopped scallions, in pea-sized pieces, including green part
⅓ cup chopped fresh coriander (leaves only)
1 small bowl thin soy sauce
1 small bowl sesame seed oil

DIRECTIONS FOR COOKING

1. Heat oil in wok to deep-fry temperature. Deep-fry peanuts until golden brown. Drain, cool, and put in a small serving bowl.*

2. Reheat oil to deep-fry temperature. Loosen noodles or rice sticks by pulling them apart. Test oil by dropping in a piece of noodle or rice stick; if it pops up and turns white, the oil is right. Deep-fry noodles; they will pop up and turn into a white nest instantly; quickly turn over the nest and fry the other side. (This takes less than 10 seconds.) Drain on paper towels. Put on a serving plate.*

3. Loosen wonton strips by pulling them apart, then deep-fry half at a time until they are golden brown. Drain on paper towels. Put on a serving plate.*

4. Bring 10 cups of water to a rapid boil. Add soaked rice. Uncover and cook over medium heat for about 2 hours or until rice becomes like a thin gruel. There should be 8 cups congee left in the pot at the end of cooking time.

5. Keep congee bubbling over medium heat. Add beef mixture and stir to separate pieces. Stir and cook until beef just loses its redness. It takes less than 30 seconds. Turn off heat. Stir in sauce mixture. Salt to taste.

6. Serve congee hot in individual bowls. Bring peanuts, fried noodles, fried wonton strips, scallions, coriander, soy sauce, and sesame seed oil to the table in small bowls. Let each person add these condiments to his or her congee. Sesame seed oil should be used sparingly. Taste the congee before adding thin soy sauce; it might not need it.

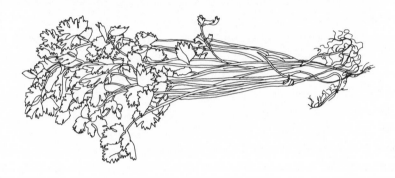

艇仔粥

SAMPAN CONGEE
8 to 12 servings

In the hot southern summer, when dusk deepened, the light of the Pearl River became more brilliant. Like millions of fireflies, the sampans' lights flickered on the water. The noise became so loud that one had to shout. Flocks of fun seekers assembled at the shore to take a boat ride in hopes of cooling off on the river while the moonbeams shone.

Like a school of fish, the sampans gathered where the fun seekers stood. Since there was never a fixed fare, bargaining preceded the ride. A good bargainer would start at a price insultingly low. The oarsman would yell back, cursing sometimes. The customer would look away, pretending not to hear. A good actor would turn slowly as if to walk away. The voice from the sampan would soften. The customer would slightly raise the price. The oarsman would be mad, spit, then plead: life had been hard; too much rain; no fun seekers; children to feed. The bargaining went on. When finally it was settled, one of them always felt cheated. But when the sampan was loaded, no grudge would be held. Then we all floated and rolled on the gentle glowing river in peace.

The highlight of the evening was not the soft rock of the Pearl River, the moon and the summer stars, or even the ladies and gentlemen in the other boats that my mother would not allow us to stare at. It was the food hawkers' boats that we desired. They would stop and pass us often, making our mouths water. At last the night snack signal would be given. The oarsman would spring from his silence, yelling and waving. In seconds, we would be almost swallowed by half a dozen boats, feeling steamed and smothered by their food. Some boats sold only congee, noodles, and wontons. Some carried only steamed clams, snails, and spiced innards. The sampan congee was always so good that we all would have some. Uncle would order his usual clams and snails. The innards would be plentiful for everyone. The children chose the noodles and wontons in soup. The oarsman graciously accepted a bowl.

Under the Milky Way in that small little boat, who cared to seize the moment of wholeness that was ours? It was so long, long ago. Now we are all scattered like those distant stars. Some have gone beyond them. But voices and laughter do remain.

PREPARATION OF INGREDIENTS

4 cups oil for deep-frying
½ cup uncooked skinless peanuts
1 ounce bean thread noodles or rice sticks
20 wonton skins: cut into strips ¼ inch wide
10 cups water
¾ cup rice: soak in water for 2 hours or more, drain before
   cooking
¾ teaspoon salt
1 tablespoon oil for rice

FISH AND SQUID MIXTURE (MIX IN A BOWL. KEEP REFRIGERATED BEFORE USE)*

   1 pound fish fillets (sea bass or flounder): cut crosswise into thin
      slices
   ½ pound fresh cleaned squid (optional): rinse in cold water,
      drain, cut crosswise into ½-inch strips

1 tablespoon sesame seed oil
1 teaspoon Chinese red vinegar
2 teaspoons thin soy sauce
¼ teaspoon white pepper
¼ teaspoon sugar
1 teaspoon finely minced fresh ginger root

1 cup canned abalone cut into strips, ¼ inch thick and wide by
   2 inches long
1 cup soaked jellyfish skin (optional) cut into strips, ¼ inch
   wide by 2 inches long
1 tablespoon sesame seed oil
⅓ cup scallions: cut into pea-sized pieces, including green part
⅓ cup fresh coriander (leaves only)
1 small dish white pepper
1 small bowl thin soy sauce
1 small bowl sesame seed oil
6 fresh eggs (optional): leave whole

DIRECTIONS FOR COOKING

1. Heat oil for deep-frying in wok. Deep-fry peanuts until golden brown. Drain and cool on paper towels. Put in a small serving bowl.*

2. Reheat same oil to deep-fry temperature. Loosen noodles or rice sticks by pulling them apart. Test oil by dropping in a piece of noodle or rice stick; if it pops up and turns white, the oil is right. Deep-fry noodles. They will pop up and turn into a white nest instantly; quickly turn over the nest and fry the other side (this takes less than 10 seconds). Drain on paper towels. Put on a serving plate. Crumble noodles slightly.*

3. Loosen shredded wonton skins, and deep-fry half at a time, until golden brown. Drain on paper towels. Put on a serving plate.*

4. Bring 10 cups of water to a rapid boil. Add rice, salt, and oil for rice. Uncover and cook over medium heat for about 2 hours or until rice becomes like thin gruel. There should be 8 cups congee left in the pot at the end of cooking time. Add boiling water to maintain the 8-cup level if necessary.

5. Keep congee bubbling over medium heat. Add fish and squid mixture. Stir to separate pieces. Cook for about 30 seconds, then turn off heat. Add abalone and jellyfish skin, and swirl in sesame seed oil. Mix well.

6. Bring cooked peanuts, fried wonton skins, fried noodles, scallions, coriander, white pepper, soy sauce, and sesame seed oil to the table in individual bowls. Break an egg into each serving bowl, according to wish of guests. Immediately add piping hot congee. Let each person add condiments to congee.

薄餅

MANDARIN PANCAKES
makes about 20

Making Mandarin pancakes is not as easy as making ordinary pancakes. But it is not hard either. They need just a little practice and patience. Don't make them when you are in a grouchy mood or in a hurry. Because the pancakes can be frozen and kept for months, the best thing to do is to make plenty of them. Wrap them in foil or in plastic bags by the dozen and freeze them. (It is not necessary to separate them.) Any time you prepare Peking duck or moo shu pork, you will then have Mandarin pancakes on hand.

Because the pancakes should be served warm and soft, it is important to steam them or reheat them in a low oven.

PREPARATION OF INGREDIENTS

2 cups all-purpose flour, sifted
¼ teaspoon salt
about ¾ cup boiling water
about 3 tablespoons sesame seed oil

DIRECTIONS FOR COOKING

1. Put flour and salt in a mixing bowl. Add boiling water gradually. Knead until mixture is soft and smooth. Cover and allow to rest for 15 minutes. Roll dough into a long sausage about 1 inch in diameter and cut off two pieces as big as walnuts. Put a damp towel over the rest of the dough to keep it moist.

2. Flour walnut-sized pieces slightly and roll into small balls. Press each ball flat with your palm to make two small round pancakes, 1½ inches in diameter. Brush sesame seed oil on one side of a pancake, then place a

second pancake on it to make a small sandwich. Roll. the two together into a very thin round pancake about 6 to 7 inches in diameter.

3. Heat a flat ungreased frying pan over low heat. Cook both sides of pancake until it turns clear and puffs up slightly; do not brown. Remove from pan and separate it into two very thin pancakes. Trim pancakes with scissors to make them round, if necessary. Wrap in foil or put in a covered container while the others are being cooked. Repeat process for the rest of the dough.

4. Steam pancakes over medium-low heat for 3 minutes, or reheat them in foil in a 275-degree oven for about 10 minutes or until they are hot. Arrange them on a serving platter just before serving. Serve hot.

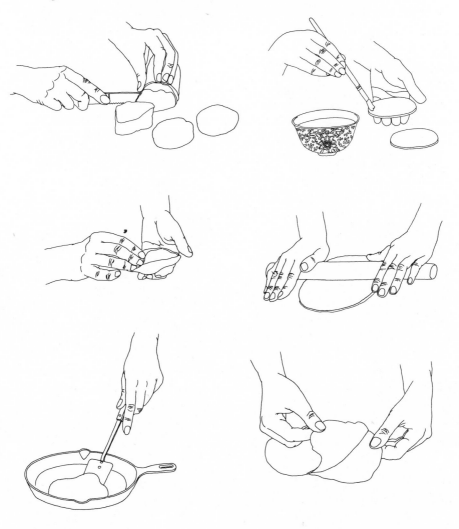

oooo

Chinese Sweets

CHINESE SWEETS

Except for banquets, the Chinese do not include dessert in their meals. Fresh fruit occasionally is served after the meal. Since milk and cream and other dairy products are not included in our diet, traditional Chinese sweets are generally heavy and quite plain; usually they are made with rice, rice powder, sugar, and sweet bean paste. But one of the very popular desserts is sweet soup, made with beans, seeds, or nuts ground up and liquefied. The pastries and tarts that are filled with cream and sold in Chinese pastry shops reflect the influence of the British colonials.

During banquets, because the endless courses may dull one's palate, light sweet dishes are served in-between and at the end to refresh one's taste buds.

Sweets that are frequently presented at banquets as desserts are almond float, eight-jewel rice pudding, and glazed apples. Almond float was served as one of the sweet dishes at the banquet given for Mr. and Mrs. Nixon in Peking.

The Chinese do like sweets, but usually eat them between meals. Pie and cake are too heavy to conclude a Chinese meal. If you are uncertain as to what to serve for dessert, fresh fruit is always welcomed.

八宝飯

EIGHT-JEWEL RICE PUDDING
6 to 8 servings

PREPARATION OF INGREDIENTS

1 pound glutinous rice: soak in cold water overnight or until plump
2 tablespoons lard
1 cup sugar
½ cup assorted candied fruit (such as fruitcake mixture)
⅓ cup glacé cherries
¼ cup raisins
1 cup sweet red bean paste

SAUCE MIXTURE

1 cup water
¼ cup water mixed with 2 tablespoons cornstarch
½ cup orange liqueur

DIRECTIONS FOR COOKING

1. Steam rice over water for 20 minutes or until it is done.

2. Put hot rice into a big mixing bowl. Immediately add lard and ½ cup sugar and mix thoroughly.

3. Grease an 8- to 9-inch ring mold. Arrange candied fruits, glacé cherries, and raisins in your own design. Spoon half the rice on fruits very gently so as not to disturb the pattern. Pack down rice firmly and evenly. Spread sweet red bean paste on rice. Spoon remaining rice on top of bean paste. Pack and smooth rice evenly and gently.*

4. Cover and steam rice pudding in wok over water for about 40 minutes. Pour more boiling water into wok from time to time to maintain water level.

5. Prepare sauce about 10 minutes before pudding is done. Mix remaining ½ cup sugar and cup of water in a small pot, and heat over medium-low heat. Cook, stirring, until sugar water boils. Then thicken sauce with cornstarch water. Add liqueur and stir to mix. Cover to keep hot.

6. Turn pudding upside down on a serving plate with the pattern on top. Slice pudding and serve with the hot sauce.

NOTE: *Pudding can be made a few days in advance and then resteamed.*

拔絲蘋果

GLAZED APPLES
4 to 6 servings

PREPARATION OF INGREDIENTS

3 firm apples: peel, cut each into 6 wedges, discard core
2 eggs: beat until slightly foamy
½ cup cornstarch
about 4 cups oil

SUGAR MIXTURE (MIX IN A BOWL)*

> *3 tablespoons oil*
> *1 cup sugar*
> *¼ cup water*

1 tablespoon black sesame seeds
1 big bowl cold water with ice cubes

DIRECTIONS FOR COOKING

1. Dip sliced apples in eggs, then roll pieces in cornstarch to coat evenly. Put aside.

2. Generously brush a serving plate with oil.

3. Heat the 4 cups of oil in a medium-sized pot to deep-fry temperature. Deep-fry half the apples at a time until golden brown. Remove with a drainer. Drain on paper towels, and keep hot in a 300-degree oven.

4. While you are frying apples, heat sugar mixture in a wok over medium heat until sugar becomes a syrup ready for glazing: it should spin a long thread when a drop falls from the tip of a chopstick, or it should form a hard ball when dropped in cold water. Add sesame seeds.

5. Quickly roll fried apples in syrup to coat evenly, then put them on the greased plate.

6. Quickly bring glazed apples and the bowl of ice water to the table. Let your family or guests have the pleasure of dipping the apples in the ice water to harden the syrup before eating. The glaze should be crisp and hard like a layer of thin glass.

炸金鈴

GOLDEN BELLS
makes 40

PREPARATION OF INGREDIENTS

2 tablespoons white sesame seeds
about 3 cups oil
1 cup walnuts: rinse in hot water, dry on paper towels
2 tablespoons sugar
4 tablespoons sweetened coconut shreds: chop coarsely
40 wonton skins

DIRECTIONS FOR COOKING

1. Heat a small pot over medium heat. Add sesame seeds and stir and roast until they are golden brown. Remove from heat to cool. Then crush them coarsely with a rolling pin. Put in a bowl.

2. Heat oil. When it is hot, deep-fry walnuts to golden brown. Drain and cool on paper towels. Then crush them coarsely with a rolling pin.

3. Combine sugar, crushed sesame seeds, coconut shreds, and walnuts to make filling.*

4. Put a heaping teaspoon of filling in the middle of a wonton skin. Make golden bells as illustrated in recipe for Fried Wontons with Shrimp or Pork Filling.

5. Heat oil to deep-fry temperature. Deep-fry golden bells, several at a time, until they are golden brown. Drain on paper towels. Serve hot or cold. They will stay crisp uncovered at room temperature for several hours.

杏仁豆腐

ALMOND FLOAT
8 to 12 servings

PREPARATION OF INGREDIENTS

2 envelopes unflavored gelatin
½ cup cold water
2 cups boiling water
¾ cup sugar
1 teaspoon almond extract
1 cup milk
a few drops food coloring (optional)
20-ounce can lychee fruit, mandarin oranges, or mixed fruit
  cocktail: chill

DIRECTIONS FOR COOKING

1. Empty gelatin into a mixing bowl. Add cold water and stir well. Add boiling water, sugar, almond extract, and milk. Stir until sugar completely dissolves. Add food coloring if you wish.

2. Pour mixture into two pie plates. Chill in refrigerator for about 6 hours.

3. Using a knife, slice almond float into small cubes and put into a serving bowl. Top with chilled lychee, oranges, or fruit cocktail and the juice from the can. Serve in small bowls.

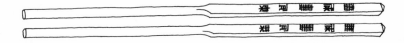

合桃酪

MRS. CHU'S WALNUT SOUP
6 servings

This sweet soup was usually a family's evening snack. Since electric blenders were twenty years in the future in those days, we ground the walnuts with water through a heavy stone grinder. We then squeezed the mixture through a thin bag to obtain only the finest paste. It took strong muscles and at least a few hours of patience in order to enjoy this sweet soup. Now, with the electric blender, it takes only a few seconds.

My family learned the method of cooking this soup from Mrs. Chu, who was a food hawker. Her specialties were this delicious walnut soup and almond soup. At the age of fifty-five, she carried on her shoulders, suspended from a thick bamboo pole, two big burning stoves with piping hot sweet soup. Her thin high voice rang through our streets every evening, in cold and in rain. The sweet soups she sold were noted for their smoothness and rich flavor. Her secret was to fry the walnuts or almonds and then grind them. The aromatic fried nuts gave a more savory flavor than those that were not fried.

Like most of the food hawkers, Mrs. Chu brought the soup in her china bowls right into our living room; then she collected and washed the bowls with water she carried. Sometimes she stood and chatted with us while we drank the soup. One of her favorite subjects was her new religion, Catholicism, which had heaven and only one hell, rather than ten. It was not a bad bargain, she said, but she really would prefer joining her relatives and friends in hell, rather than going to heaven to be lonely among the blue-eyed foreigners who did not speak her tongue.

PREPARATION OF INGREDIENTS

2 cups oil
1½ cups uncooked walnuts or almonds: rinse in hot water, drain,
    dry on paper towels
2½ cups water
½ cup sugar
⅛ teaspoon salt
2 teaspoons cornstarch mixed with 1 tablespoon water

DIRECTIONS FOR COOKING

1. Deep-fry walnuts or almonds until golden brown. Drain and cool.

2. Add fried walnuts or almonds to 1½ cups of water in a blender and blend into a smooth liquid. Pour liquid into a 3-quart pot. Add sugar and salt. Set aside.*

3. Pour 1 cup of water into the blender and blend to rinse out the blender. Add this water to the liquid in the pot.

4. Bring liquid to a gentle boil over medium-low heat. Stir in the cornstarch water. Stir and cook until it is thickened. Pour into a serving bowl. Serve hot in small individual serving bowls.

合桃酥

ALMOND COOKIES
makes about 30

The Chinese call these walnut cookies, and they are at least twice as large as the American-made almond cookies. A walnut is pressed on each cookie instead of an almond, but you may use either walnuts or almonds.

Walnut cookies are among the traditional wedding pastries which the groom's family gives by the hundreds to the bride-to-be. Her family gives them to relatives and friends as a way of announcing the coming wedding and showing pride that their daughter is well-considered by her new family.

This tradition is still very strong among many Chinese. My family, especially my grandmother, felt very sorry when I told them that I was not going to ask for wedding pastry from my American groom-to-be. Grandmother, then seventy-two, had always been open-minded and considerate. But the notion of marrying off her eldest granddaughter without the wedding pastry was a shame that she could not bear. Even her maids received pastry, she said; how could she face the spirits of her ancestors?

Already in a daze from learning that he had to provide twenty tables of wedding banquet, my groom-to-be was too numb to run or to fight. We compromised. I received one hundred dozen Chinese pastries and one hundred dozen Western cream-filled pastries, which were much cheaper than the Chinese pastry.

My grandmother was pleased. So were my parents. My groom-to-be gained his first respect and acceptance, being complimented that he did look Chinese, if one did not notice his eyes and nose.

PREPARATION OF INGREDIENTS

1½ cups sugar
1 teaspoon vanilla extract or almond extract
8 ounces lard
4 cups sifted all-purpose flour
2 teaspoons baking soda
3 eggs: beat until slightly foamy
½ cup uncooked walnuts or almonds
1 egg (for brushing cookies): beat until slightly foamy

DIRECTIONS FOR COOKING

1. In a mixing bowl, cream together sugar, vanilla or almond extract, and lard.

2. Combine flour and baking soda, and mix with the creamed sugar and lard. Pour in the 3 beaten eggs. Mix until dough forms into a smooth ball.

3. Roll dough into a 2-inch-diameter sausage (a smaller-diameter sausage will give smaller cookies), then cut into ½-inch-thick rounds. Slightly flatten the edge of each round with your hand. Gently press a walnut or almond in the center of each cookie. Brush cookies with the beaten egg.

4. Arrange cookies on cookie sheet lined with aluminum foil. Do not preheat oven. Put cookies in cold oven, turn oven to 325 degrees, and bake for 20 to 25 minutes or until cookies are golden brown. Let oven cool completely before baking the remaining cookies. Repeat procedure. Cool before storing in cookie jar.

✿✿✿✿

Sauces and Dips

SAUCES AND DIPS

BEAN SAUCE DIP
makes about ⅓ cup

4 tablespoons Szechwan sweet bean sauce or ground bean sauce
4 teaspoons sugar
4 teaspoons sesame seed oil

Heat all the ingredients in a small pot over low heat. Stir constantly until it is smooth and hot. Put in individual serving dishes. Serve warm.

CHILI OIL

The hotness of a Szechwan or Hunan dish completely depends on the chili peppers and the chili oil. For the past few years, the chili oil that has been available in Chinese grocery stores is too mild to be effective in cooking. Therefore, if you enjoy peppery food, it is best to make your own chili oil.

For persons who like extremely hot food, I suggest Chili Oil II for dipping as well as for cooking. For most people, it is safer to try Chili Oil I first.

CHILI OIL I (HOT)
makes about 1½ cups

For this chili oil, use regular chili peppers, those the size of your little finger. They are hot but not unbearable if you swallow one. Most Chinese and Italian grocery stores sell them in packages.

2 cups oil
1½ cups dried red chili peppers: tear or chop into small pieces,
do not discard seeds
5 teaspoons cayenne pepper

1. In a small pot, heat oil over medium-low heat. The oil should be hot, but not yet to deep-fry temperature. (Test by dropping a pepper in oil. If pepper sizzles gently, then oil is right. If pepper turns black quickly, oil is too hot; cool it down before adding rest of peppers.) Add peppers and their seeds. Cover and cook gently over low heat, stirring from time to time, until all the peppers turn black. Turn off heat and let oil cool a little, about 15 minutes, before adding cayenne. (If oil is too hot, it will burn the cayenne.)

2. Add cayenne, stir, and mix well. Cover and let peppers, cayenne, and oil stand at room temperature overnight.

3. Strain chili oil, which is orange-red in color, through cheesecloth into jar. Cover and keep in refrigerator—it will last for years! (The chili oil will become cloudy in the refrigerator, but it will clear up quickly at room temperature.)

CHILI OIL II (VERY HOT)
makes about 1⅓ cups

The chili peppers in this recipe are very different from the regular ones in the preceding recipe. These dried red chili peppers are tiny and extremely hot. They look like very big long-grain rice. The Chinese use them in making chili oil, but do not put them in dishes because they are too small to detect in food and would bring tears if swallowed. They can be obtained in Chinese grocery stores.

2 cups oil
1½ cups tiny dried red chili peppers: leave them whole
5 teaspoons cayenne pepper

Follow instructions for Chili Oil I.

FIVE-FRAGRANCE SALT DIP
makes about ⅓ cup

6 tablespoons salt
¼ teaspoon five-fragrance powder
½ teaspoon ground pepper

Heat a small dry pot. Put in salt and stir it constantly. When salt is very hot, add five-fragrance powder and ground pepper. Mix well and turn off heat. Cool; put in a covered jar. It will keep for months. Use sparingly. Put small amount into small dishes and serve as a dip. It is also very good to use as a table salt.

FLOWER PEPPERCORN POWDER
makes about ⅓ cup

6 tablespoons flower peppercorns or more

Heat a small dry pot over medium heat. Add flower peppercorns. Stir constantly until peppercorns turn deep brown and become aromatic. (They smoke slightly.) Remove from heat.

Grind roasted peppercorns to a powder in a pepper mill. Put in a covered jar. It will keep for months.

FLOWER PEPPERCORN AND SALT DIP
makes about ⅓ cup

2 teaspoons flower peppercorn powder (*see preceding recipe*)
4 tablespoons salt
1 teaspoon ground pepper

Mix all the ingredients. Store in a covered jar; it will keep for months. Use sparingly. Put small amount into small dishes and serve as a dip.

FRESH CHILI-SOY DIP
makes 4 servings

¼ *cup fresh hot chili peppers cut into small rings, do not*
   discard seeds
6 *tablespoons black soy sauce*
2 *tablespoons Chinese red vinegar*
2 *tablespoons peanut oil or corn oil*

Put peppers, soy sauce, and vinegar in a serving bowl. Heat oil and pour over mixture.*

GINGER-SCALLION DIP
makes 4 servings

3 *tablespoons peanut oil or corn oil*
2 *tablespoons sesame seed oil*
3 *tablespoons finely minced fresh ginger root*
1 *cup finely shredded scallions*
1 *teaspoon salt*

Heat peanut or corn oil. Add sesame seed oil, cool, then pour over ginger, scallions, and salt in a serving bowl.*

GINGER-VINEGAR DIP
makes 4 servings

3 *tablespoons finely shredded fresh ginger root*
6 *tablespoons Chinese red vinegar or cider vinegar*

Mix together and serve.*

HOISIN SAUCE DIP
makes 4 servings

8 tablespoons hoisin sauce
1 tablespoon sesame seed oil

Heat hoisin sauce and sesame seed oil in a pot over low heat. Stir constantly until it is hot. Put in individual serving dishes. Serve warm.

MUSTARD-OIL DIP
makes about 4 servings

2 tablespoons Colman's mustard powder
1 teaspoon sesame seed oil

Mix mustard with enough water to make a thin paste. Then put in a serving bowl and top with sesame seed oil.

PLUM SAUCE DIP
makes about 2 cups

4 tablespoons sugar (optional)
4 tablespoons water
1-pound can plum sauce

Dissolve sugar in water over low heat. Mix sugar water with plum sauce. Put in a container and refrigerate. Serve at room temperature.*

SOY-CHILI DIP

makes 4 servings

4 tablespoons black soy sauce
2 teaspoons chili oil

Mix in a serving bowl and serve.*

SOY-SESAME DIP

makes 4 servings

4 tablespoons black soy sauce
1 tablespoon sesame seed oil

Put soy sauce in a small serving dish. Add oil and serve.*

OIL-OYSTER SAUCE DIP

makes 4 servings

6 tablespoons oyster-flavored sauce
1 tablespoon peanut oil or corn oil
1 teaspoon sesame seed oil

Put oyster-flavored sauce in a serving bowl. Heat oils in a small pot, pour it over oyster-flavored sauce, and serve warm.

SOY-VINEGAR DIP

makes about 4 servings

4 tablespoons Chinese red vinegar or cider vinegar
4 tablespoons black soy sauce

Mix in a serving bowl and serve.*

甜酒釀

SWEET WINE SAUCE

(SWEET FERMENTED RICE)

makes about 4 cups

1 pound glutinous rice: soak in water overnight until plump,
    drain before steaming
1 wine ball: grind into fine powder with a rolling pin

1. Steam rice over water for 15 minutes or until it is done. Transfer hot rice to a colander, and rinse with warm water until each grain is separated and not sticky. Drain thoroughly; mix gently with wine ball powder. (Do not overmix.)

2. Put rice in a clean, dry container. Make a well, 1½ inches in diameter, in the center. Smooth out rice around the well. The rice should be slightly warm. (If it is cold, the rice will not ferment. If it is too hot, the fermented rice will be sour, not sweet.) Cover rice tightly and wrap with blankets or quilts. Put in a warm (not hot) place for 48 hours.

3. If everything goes well, when the rice is uncovered, there is liquid collected in the well. The sauce is sweet, and the rice is juicy and spongy. Put in covered glass jars, and keep refrigerated. It will keep for months.

Menu Suggestions

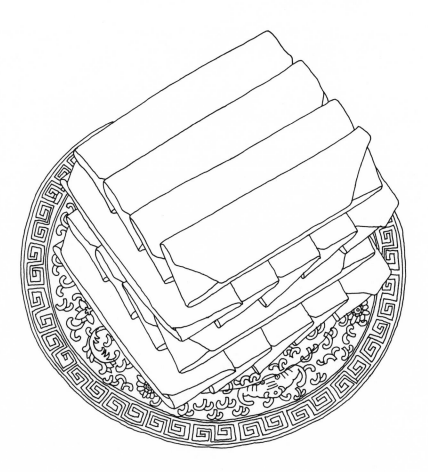

✹✹✹✹

MENU SUGGESTIONS

THE FAMILY-STYLE DINNER

A Chinese family-style meal will include a few dishes served simultaneously or in pairs, with rice, rather than a central main dish as in American meals. We achieve a balanced meal with meat, fowl, soup, seafood, and vegetable dishes. The following sample menus are for six to eight people—a family or an informal dinner party. If you wish a more elaborate meal, see The Formal Dinner.

Menu 1
   Orange-Flavored Beef
   Salt Roast Chicken
   Jade Green Broccoli in Ginger and Wine Sauce
   Shrimp Balls and Straw Mushroom Soup

Menu 2
   My Mother's Lettuce Packages
   Hunan Changsha Crisp Whole Sea Bass
   Peking Crisp String Beans with Garlic
   Hot and Sour Soup

Menu 3
   Deep-Fried Shrimp Balls
   Cantonese Roast Duck
   Sliced Leg of Lamb, Hunan Style
   Subgum Soup

Menu 4

Cantonese Barbecued Spareribs
Szechwan Spiced Beef Shreds on Fried Noodles
Fish Slices in Hot Vinegar Sauce, Peking Style
Sizzling Rice Soup with Shrimp and Chicken

Menu 5

Moo Shu Pork with Mandarin Pancakes
Szechwan Spiced Shrimp
Beef in Oyster Sauce
Stir-Fried Lettuce or Bean Sprouts

Menu 6

Lobster Cantonese or Shrimp Cantonese
Sweet and Sour Pork
The Empress Dowager's Lamb
Stir-Fried Fresh Snow Peas, Water Chestnuts, and Bamboo Shoots

THE FORMAL DINNER

If you wish to give a formal Chinese dinner party in your home, there are several considerations you will want to keep in mind. At a formal dinner the dishes are presented one at a time. Rice and tea are not served during the meal; fried rice or noodles might be served at the end before the sweet dish. Beer or wine may be served throughout dinner. It will help to list all the dishes on a card and put the card on the dining room table. Otherwise, your guests may fill themselves up with the first few courses.

When you plan your menu, choose dishes that vary in ingredients, sauces, and tastes. A good menu should include variations in flavors and textures. A sweet and sour dish and a salty one complement each other. The soft should go with the hard. The mild will smooth the peppery. A dish with sauce will enhance a dry one.

Fried wontons, wontons in soup, spring rolls, and spareribs are good, but they are too common. You might like to know that the Chinese do not include them in a formal dinner.

Following are some menu suggestions for eight to ten persons. All these dishes can be prepared in your own kitchen.

Menu 1 (serve sequentially)
Chicken Shreds and Cucumber Salad
Puffed Butterfly Shrimp
Orange-Flavored Beef
Peking Duck with Mandarin Pancakes
Asparagus in Crabmeat Sauce
Sizzling Rice Soup with Shrimp and Chicken
Yangchow Fried Rice
Mrs. Chu's Walnut Soup

Menu 2 (serve sequentially)
Jellied Lamb
Szechwan Spiced Beef Shreds on Fried Noodles
Cantonese Roast Duck
Whole Fish in Sweet and Sour Sauce
Peking Crisp String Beans with Garlic
Shrimp Balls and Straw Mushroom Soup
Noodles of Longevity
Fresh Fruit

THE BANQUET

When Chinese use the word "banquet," we mean a formal occasion in a restaurant. A normal banquet meal for ten to twelve persons includes four cold dishes, four quick stir-fried dishes, four to six main dishes, a soup, a dish of rice or noodles, and a sweet dish. It requires a chef and a staff and a large, fully equipped kitchen. At such a banquet the menu might look like this:

Cold Dishes (serve simultaneously)
Jellied Lamb   Drunken Chicken
Smoked Fish   Pong-Pong Chicken, Szechwan Style (Hacked Chicken)

Quick Stir-Fried Dishes (serve sequentially)
 Crabmeat Fu Yung Eggs on Fried Noodles
 Pork Dings and Walnuts
 Peking Pure Shrimp
 Happy Union

Main Dishes (serve sequentially)
 Orange-Flavored Beef
 Peking Duck with Mandarin Pancakes
 Hunan Changsha Crisp Whole Sea Bass
 Crisp Lemon Chicken
 Stuffed Prawns
 Tung Po Pork

Soup: Eight Precious Jewels Whole Winter Melon Soup

Rich Dish: Yangchow Fried Rice

Sweet Dish: Glazed Apples

CHINESE COOKING INGREDIENTS
WITH INFORMATION ON STORING

鮑魚

ABALONE

The canned variety mostly comes from Japan or Mexico. It is already cooked and ready to be served from the can. It is best to use it in stir-fry dishes, congee, or as an appetizer. Cooking time should be short. Excessive heat will toughen it, and it becomes chewy. Liquid from the can is good for soup and congee.

STORING: *Drain and rinse. Store in covered jar with enough fresh cold water to cover. Refrigerate. Change water every day. Will keep for about 2 weeks.*

東洋大菜

AGAR-AGAR (tai choy)

A dried seaweed with no flavor. Sold in packages, mostly from Japan. Resembles a cross between rice sticks and bean thread noodles. Functions like unflavored gelatin in sweet dishes. Cook in water until dissolved, then chill. For use in salad dishes, soak in cold water and cut into 1½-inch lengths.

STORING: *Needs no refrigeration. Keeps forever.*

八角

ANISE (star)

Chinese spice, looks like a ½-inch eight-pointed star, reddish-brown, hard and dried, smells like licorice. Used to flavor meat and poultry. Sold by weight (usually with the points apart).

STORING: *Store in covered jar at room temperature; will keep forever.*

玉筍

BABY CORN

(See recipe Beef with Baby Corn and Chinese Mushrooms in Black Bean Sauce.)

STORING: *Keep in water in refrigerator; change water daily. Will keep for weeks.*

竹筍

BAMBOO SHOOTS

Young shoots of tropical bamboo. Ivory-colored and delicious when fresh and young. In the United States, usually imported in cans.

The canned variety: canned in plain water in chunks or slices. Rinse in fresh cold water to get rid of the sour odor before using.

STORING: *Store in covered jar with enough water to cover. Refrigerate. Change cold water every day. Will keep for a few weeks.*

豆腐

BEAN CURD (fresh)

(See Vegetables and Bean Curd chapter.)

紅南乳

BEAN CURD CHEESE (red)

Labeled as red bean cheese, brick-red, 2 inches square and about 1 inch thick. Fermented with beans, red rice, salt, water, and rice wine. Strong, pungent, and salty in taste. Mostly used as seasoning. Sold in cans or jars.

STORING: *Place in clear glass jar and refrigerate. Will keep for several months.*

炸豆腐泡

BEAN CURD PUFFS (fried)

Golden color, fluffy and spongy, cushionlike square cakes.

STORING: *Store in plastic bag. Will keep at least two weeks if refrigerated. If frozen, will keep for months.*

大腐皮

BEAN CURD SKINS (plain, dried)

Shiny, light yellow, approximately 6-by-10-inch paper-thin skin, dried and brittle. It is the rich cream that floats on top of the yellow soybean milk and is also called "floating bean curd skin." Commonly cooked in sugar water with ginger and lotus seeds or ginkgo nuts as snacks in the south. Also used in soup, for pastry skin, and for vegetable dishes. Sold in packages.

STORING: *Store in plastic bags. No refrigeration needed. Will keep for months.*

紅豆沙

BEAN PASTE (sweet red)

Dark red color, thick, and quite sweet. Made from puréing Chinese red beans, sugar, and shortening. Widely used in sweet pastries and sweet dishes. Sold in cans or by weight in Chinese pastry stores.

STORING: *Will keep for weeks if refrigerated in covered jar.*

❀❀❀❀

BEAN SAUCES
磨原豉

Ground Bean Sauce

Also known as brown bean sauce or brown bean paste. Brown, thick, puréed sauce made from yellow soybeans, flour, salt, and water; salty and pungent. Sold in cans.

STORING: *Refrigerate in a covered jar; will keep for months.*

四川辣豆瓣醬

Szechwan Chili Bean Sauce

Orange-brown color, very salty, pungent, spicy, and hot. Used in Szechwan dishes. Available in 6-ounce cans.

STORING: *Store as ground bean sauce.*

四川甜麵醬

Szechwan Sweet Bean Sauce

Labeled as sweet bean paste sometimes. Not sweet, but salty and pungent; tastes very much like ground bean sauce (which can be used as a substitute). Used in many Szechwan dishes. Available in 6-ounce cans.

STORING: *Store as ground bean sauce.*

綠豆芽

BEAN SPROUTS (green, fresh)

The sprouts of mung beans (called green beans by the Chinese), with white body, yellow heads, green hoods, and small tails. Green hoods should be removed when washing. Chinese people spend hours leisurely pinching off the tails, so that the sprouts look neater.

If bean sprouts look slightly brownish and have some odor, they are not fresh. The canned ones, primarily for non-Chinese, are limp, almost mushy, and have completely lost their delicacy. Chinese do not like to eat them. If you want to grow bean sprouts yourself, see Chapter on Vegetables.

STORING: *Rinse well in cold water. Keep refrigerated. Will keep for about 4 days.*

燕窩

BIRDS' NESTS

(See recipe Fu Yung Bird's Nest Soup.)
STORING: *Will keep indefinitely.*

豆豉

BLACK BEANS (salted)

Black beans preserved in ginger, garlic, salt, and spices; used as seasoning. Before cooking, they are strong, pungent, and salty in taste; must be rinsed in hot water before use. After cooking, they give a delicious flavor to food. Sold in cans or bags.

STORING: *Keep in covered jar; no refrigeration needed; will keep for months.*

白菜

BOK CHOY

In English, "white vegetable"; a leafy vegetable with long white stems and large ruffled green leaves; used to stir-fry with meat or seafood or to simmer with meat in soup. Sold fresh.

STORING: *Will keep at least 5 days if refrigerated.*

天津白菜

CELERY CABBAGE

Also known as Tientsin cabbage; shaped like a short, stout celery. Has wide, yellow-white, tightly packed stalks, about 9 to 10 inches long. The kind that is commonly sold in supermarkets has longer stalks, about 12 to 14 inches; color is less yellow and more green. Choose the one that is light yellow or pale green.

STORING: *Wrap and refrigerate; will keep 2 weeks or more.*

猪網油

CAUL (lace fat)

Big sheets of fat that look like a net or lace, caul encases the inner organs of the pig; sold in Chinese or Italian meat stores.

STORING: *Will keep for a few days in the refrigerator or for months in the freezer; thaw before use.*

清鷄湯

CHICKEN BROTH (clear)

If you prefer, make your own chicken broth. But many Chinese like to use College Inn clear chicken broth, which is clear and tasty. You can use it straight or mix it with water.

辣椒油

CHILI OIL

(See Sauces and Dips.)

乾辣椒

CHILI PEPPERS (dried)

Dried hot peppers, orange-red, and the size of a small finger. Use with the seeds, which are essential for the hotness.

STORING: *Store in covered jar. Will keep for months.*

椰汁

COCONUT MILK (unsweetened)

Also called coconut cream; thick cream extracted from fresh coconut meat. Imported from the Philippines.

STORING: *Leftovers can be frozen; will keep for months.*

芫荽（香菜）

CORIANDER (fresh)

Also called Chinese parsley; a very fragrant herb with long thin stalks and delicate leaves. Used as a seasoning and for garnishing. Sold in Chinese and Spanish grocery stores. Also known as Spanish parsley or cilantro.

STORING: *Wrap and refrigerate. Will keep about 4 days.*

咖哩醬

CURRY PASTE

Buy the brands made in India or packed and bottled in India, such as the American Roland Food Company's curry paste.

STORING: *Will keep for months without refrigeration.*

紅棗

DATES (Chinese red)

Chinese red dried dates, the size of small prunes; used in cooking.
STORING: *Store in covered jar; will keep for years.*

春卷皮

EGG ROLL SKINS

Machine-pressed 8-inch-square thin sheets, made from eggs, flour, and water; soft and elastic, yellowish, the color of egg noodles. Used in wrapping meat, shrimp, or vegetables, then deep-fried. Can be quartered to make fried wontons or wontons for soup. Sold in stacks by weight, usually in 2-pound packages. You may make your own (see recipe).

STORING: *Wrap by the dozen in plastic wrap. Seal well and freeze. Will keep for months. Thaw at room temperature for an hour or until soft. If refrigerated, will keep 4 to 5 days.*

皮蛋

EGGS (preserved)

Also known as thousand-year-old eggs. They are uncooked duck eggs coated with clay mixed with lime, ashes, and rice husks, then buried in an earthen pot for about three months. The egg whites become firm, amber-colored, and transparent, sometimes dotted with feather designs. The yolks turn dark green, firm but moist.

STORING: *Will keep a couple of weeks; no refrigeration needed.*

魚露

FISH SAUCE

Thin, topaz-colored extract from fish; salty but savory in taste. Used in cooking or for dipping. Sold by the bottle.

STORING: *Keep in refrigerator in hot weather. Will keep for months.*

五香粉

FIVE-FRAGRANCE POWDER

Mixture of five ground spices (star anise, clove, fennel, cinnamon, and peppercorns), cinnamon-colored, fragrant. Used sparingly to flavor food.

STORING: *Will keep indefinitely in a covered jar.*

花椒粉

FLOWER PEPPERCORN POWDER

(See Sauces and Dips.)

花椒

FLOWER PEPPERCORNS

Also called wild peppercorns; reddish-brown, gentle and delicate in hotness and scent.

STORING: *Will keep indefinitely in tightly covered jar.*

紅蘇薑

GINGER (sweet red in syrup)

Ginger chunks dyed a red color, then preserved in syrup. Sweet, hot, and crunchy. May be used in sweet and sour dishes for color or just eaten like candy. Sold by the bottle.

STORING: *Will keep indefinitely in jar at room temperature.*

薑汁

GINGER JUICE

Not available in Chinese grocery stores. The simplest way to make it is to press a small chunk of fresh ginger root with a garlic press. Catch the juice in a small bowl. If you do not have a garlic press, just finely mince the ginger root.

薑

GINGER ROOT (fresh)

A very important seasoning in Chinese cooking, especially seafood. Eliminates fishy and gamy odors and adds flavor to meat, poultry, and seafood. Comes in a variety of shapes, like a thin potato covered with knobs. When it is young, the skin is smooth and has the color of a young potato; darker skin indicates an older root which is dry and fibrous. The meat is ivory in color and has a clear fresh smell as well as a hot and spicy taste. Some old Chinese place slices of ginger root on the forehead to draw out bad air in the head (to cure headache)! Also, ginger is eaten to help regain blood after childbirth (see recipe).

Do not (ever!) substitute ginger powder or dried ginger. If you cannot find it fresh in local stores, beg your friendly Chinese laundryman or Chinese restaurateur to sell you a small piece.

STORING: *Wrap in plastic wrap; will keep many weeks without refrigeration. Can also be sliced and frozen, but use it without thawing (it becomes spongy when thawed). Or bury it in moist soil or sand (too much water will rot the root), and it will last for months. With luck, it might grow into a ginger plant!*

白果

GINKGO NUTS

Nuts with hard white shells. Available fresh or canned. Since fresh ones are often dried out inside or rotted, I suggest buying the canned kind.

STORING: *Keep canned nuts covered with water in refrigerator. Change water daily; will keep for a week. Frozen, they will keep for months.*

火腿

HAM (Smithfield)

Cured and smoked in Smithfield, Virginia; tastes almost like Chinese ham, salty and very tasty. Used as a substitute for Chinese ham. Sold by weight.

STORING: *Wrap and refrigerate; will keep for months. Can also be frozen.*

海鮮醬

HOISIN SAUCE

Means "seafood sauce" in Chinese. Thick, brownish-red paste, spicy, salty, and moderately sweet; made from soybeans, water, garlic, chili, flour, and spices. Used in many dishes.

STORING: *Keeps for months refrigerated in covered jar.*

四川榨菜

JAH CHOY (Szechwan)

Sometimes labeled Szechwan cabbage or Szechwan vegetables. Comes in chunks in cans. Hot, spicy, and salty; rinse before cooking.

STORING: *Do not rinse off salt and spices. Put in a tightly covered jar. Will keep for months in refrigerator. Also can be frozen.*

海蜇皮

JELLYFISH SKIN

A sea organism (not the kind we see on beaches), dried, salted, and pressed into thin circles, about 14 to 16 inches in diameter. Crunchy and resilient, more texture than flavor. Must be rinsed and soaked before use. Used mostly in cold dishes. Sold by weight.

STORING: *Will keep for months in refrigerator if salt is not removed. If already soaked, immerse in cold water, cover, and refrigerate. Change fresh water every two days. Will keep for weeks.*

金針

LILY BUDS (dried)

Also known as golden needles or dried tiger lily buds. They are 2 to 3 inches long. The better kinds are still flexible, not brittle, and have a very pale gold color. Add delicate flavor in soup, poultry, meat, and fish.

STORING: *Put in a sealed jar; will keep indefinitely without refrigeration.*

豆角

LONG BEANS (fresh)

(See recipe Long Beans with Barbecued Pork.)

蓮子

LOTUS SEEDS (dried)

Represent fertility and birth. Used in many dishes. Must be soaked and cooked.

STORING: *Will keep indefinitely in a jar.*

荔枝

LYCHEE

A tropical fruit grown in the southern part of China; crimson red like a giant strawberry with tough inedible skin and small brown pit. Meat is succulent and almost translucent, crisp, sweet, and delicious. Seldom available fresh in the North and Midwest states.

The canned variety: Pitted and canned in light syrup, they have lost most of the fresh fruit taste but are still sweet and crisp.

STORING: *Put in covered jar; will keep for several days in the refrigerator.*

苦瓜

BITTER MELON

Shaped like a big sweet potato, green with a very lumpy body, slightly bitter in taste.

STORING: *Refrigerated, will keep about a week.*

冬瓜

WINTER MELON

Shape is between a watermelon and a pumpkin; green, frosty tough skin and soft white meat; mild and delicate in flavor. Sold fresh by weight, whole or in wedges.

STORING: *Wrap with plastic wrap; will keep about 4 days in refrigerator.*

☀☀☀☀

MUSHROOMS

Abalone Mushrooms (see recipe Mai's Surprise)

STORING: *Keep in water in refrigerator; change water daily. Will keep for weeks.*

蘑菇

Button Mushrooms (canned)

Identical to American button mushrooms canned in water. You may use the domestic or imported kind. Rinse before use.

STORING: *Store as abalone mushrooms.*

冬菇

Chinese Dried Mushrooms

Dried, black, aromatic, and luscious; sizes range from ½ inch to 2¼ inches in diameter. Used in innumerable ways. Must be soaked before use.

STORING: *Will keep indefinitely in tightly covered container.*

雲耳

Cloud Ears

Also known as tree fungus or tree mushrooms; black, small, crinkled dried tree fungus. Must be soaked in hot water before use; will expand two to three times original size. They resemble a cluster of clouds or human ears; soft and resilient in texture, subtle and dainty in taste. Used to cook with chicken, meat, vegetables, or in soup. Sold by weight.

STORING: *Will keep indefinitely in a covered jar at room temperature.*

草菇

Straw Mushrooms (canned)

Also called grass mushrooms; very delicate, some small and some big, canned in water. Rinse before use.

STORING: *Store as abalone mushrooms.*

✿✿✿✿

NOODLES

粉絲

Bean Thread Noodles

Also known as pea-starch noodles or cellophane noodles; wiry, hard, clear, white noodles; made from mung beans. If used in soup, must be presoaked. They are very absorbent and become soft, translucent, and gelatinous after soaking. Almost tasteless, but they easily absorb flavor of other ingredients. Should not be overcooked or they will become mushy. When deep-fried, no need to presoak; they pop up from oil like a snow-white nest. Sold in 2- or 6-ounce packages.

STORING: *Will keep indefinitely.*

新鮮沙河粉

Fresh Rice Noodles

Chinese means "sand river noodles." Made daily in noodle stores with finely ground rice powder and water. The dough is spread thinly over greased metal trays and steamed to be set in ⅛-inch-thick gelatinous white sheets. Then each sheet is rolled and cut into ½-inch-wide noodles. Used in soup or in stir-frying. Cook briefly; otherwise they become mushy. Sold by the sheet or by the pound. Available fresh in some Chinese noodle or bean curd stores.

STORING: *Put in a plastic bag, they will keep in refrigerator for about 5 days. Can be frozen for months. Thaw at room temperature before use.*

新鮮麵

Lo Mein Noodles

Made with flour and eggs, golden in color, elastic and usually thin. Sold by the pound.

STORING: *Will keep in refrigerator for about 5 days. Can be kept frozen for a couple of months.*

油

OIL (peanut oil, corn oil, vegetable oil)

Among the Chinese, we prefer to use peanut oil. But I find corn oil equally good in the United States. It is best to use peanut oil or corn oil for stir-fry cooking. For deep-frying, corn oil is the best choice. But vegetable oil will do, and it is more economical.

STORING: *Oil can be reused many times. Keep it refrigerated. To remove odor from oil: Heat the used oil to deep-fry temperature. Add 2 quarter-sized slices of fresh ginger root or raw peeled potato. Fry until they turn golden. Remove them from oil and discard. Discard oil when it becomes dark and heavy with residues. Oil used for cooking fish should be kept in a separate bottle. Remove odor as above.*

蠔油

OYSTER-FLAVORED SAUCE

A thick, caramel-colored sauce made from oyster extract, water, salt, and starch; salty, pungent, and tasty. Adds flavor to meat and poultry and is also used as a table condiment. There are many grades. The best kind is thinner and more runny than the inferior kind, which is usually too thick to pour and sometimes foamy.

STORING: *Cover and refrigerate. Will keep indefinitely.*

蘇梅醬

PLUM SAUCE

Also known as duck sauce. A thick, chutneylike sauce, spicy, sweet, and sour, made from plums, ginger, apricots, chilis, vinegar, sugar, and water. Used as a table condiment for duck, fried wontons, egg rolls, or spring rolls. For thinner dip, dilute the whole can with sugar and water, see Plum Sauce Dip.

STORING: *Will keep for months refrigerated in a covered jar.*

义燒肉

PORK (Cantonese barbecued)

Marinated pork chunks roasted on skewers; sweet, tender, and savory. Can be made at home (see recipe) or bought in Chinese grocery stores. Used in many dishes or eaten as cold meat.

STORING: *Wrap and refrigerate; will keep 4 to 5 days. May also be frozen.*

糯米

RICE (glutinous)

Also known as sweet rice. Short, plump, milk-white rice, sticky and glutinous when cooked. Used in making dumplings, pastries, and puddings or as stuffing for poultry.

STORING: *Store as rice.*

粘米粉

RICE POWDER

Powder ground from rice. Used in pastries and sweet dishes.
STORING: *Store as flour.*

糯米粉

RICE POWDER (glutinous)

Fine powder ground from glutinous rice; whiter than wheat flour. When cooked, becomes soft, sticky, and chewy. Used in making dumplings, sweet dishes, and pastries.
STORING: *Store as flour.*

乾米粉

RICE STICKS (dried)

Brittle, long, thin white sticks, they look almost like bean thread noodles except that they are whiter and more brittle. Used in soup, stir-frying, deep-frying, and as a garnish for many dishes.
STORING: *Will keep indefinitely without refrigeration.*

腊腸

SAUSAGE (Chinese pork)

Minced pork cured with seasonings, stuffed in casings, then tied in pairs to air-dry. Each link is 5 to 6 inches long and ½ inch in diameter. Red and white in color, savory and rich in taste. Used in stuffing, rice, soup, or steamed and served as a dish.
STORING: *Wrap and refrigerate or hang in cool place; will keep for weeks.*

葱

SCALLIONS

Also known as spring onions; in a Chinese kitchen, scallions, fresh ginger root, and garlic are as essential as salt and pepper. The scallions are used like your onion, which we call "foreign scallion." When we use scallions, we use not only the white part but also the green part. But do pinch off the tired ends and discard the roots.

麻油

SESAME SEED OIL

Savory, aromatic, topaz-colored oil made from roasted white sesame seeds. Used sparingly to flavor food.

STORING: *Will keep indefinitely if refrigerated.*

芝蔴醬

SESAME SEED PASTE

Since most of the imported sesame seed paste has lost its flavor, it is much better to use peanut butter. In China, peanut butter and sesame seed paste are used interchangeably in cooking; and peanuts are eaten as a snack, as they are in the United States.

STORING: *Store as peanut butter.*

芝蔴

SESAME SEEDS

Tiny seeds with nutty flavor; there are two varieties: black and white. Used in making oil, pastries, and dumplings.

STORING: *In covered jar, will keep for many months.*

山楂餅

SHAN JAH BENG

Also labeled as preserved plums, shan cha beng, or san jan cakes; made from sugar, plums, or apples, pressed into quarter-sized thin wafers. Red in color, sweet and sour in taste. Believed to enhance appetite; therefore, many old Chinese prefer children to eat shan jah beng rather than candies. Used in making sweet and sour sauce before ketchup became popular.

STORING: *In covered jar, will keep indefinitely.*

魚翅

SHARK'S FIN

Cartilage from the fins of sharks, dried and already cooked. Very expensive and very celebrated; often served in soup at formal Chinese banquets. After being recooked until smooth and resilient, looks like long translucent needles. Regarded as highly nutritious by the Chinese, although it becomes quite tasteless after cooking. Must be cooked in good broth and flavored by other ingredients.

STORING: *Will keep indefinitely in dried form. If soaked, put in cold water and refrigerate; will keep up to 5 days.*

蝦米

SHRIMP (Chinese dried)

Shelled and dried under the sun, they have a sharp flavor. They are used in small amounts for stuffing, with rice, or in soup. Best variety is light orange-pink and about 1 inch long. If color is dark and texture is powdery, they are no longer good.

STORING: *Will keep for months in a tightly covered jar without refrigeration.*

蝦片

SHRIMP CHIPS

Thin, hard, quarter-size chips in assorted colors, made with shrimp, flour, and seasonings. Must be deep-fried to puff up and double in size; tasty and crisp. Eaten as a snack like potato chips or used as a garnish for dishes.

STORING: *Will keep indefinitely. Need no refrigeration.*

雪豆

SNOW PEAS (fresh)

Also known as Holland peas among the Chinese. It was said that they originated in Holland. Flat and light green in color, crisp and juicy if they are not overcooked. Eat pods and all. Use frozen ones only as a last resort.

STORING: *Will keep in refrigerator for about 10 days.*

❀❀❀❀

SOY SAUCES

The most important seasoning in Chinese cooking. Varieties and grades are many. Thin or black, good or bad, domestic or imported, all are labeled under the name "soy sauce" in English. Knowing their differences and using the right kind is the key to good-tasting dishes. The two most frequently used types are black soy sauce and thin soy sauce.

醬油 (老抽)

Black Soy Sauce

Also known as dark soy sauce; extract from fermented soybeans, caramel, flour, salt, and water; darker and heavier than thin soy sauce, salty but with a slightly sweet taste. Do not buy the one labeled "double dark soy sauce." It is too salty.

STORING: *Keep in refrigerator in hot weather. Will keep for months.*

生抽

Thin Soy Sauce

Also known as light soy sauce; liquid extract from soybeans, flour, salt, and water after slow fermentation under the sun. The first extraction, which is commonly sold in the States, is the best: topaz-colored, salty and savory in taste. Used in stir-frying, in soup, as marinade, as table condiment. Imported from China, Hong Kong, and Taiwan.

STORING: *Store as black soy sauce.*

上海春卷皮

SPRING ROLL SKINS (Shanghai)

Confusingly labeled as egg roll skins in America. Cooked, translucent crepes, paper-thin and delicate, mostly handmade. Come in round or square sheets, 9 inches in diameter; made from thin flour batter or marshmallow-like dough adhered to a hot iron skillet. Used to wrap cooked meat, vegetables, seafood, or stuffed and then deep-fried. Will dissolve or turn mushy if put in soup. Sold in stacks by weight.

STORING: *Wrap and freeze. Will keep for months. Thaw at room temperature an hour or until soft.*

陳皮

TANGERINE PEEL (dried)

Also known as old tangerine peel or mandarin orange peel; dried tangerine skin with coffee color and a condensed sweet fragrance. Used to flavor food.

STORING: *Keeps indefinitely in a tightly covered jar. The longer it is kept, the better it is.*

芋頭

TARO

A potatolike starchy root with dusty rough skin. Comes in many sizes and varieties. Can be slow-cooked with meat, deep-fried, steamed, or used in making pastry. The most starchy kind is considered the best, especially in pastry-making.

STORING: *Will keep about a week or more. Needs no refrigeration.*

大蘿蔔

TURNIP (white giant)

Shaped like a big sweet potato; has a white body and translucent skin. Mild in taste. Choose one that is firm and heavy.

STORING: *Refrigerated, will keep about 2 weeks.*

❀❀❀❀

VINEGARS

大紅浙醋

Chinese Red Vinegar

Made from rice; has a clear color in the bottle but turns red within hours after bottle is opened. Used in cooking as well as in dips.

STORING: *Store at room temperature; will keep indefinitely.*

漆丁甜醋

Chinese Sweet Vinegar

Made from sugar and black vinegar; sweet, black, and pungent; also known as childbirth vinegar. Used primarily in cooking with ginger, pig's feet, and eggs. A nutritious, popular folk tonic (delicious too) of southern China; specially cooked and served to women after childbirth to help them regain strength (see recipe).

STORING: *Store at room temperature; will keep many months.*

白醋

Chinese White Vinegar

Made from rice; sharp and tastes like American-made vinegar, which can be used as a substitute.

STORING: *Store as distilled white vinegar.*

馬蹄粉

WATER CHESTNUT POWDER

Lumpy, grayish flour made from water chestnuts. Used in making sweet pastries or as batter to coat deep-fried foods for crispness. Sold by weight.

STORING: *Store as flour.*

馬蹄

WATER CHESTNUTS

The fresh variety are quarter-sized buttonlike bulbs, with deep purple skins. They grow in shallow, muddy water. When fresh and young, the meat is crystal white, sweet, juicy, and crisp. If old, they become starchy and less sweet. Must be skinned; eat fresh as fruit, or as vegetable cook with meat and poultry. Also can be glazed in sugar or ground into powder to make sweet pastry.

The canned variety are peeled and in water; crisp, but have lost sweetness in canning. Used as a vegetable; cook with meat and poultry.

STORING: *Let the mud stay on the skin to protect fresh water chestnuts from drying out; if refrigerated, will keep for 4 to 5 days. Or you may wash and peel them, put in a jar, cover with cold water, refrigerate, and change water every other day. Canned water chestnuts should be stored in the same way. Will keep for weeks. Freezing is not desirable; the meat becomes spongy.*

澄麵粉

WHEAT STARCH

Wheat flour with gluten removed. Used in making dim sum. No substitutes.

STORING: *Store as flour.*

紹興酒

WINE (Chinese Shaohsing wine and pale dry sherry)

The purpose of using a small amount of wine in many dishes is not just for the flavor, but also to eliminate the odor in seafood, poultry, and meat. Shaohsing wine is a rice wine widely used by the Chinese in cooking. We drink it warm. If Shaohsing wine is not available, pale dry sherry is the best substitute.

洒餅

WINE BALLS (wine cubes)

Also called wine cake; white and round, the size of a Ping-Pong ball. It is a wine starter.

STORING: *Must be stored in a tightly covered jar; will keep for years in a cool, dry place.*

甜酒釀 (酒糟)

SWEET WINE SAUCE (fermented wine rice)

Glutinous rice fermented with wine balls. Sweet wine sauce is sold in jars; the rice is spongy and the sauce is sweet. You may make your own (see recipe).

STORING: *Needs to be refrigerated; will keep for months.*

餛飩皮

WONTON SKINS

Also known as shao-mai skins; 3½-inch squares, thinner than egg roll skins, but made with the same ingredients. Stuffed with shrimp, crabmeat, meat, or vegetables, then cooked in broth, steamed, or deep-fried. Sold by weight. You may also make your own (see recipe).

STORING: *Will keep refrigerated for 4 to 5 days. Will keep frozen, sealed by the dozen in plastic wrap, for months. Thaw at room temperature for an hour or until soft.*

○○○○

SHOPPING LIST

Shopping for Chinese foods is usually difficult if you do not speak the language. Even if you do speak some Chinese, you may not speak the grocer's dialect. Although we have hundreds of dialects in China, fortunately we have only one written language. So communication is possible for eight hundred million of us.

In addition to the problem of language, the labeling of imported Chinese ingredients is very confusing to the non-Chinese. Different varieties of soy sauces are simply labeled in English as "Soy Sauce." If you do not read Chinese, you are likely to pick up the wrong kind. Even though most Chinese grocers are friendly, if you cannot make it very clear to them what you want, they may shake their heads or say they don't have it.

For your shopping convenience, I have listed the Chinese cooking ingredients in English and Chinese. Make Xerox copies of the list. When you go to shop or order by mail, simply indicate the items you want to the grocer. You should have no difficulty in obtaining the desired ingredients.

ABALONE (CANNED) 罐頭鮑魚

AGAR-AGAR (TAI CHOY) 東洋大菜

ANISE (STAR) 八角

BABY CORN (CANNED) 罐頭玉筍

BAMBOO SHOOTS (CANNED)   竹筍

BEAN CURD (FRESH)   豆腐

BEAN CURD CHEESE (RED)   紅南乳

BEAN CURD PUFFS (FRIED)   炸豆腐泡

BEAN CURD SKINS (DRIED)   大腐皮

BEAN PASTE (SWEET RED)   罐頭紅豆沙

BEAN SAUCE (GROUND)   磨原豉

BEAN SAUCE (SZECHWAN CHILI)   四川辣豆瓣醬

BEAN SAUCE (SZECHWAN SWEET)   四川甜麵醬

BEAN SPROUTS (FRESH)   綠豆芽

BIRDS' NESTS   燕窩

BLACK BEANS (SALTED)   豆豉

BOK CHOY   白菜

CAUL (LACE FAT)   網油

CELERY CABBAGE (TIENTSIN)   天津白菜

CHILI OIL   辣椒油

CHILI PEPPERS (DRIED)   乾辣椒

CHILI PEPPERS (TINY DRIED)　指尖椒

CLOUD EARS　雲耳

COCONUT MILK (UNSWEETENED)　椰汁（不甜的）

CORIANDER (FRESH)　芫荽

CURRY PASTE　咖哩醬

DATES (CHINESE RED)　紅棗

EGG ROLL SKINS　春卷皮

EGGS (PRESERVED)　皮蛋

FISH SAUCE　魚露

FIVE-FRAGRANCE POWDER　五香粉

FLOWER PEPPERCORNS　花椒

GINGER (SWEET RED IN SYRUP)　紅蘇薑

GINGER ROOT (FRESH)　薑

GINKGO NUTS (CANNED)　罐頭白果

HOISIN SAUCE　海鮮醬

JAH CHOY (SZECHWAN)　四川榨菜

JELLYFISH SKIN　海蜇皮

LILY BUDS (DRIED)　金針

LONG BEANS (FRESH)   豆角

LOTUS SEEDS (DRIED)   蓮子

LYCHEE (CANNED)   罐頭荔枝

MELON (BITTER)   苦瓜

MELON (WINTER)   冬瓜

MUNG BEANS   綠豆

MUSHROOMS (ABALONE)   罐頭鮑魚菇

MUSHROOMS (BUTTON)   蘑菇

MUSHROOMS (CHINESE DRIED)   冬菇

MUSHROOMS (STRAW)   罐頭草菇

NOODLES (BEAN THREAD)   粉絲

NOODLES (LO MEIN)   新鮮拷麵

NOODLES (RICE, FRESH)   沙河粉

OYSTER-FLAVORED SAUCE   蠔油

PLUM SAUCE   蘇梅醬

PORK (CANTONESE BARBECUED)   义燒肉

RICE (GLUTINOUS)   糯米

RICE POWDER　粘米粉

RICE POWDER (GLUTINOUS)　糯米粉

RICE STICKS (DRIED)　乾米粉

SAUSAGE (CHINESE PORK)　臘腸

SCALLIONS　葱

SESAME SEED OIL　蔴油

SESAME SEED PASTE　芝蔴醬

SESAME SEEDS (BLACK)　黑芝蔴

SESAME SEEDS (WHITE)　白芝蔴

SHAN JAH BENG　山楂餅

SHARK'S FIN　魚翅

SHRIMP (CHINESE DRIED)　蝦米

SHRIMP CHIPS　蝦片

SNOW PEAS　雪豆

SOY SAUCE (BLACK)　醬油（陶大）

SOY SAUCE (THIN)　生抽

SPRING ROLL SKINS (SHANGHAI)　上海春卷皮

TANGERINE PEEL (DRIED) 陳皮

TARO (FRESH) 芋頭

TURNIP (WHITE GIANT) 大蘿蔔

VINEGAR (CHINESE RED) 大紅浙醋

VINEGAR (CHINESE SWEET) 漆丁甜醋

VINEGAR (CHINESE WHITE) 白醋

WATER CHESTNUT POWDER 馬蹄粉

WATER CHESTNUTS 馬蹄

WHEAT STARCH 澄麵粉

WINE (CHINESE SHAOHSING) 紹興酒

WINE BALLS 酒餅

WINE SAUCE (SWEET) 甜酒釀

WONTON SKINS 餛飩皮

INDEX